Economic Aspects of the Sustainability Transition in Europe

This book comprehensively examines the financial and economic aspects of the 'sustainability transitions' demanded by the primary components of the European Green Deal.

It asks how the EU has been dealing with the allocation of resources to foster the sustainability transition, how the additional transformations required by the 'climate emergency' will be financed and which actors (businesses, governments, citizens) will pay and how. Looking at how the EU has been managing this over time, through changes in the Environment Action Programmes, Structural Funds, or the Multiannual Financial Framework, this book examines policy priorities and analyses the different instruments proposed as part of this evolving context, including market support instruments for renewable energies and the creation of new instruments, such as Climate Awareness Bonds. It also highlights new developments, such as the debate on the role of environmental taxes, or the uneven development across Member States of green financial instruments. This book presents an evolving puzzle into the limited possibilities of the EU to deploy resources that contribute to the overarching goal of achieving a low-carbon economy and illustrates the need for acceptance towards changes and compromises that are required from all affected stakeholders.

This book will be of key interest to scholars, students and practitioners of sustainable development, climate governance and EU politics, and more broadly to those working on European Studies, economics, politics, international relations or public policy.

Rosa Maria Fernandez Martin is Associate Professor in Economics and Finance, the Sustainability Lead, PGR Lead and Director for Masters in Economics at Keele Business School, Keele University, UK.

Routledge Studies on the Governance of Sustainability in Europe

Series editors: *Thomas Hoerber, ESSCA School of Management, France, Jenny Fairbrass, University of East Anglia, UK, Kristina Kurze, University of Göttingen, Germany, and Helene Dyrhauge, Roskilde University, Denmark*

At the beginning of the twenty-first century the EU is faced with major economic, environmental and societal challenges. Climate change is at the forefront of these challenges having a wide-ranging impact on the economy and society. This series will examine tensions and ambiguities in European sustainable development from an interdisciplinary and multidisciplinary background, covering the impact of sustainable development policies on European integration, and sustainability issues in energy, environmental, transport, development and agricultural policies.

Comparative Renewables Policy
Political, Organizational and European Fields
Edited by Elin Lerum Boasson, Merethe Dotterud Leiren and Jørgen Wettestad

The European Environmental Conscience in EU Politics
A Developing Ideology
Edited by Thomas Hoerber and Gabriel Weber

Making the European Green Deal Work
EU Sustainability Policies at Home and Abroad
Edited by Helene Dyrhauge and Kristina Kurze

The EU in a Globalized World
Edited by Thomas Hoerber, Alexandre Bohas and Stefano Valdemarin

EU Energy and Climate Policy after COVID-19 and the Invasion of Ukraine
Decarbonisation and Security in Transition
Edited by Matúš Mišík and Andrea Figulová

Economic Aspects of the Sustainability Transition in Europe
Rosa Maria Fernandez Martin

Economic Aspects of the Sustainability Transition in Europe

Rosa Maria Fernandez Martin

Routledge
Taylor & Francis Group
LONDON AND NEW YORK

First published 2025
by Routledge
4 Park Square, Milton Park, Abingdon, Oxon OX14 4RN

and by Routledge
605 Third Avenue, New York, NY 10158

Routledge is an imprint of the Taylor & Francis Group, an informa business

British Library Cataloguing-in-Publication Data
A catalogue record for this book is available from the British Library

Library of Congress Cataloging-in-Publication Data
Names: Fernandez Martin, Rosa Maria, author.
Title: Economic aspects of the sustainability transition in Europe /
Rosa Maria Fernandez Martin.
Description: Abingdon, Oxon ; New York, NY : Routledge, 2025. |
Series: Routledge studies on the governance of sustainability in Europe |
Includes bibliographical references and index.
Identifiers: LCCN 2024036883 (print) | LCCN 2024036884 (ebook) | ISBN 9781032124827 (hardback) | ISBN 9781032124889 (paperback) | ISBN 9781003224785 (ebook)
Subjects: LCSH: Sustainable development—European Union countries—Finance. | Environmental protection—European Union countries—Finance | Environmental policy—Economic aspects—European Union countries.
Classification: LCC HC240.9.E5 F47 2025 (print) | LCC HC240.9.E5 (ebook) | DDC 338.94/07—dc23/eng/20241026
LC record available at https://lccn.loc.gov/2024036883
LC ebook record available at https://lccn.loc.gov/2024036884

ISBN: 978-1-032-12482-7 (hbk)
ISBN: 978-1-032-12488-9 (pbk)
ISBN: 978-1-003-22478-5 (ebk)

DOI: 10.4324/9781003224785

Typeset in Times New Roman
by codeMantra

To the memory of my father, whom I deeply miss every day.
To my mother and my brothers, who have demonstrated the strength of togetherness, even in the distance.
To my nephews and niece, for bringing a smile to my face. They are the generation the topic of this book will affect the most.
And to my husband, my rock and the love of my life. Thank you for believing in me.

Contents

Illustrations

Figures

Tables

Boxes

Preface

From a very early stage of my PhD I knew I wanted to focus my research around environmental issues, climate change and sustainability, and one of my early works covered EU environmental policy. However, being an economist that was not an easy task, since it was mainly politics the discipline with more research in the area, apart from environmental sciences. In economics, other topics such as fiscal or monetary policies or big macroeconomic problems such as unemployment were expected to be given priority by researchers, in a country like Spain, behind the big European economies at the time (early 2000s) and with significant structural problems.

To my surprise, attending international conferences on European topics revealed that one of the main barriers for economists' messages to be understood was the use of the very specific language associated with economic analysis, particularly if one was using econometrics.

I took it to heart to make economic concepts and topics better understood by the general public and any non-economist academic, while making sure that the importance of said concepts was not underestimated.

This book is the product of years of research and an attempt to marry my expertise with my commitment to make the economics behind what we see happening around us every day accessible to all. I hope it will contribute to a better understanding of the conundrum policymakers face when making decisions on the path towards a more sustainable future in Europe and beyond.

1 Concepts and context

Introduction: Book justification and structure

When I tell people that I am an economist, most reactions (out of a university campus in particular) tend to include expressions such as 'that's very difficult', 'better you than me' or 'I don't understand a word of it'. So, if someone sees *Economic aspects of the sustainability transition in Europe* as the title of a book, they may assume it is going to be a subset of content related to Environmental Economics, full of complicated formulas and as such difficult to grasp by a non-economist. But this is far from being the case. This book is aimed at introducing readers to some questions posed by the double blow we are experiencing as a society, and their possible responses. On the one hand, the Covid-19 pandemic has created unprecedented levels of public, corporate and private debt (Capo McCormick et al., 2021) and thus scarcity of resources in most countries around the world. At the same time but very importantly, for a good number of years before the pandemic started, the world has also been facing a climate emergency (Ripple et al., 2020). Both situations call for the transformation of our lifestyles and require action from everyone and everything, including our governance systems. Transformations, changes and adaptations require not only time but also money, so one of the main questions one asks in the current situation is: How are we going to pay for the necessary changes if we do not have the resources? This is, of course, notwithstanding that the situation of climate emergency makes both doing nothing and delaying the changes no-go options. To complicate matters further, increases in the price of energy created by surges in demand as economies rebound from Covid-19, coupled with decrease in supply (Fernandez Alvarez and Molnar, 2021), are squeezing everyone's pockets, and Russia's invasion of Ukraine has made the increase even higher – at least temporarily, which added difficulties to the functioning of global food supply chains, creating what many are calling a 'cost of living crisis' worldwide (*The Guardian, 2022*). This may translate in little appetite to commit resources, no availability of said resources and the risk of lowering the level of priority given to the climate emergency. On a more forward-thinking and positive side, this new energy crisis should encourage governments and everyone else to take measures that decrease countries' fossil fuel dependence, opting for an expansion of renewable sources'

DOI: 10.4324/9781003224785-1

participation in the energy mix. However, in some circles there has been a call to allow fracking activities, and in others the priority is given to find alternative suppliers for the same fossil fuels.

Research questions and methodology

Where does the European Union (EU) sit in this puzzle? The EU has been an advocate of more sustainable practices for a long time, and many consider it a world leader. In fact, its communications and policy proposals often include a rhetoric around the lines of positioning itself as a leader, keeping, cementing or extending its leadership role (see for instance the 'Fit for 55' European Commission Communication [EC, 2021]: 2). It then becomes justified to look into how the EU has been doing over time and what its plans are for the future in this key issue. The questions that emerge from an economic point of view are: where does the money that Member States send to the EU go? How is the EU budget spent? How much is it going to cost to move towards more sustainable practices? Who is going to pay for it? What are the trade-offs involved? Those questions can be formulated using more specific (economic) terminology, which will be explained along the way: How has the EU been dealing with the allocation of resources to foster the sustainability transition? How are the additional transformations required by the 'climate emergency' going to be financed? Which actors (businesses, governments, citizens) are going to pay for it and how?

This book will provide possible responses to those questions conducting an extensive review of the EU policies and programmes (Part I), the instruments associated to those policies (Part II) and the latest developments (Part III). Policies, instruments, actors and institutions are all part of the EU governance system, a system that has been changing overtime but, as it will be seen very early on, requires further transformation.

The research approach used to answer these questions is that of a narrative enquiry, understood as a qualitative research method (Creswell, 2013), which departs from the mere storytelling to contributing to knowledge creation or construction (Webster and Mertova, 2007: 20). It does so by adding critical reflection (Hickson, 2016: 380–381) along the way, inviting the reader to reach own conclusions about the merits of the EU sustainability transition pathway used to date, particularly about its alignment (or lack thereof) with a strong sustainability approach (term that will be explained in the next section). This methodological approach involves reviewing specific aspects of the historical evolution of EU economic-related policies and institutional developments in connection with environmental protection and sustainability actions. It will be reinforced by the exemplification of the effects of said actions in different Member States, added to each chapter as case studies in the relevant text boxes. With the evidence presented this way, the reader will be invited to reflect on the significance of the approaches taken, in relation to the conceptual ideas introduced by this first chapter.

In this sense, this chapter will introduce the current framework for EU actions: the European Green Deal (EGD), as the flagship initiative of the Von der Leyen

Commission (EC, 2019a), where the plans of the previous Commission with regard to an Energy Union Package have been embedded.

Before looking into that however, it is important to understand the plethora of terms associated to 'sustainability transitions'. The term 'sustainability transition' itself is widely used these days in policymakers' and academic forums alike, but there are multiplicity of definitions and it is not a particularly simple concept. The following section of this chapter will be focused on clarifying the terminology used around 'sustainability transition or transitions', and subsequent sections will review the context in which said transition is happening, that is, the EU committed to international targets related to climate change, through the 2030 UN Sustainable Development Goals (SDGs) (UN, 2015a) as well as the Paris Agreement (UN, 2015b) and the United Nations Framework Convention on Climate Change (UNFCCC) Conferences of the Parties (COPs).

The rest of this book is structured in three parts: the first one is dedicated to the main policies and programmes that the EU has implemented over time to achieve sustainability-related targets, without limiting the scope to energy or climate ones. The second part will be focused on other elements of the governance system, particularly the instruments that said policies have used and the institutions playing relevant roles, such as the European Environment Agency (EAA) or the European Investment Bank (EIB), with the third part looking into the latest options within policies and instruments to move forward, including how to organise the necessary investments around green economy and green finance.

Concepts related to 'sustainability transitions'

Sustainable development and sustainability

The term 'sustainable development' has received multiple definitions, but the one that remains widely used by international institutions, governments, policymakers and academics (even if on many occasions to criticise it) is the one coined in 1987 by the UN World Commission on Environment and Development (Bruntland Commission), as *development that meets the needs of the present without compromising the ability of future generations to meet their own needs* (WCED, 1987).

If one tries to understand the concept by looking into its components, 'sustainable' and 'development', it becomes apparent why its meaning can be problematic. A simple online search on dictionary definitions presents 'sustainable' sometimes as interchangeable with 'sustained', that is *continuing for a long time* (Cambridge Dictionary, 2022a) and only within a specialised meaning is considered as *causing, or made in a way that causes, little or no damage to the environment and therefore able to continue for a long time* (Cambridge Dictionary, 2022b). The term 'development' is not free from problems either, mainly because it is widely identified with economic growth, but its meaning is much deeper. Development involves the improvement of the living standards of a country's citizens, looking at socio-economic factors and not just an increase in production. This is why the 'Human Development Index' (HDI) includes indicators measuring life expectancy at birth, years of schooling and Gross National Income (GNI) per capita (UNDP, 2011). The HDI is still an imperfect measure, with additional indexes trying to account for inequality, gender and multidimensional poverty (UNDP, 2011).

UNESCO (n.d.) includes four dimensions in sustainable development: society, environment, economy (usually identified as the three pillars of sustainability by other authors) and culture. In that regard, sustainability is seen as the long-term goal (a more sustainable world), and sustainable development would refer to the set of processes and pathways to achieve it, which would involve a reconciliation of the ecological, economic and social dimensions of life (Baker, 2016). Examples of what this could include range from sustainable production and consumption (one of the SDGs – SDG12 [UN, 2015a]), good government, research and technology transfer, education (SDG4) and training or recognition of cultural values and different forms of knowledge (Baker, 2016).

As previously stated, the Bruntland definition of sustainable development has been criticised. The main criticism emerges from the assignment of equal weight to the three elements or pillars of development: environment (nature), society and economy, following what is considered a *weak sustainability* approach. This involves the belief that economic growth and technological development could solve both social and environmental issues, considering that natural resources can be replaced by man-made capital (Giddings et al., 2002). The bulk of international initiatives and governmental responses to solve environmental, climate, and poverty issues has followed this approach over the past three decades (Morandin-Ahuerma et al., 2019). On the other side of the spectrum, *strong sustainability* makes both society and economy dependent of the ecosystem in which they live, understanding that without the biosphere nothing can be developed. This approach presents the three themes as nested and uses an eco-centric perspective instead of an anthropocentric one, moving away from the belief that economic growth is an irreplaceable need (Giddings et al., 2002; Morandin-Ahuerma et al., 2019). Figure 1.1 shows visually the difference between the two approaches.

It is not the purpose of this book to take sides on this debate, but different options will be made visible in subsequent chapters to reflect on alternative pathways to sustainable futures. In this regard, a common thread that this book will try to develop is the provision of elements for reflection over which pillar of sustainability (economic, social or environmental), if any, is given prominence throughout the transition journey, which will inform the reader on how far we may be (or not) from a strong sustainability approach, and decide if that is a desirable or feasible path.

Sustainability transitions

One of the multiple definitions that can be found on sustainability transitions describes them as 'radical transformations towards a sustainable society, as a response to a number of persistent problems confronting contemporary modern societies' (Grin et al., 2010). Said transformations affect multiple dimensions of everyone's life: technologies, markets, user practices, infrastructures, policies, etc. and it is important to acknowledge that such comprehensive volume of change

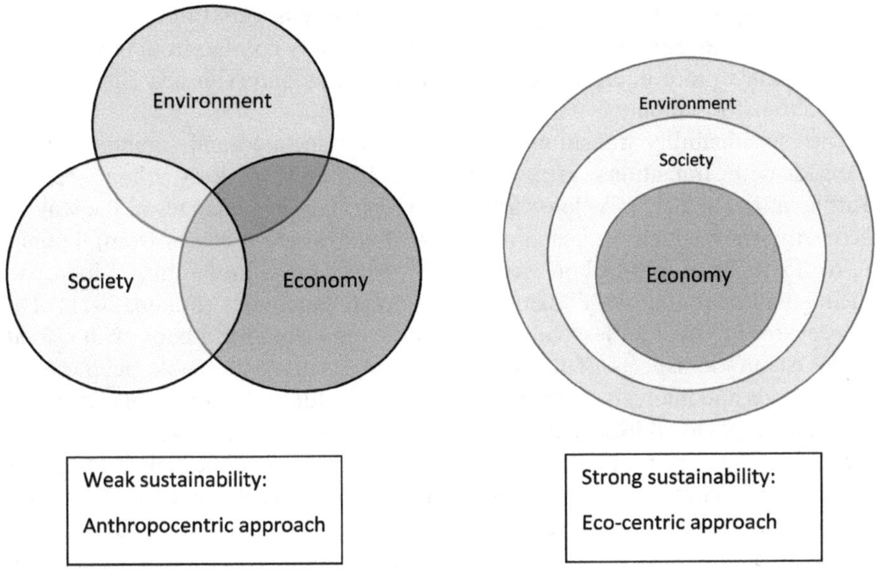

Figure 1.1 Weak vs strong sustainability
Source: Adapted from Giddings et al. (2002).

requires time (Köhler et al., 2019). Therefore, it is useful to understand sustainability transitions as processes of reconfiguration that will gradually modify our practices (Laakso et al., 2021). However, while for other transitions it may be advisable and even desirable to let transformations happen over a long period of time, in the case of sustainability transitions a slow pace would be detrimental, as the long-term environmental costs would be too high (Hess, 2014).

Using similar arguments to the ones outlined above, many describe sustainability transitions as the transformations of the existing 'socio-technical' regimes (Köhler et al., 2019), and technology plays a key role in transforming our current practices into low-carbon ones. For this reason, technological innovation has been brought to the forefront of policy priorities. The Kyoto Protocol already mentioned the sharing and transfer of technology as one of the key actions to allow emission reductions across the globe, particularly to enable access to developing countries (UN, 1997). However, innovation policy needs a change in orientation too. Note that the regimes above mentioned are 'socio-technical', which means that a change in society's behaviour is required too. So far, innovation policies have focused on the producer side of the equation, but it is time to look into consumers and their decisions, if we want everyone's behaviour to shift towards more sustainable futures, and as such, innovations to be successful (Fagerberg, 2017). The reference to changes needed in 'society' implies that everyone should be involved, which means a multi-stakeholder approach for both policy formulation and policy implementation. However what most countries have experienced up to now is top-down approaches in which governments/policymakers impose new regulations, and the feedback loop from the private sector or civil society is very limited, particularly in the case of the latter, with lobbying activities usually coming from powerful big multinationals more interested on keeping the status quo (van den Broek, 2021) than on transformation.

The 'sustainability transitions' term appears associated and sometimes interchanged with transitions to low-carbon economies or low-carbon societies (Turnheim et al., 2015). A 'low-carbon economy' requires changes in the way we use energy (how much we use, how we use it and where it comes from), but also the deployment of low-carbon technologies and changes in the mix of industries existing and operating within national and global economies (Foxon, 2011). This requirement for such a massive change justifies the need for a book with a focus on the economic aspects of the sustainability transition, to enable people of all backgrounds and interests gain awareness of the multiple challenges ahead and the current attempts to address them.

In this context, something that can confuse the general public is the use of some terminology related to the commitments that many governments and institutions are taking in the path to making their economies more sustainable. Targets and initiatives are many times linked to international commitments, since most countries are signatories of the UN Sustainable Development Agenda for 2030 (UN, 2015a) and the Paris Agreement to tackle climate change (UN, 2015b). More details of said international agreements will be provided later in the text. But it is important to understand first what some of that wording entails. In connection with the goal of achieving a 'low-carbon economy', pledges have been announced to reach 'carbon neutrality' or 'net zero'. The terms are similar, but not the same. When the term 'carbon neutrality' is used, it refers to net-zero carbon dioxide[1] (CO_2) emissions, through balancing the emission of CO_2 with its removal, so that its concentration in the atmosphere does not increase, and thus, it would not contribute to additional global warming (Chen, 2021). *Net-zero emissions* would involve the balance of all the greenhouse gases (GHGs) released to the atmosphere with the amount removed. *Net-zero carbon* however, would involve that no carbon has been emitted from the beginning of the activity we are measuring, so no carbon would need to be captured or offset (Bernoville, 2021). If one company's buildings were to be run entirely on renewable energy (solar, for instance), with no use of fossil fuels for anything, they would be able to label their energy as 'zero carbon'. But realistically, we are far from achieving something like this for every single activity in every single country, hence the need for more innovation and for the moment, the need to capture or offset emissions. In case this term is not clear, carbon offsetting refers to the remediation of emissions through paying another actor to facilitate a matching emissions' reduction elsewhere, but its effectiveness (Dalsgaard, 2022) as well as its ethical credentials have been put into question.

Not connected with its economic or financial equivalent, and to signify the emergency of taking action, the term 'carbon budget' has been introduced in policymaking. It essentially represents the maximum amount of carbon or GHG emissions that can take place to avoid reaching the threshold of temperature increase, 1.5°C or 2°C, as established by the Paris Agreement (MCC, 2022).

Another related term that will feature in this book, connected to those highlighted above, is that of *climate neutrality*. As with the previous concepts, there is confusion about its true meaning and there can be multiple interpretations. Generally, existing literature uses the term to refer to the moment in which we reach 'net zero greenhouse gas emissions' as defined by the Kyoto Protocol (see note 1), which would involve that all CO_2 and non-CO_2 emissions are compensated by negative emissions of CO_2. Using a broader approach, emissions would not only be the ones considered by Kyoto but all anthropogenic influences, such as other air pollutants or the modification of Earth's surface due to land-use changes (Rogelj et al., 2015).

What is the EU, as a supranational entity, doing about this? This book will give a comprehensive picture of it, with an introduction in the following sections.

The European context for the current transition

Nobody can say that the European integration process has been plain sailing. Since the 1950s, when the first Member States joined the then European Community, more policies have been added to the portfolio of responsibilities that the EU takes care of, as main regulator, but more often than not, exercising shared powers together with the Member States. The enlargement processes of the early 2000s doubled the number of Member States, and even if not all decisions are taken by unanimity, reaching majority votes is not easy, with what until very recently were 28 very different countries (27 since Brexit), not always having convergent ideas towards the direction that the EU should take.

Environmental protection on the other hand is a policy area where less conflicting views have emerged. The starting point was timid, but now environmental policy is at the forefront of EU strategies; environmental protection is one of the main objectives of the EU as a whole; it relies on specific institutions to oversee its functioning, and it enjoys wide support from political parties and other stakeholders (Jordan et al., 2021). Bearing in mind the convulse decade that the EU has recently endured, not only with Euroscepticism and the Brexit vote (2016), or the Syrian refugee crisis (2015/1016) (Niemann and Zaun, 2018), but also with emerging doubts over the democratic functioning of some Member States (Hungary's new constitution in 2013 or several regulatory changes in Poland in 2016) [See Fernandez, 2018 for examples], the EU needed a turning point towards a more positive and integrative agenda. The increase in climate change awareness and public interest in sustainable development, particularly young activism (Han and Ahn, 2020), provided the perfect opportunity.

The year 2019 started showing the first signs of change. There were elections to the European Parliament in May, and despite a traditionally perceived disconnection between citizens and the so-called 'political elite', said elections showed the highest citizens' participation in European elections (more than 200 million people) in 25 years (EC, 2020a). November brought the end of the Junker's Commission, with Angela von der Leyen taking over from December 1st. The Presidency of the European Council also changed at the same time (EC, 2020a). The flagship

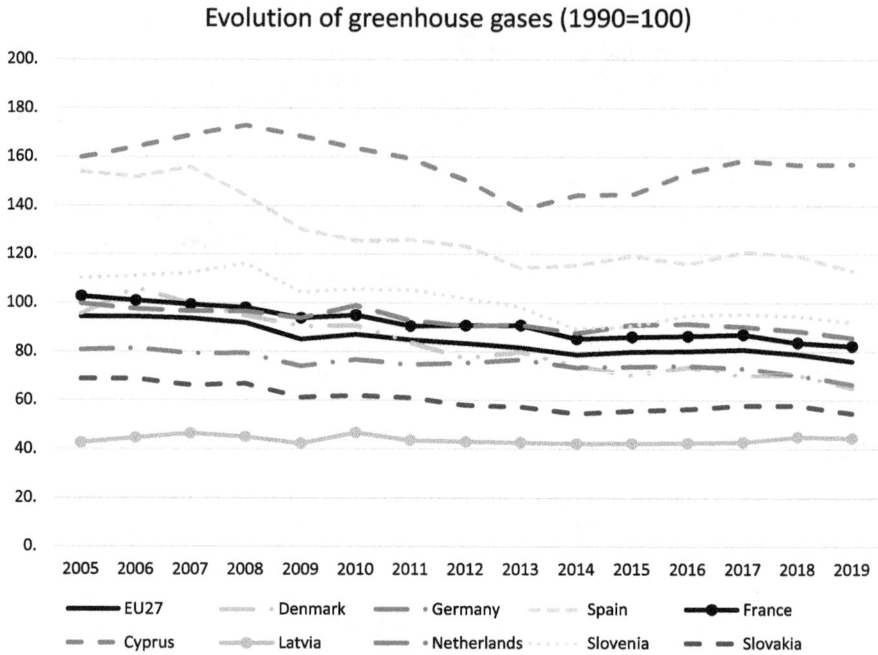

Figure 1.2 Evolution of greenhouse gas emissions in a sample of EU Member States 2005–2019

Source: Eurostat, Net greenhouse gas emissions [SDG_13_10] Extracted 06.06.2022.

initiative of the new Commission is the EGD (EC, 2019a), and since it is at the centre of every new legislative and policy initiatives, this book will use it as its overarching framework.

But it is necessary to look at what was the situation regarding climate change and environmental protection commitments up to that point. It cannot be forgotten that 2020 was the deadline for the famous '20-20-20 for 2020' targets, that is, a reduction of GHG emissions by 20% over the 1990 levels; an increase in the share of renewable energy use to 20% of the energy mix; and an improvement of energy efficiency by 20% (EC, 2008). The initial assessment of the EEA is that the three targets were actually reached (EEA, 2021), but with caveats. For years there were doubts about the energy efficiency target, and it was the fact that 2020 was the first year of the Covid-19 pandemic which made the figures add up, as lockdowns reduced economic activity, resulting in primary and final energy consumption below target levels. It is also worth mentioning that not all Member States reached their individual country targets, with Bulgaria, Cyprus, Finland, Germany, Ireland and Malta needing to make use of flexibility mechanisms such as buying emissions allowances (permits) from other EU countries, to reach their legal obligations (EEA, 2021). See Figure 1.2 for a summary of progress on emissions reduction since 2005.

It was before the new Commission was appointed that the EU had already made decisions about the way forward regarding how to tackle climate change beyond 2020. Already in 2011, the Commission had set a target for emissions reduction of 80–95% by 2050, over the levels of 1990 (EC, 2011), as part of a roadmap to transform the EU into a 'low-carbon economy'. The estimation at the time was that to make this transformation possible, there was a need for major public and private sustained investment over the subsequent 40 years, and this would mean an increase on existing investment of around €270 billion per year, which was 1.5% of the EU GDP per year in addition to the then existing investment (around 19% of GDP in 2009) (EC, 2011). In order to achieve the 2050 targets, there was also a need to review the progress towards the 2020 goals, and set intermediate targets, so a framework was designed with specific objectives for 2030 (EC, 2014). These included a reduction of GHG emissions of 40% over the 1990 levels, with specific reductions of 43% and 30% respectively for sectors in and outside the European Emissions Trading System (ETS) [which we will explain later in this book], with respect to 2005. It also included the goal to reach an EU level of 27% share of renewable energies in the energy mix, but this was criticised because the target was only indicative and non-binding for the individual Member States. The last target was related to energy efficiency, but since at the time there were doubts about the feasibility of the 20% improvement for 2020, there was just an estimation that to achieve the reduction in GHGs, energy savings should reach 25% (EC, 2014). In the end, another indicative target to achieve an improvement of 27% in energy efficiency was set up by the Council, with the aim to review said target in 2020 having in mind a 30% one (European Council, 2014). It is important to note that at this point it was acknowledged that those Member countries with GDP levels below 90% of the EU average would need to make higher investment efforts between 2021 and 2030, of around €3 billion per year higher than the EU average for the period, due to their relatively higher carbon intensity and lower energy efficiency, together with smaller capacity to invest (EC, 2014). The latter was one of the reasons to put emphasis at the time in the need to work on how to improve finance mechanisms and create innovative financial instruments, but there was also a hint that new governance structures would be required, given the complexity of the challenges ahead.

In the transition to a low-carbon economy energy is not all, but it plays a prominent role due to its extensive use both in production and consumption, affecting everyday life. Hence the large number of initiatives to encourage action in this sector, which reached a peak with the proposal for the establishment of an Energy Union (EC, 2015), outlining the need for investments both by the private sector and governments, including through European funds. It was in this context that the efforts on climate change were reviewed, with a 'Clean Energy for All' Package proposed in 2016 (EC, 2016a). Said proposal included the transformation of the renewable energy target for 2030 to a binding one, and also a binding target of 30% for energy efficiency. From an economic standpoint, two key arguments made by these initiatives were the creation of additional employment in a variety of sectors, and the reduction in the bill for imported fossil fuels (EC, 2015, 2016a), given the fact that the EU was and still is heavily dependent on imported energy sources (something that the current conflict in Ukraine has made even more visible, and the need for change even more urgent). From the governance point of view, it was openly recognised that the existing governance system was inadequate, thus the need to include a new governance mechanism as part of the Energy Union Package (EC, 2016b).

This was not the last modification of the targets, and indeed they are continuously under review, posing questions about the ever-changing regulatory environment in which private companies need to operate and the regulatory adaptations that national governments need to undertake. Interestingly, already in 2014, there was a stated commitment to improve the level of certainty for investors 'by providing clear signals now on how the policy framework will change after 2020 and by ensuring that substantial changes to existing objectives and instruments do not take effect before this date' (EC, 2014). From what followed it could be inferred that this commitment has not been kept. In 2018, an agreement between the European Parliament and the Council increased the ambition of the renewables target to 32% (European Parliament, 2018), which was reflected in a modification of the Renewables Directive (2018/2001/EU). It could be argued that this movement towards greater ambition on climate and environmental targets was in part triggered by wider public pressure, with 2018 being the year when Greta Thunberg's campaigning activities started (Kraemer, 2021), spearheading young climate activist movements across the world. It was also 2018 when the Energy Efficiency Directive was modified (2018/2002/EU), setting up an even more ambitious target of 32.5% improvement for 2030. Both directives were part of the actions envisioned by the Clean Energy for All Package, which was finally adopted in 2019 (EC, 2019b). Furthering the vision for a low-carbon economy outlined in 2011, 2018 was also the year in which the Commission set out its plan to achieve 'climate neutrality' by 2050 (EC, 2018).

The European Green Deal

Following this pattern of continuous change, it was not a surprise that a new set of EU governing bodies' leadership would embark on further plans to achieve the targets set for 2030 and the longer-term goals for 2050. The EGD is a strategy for economic growth, but growth that is achieved through a transformation towards sustainable futures. It acknowledges that this requires changes in policies not only related to energy, but also 'industry, production and consumption, large-scale infrastructure, transport, food and agriculture, construction, taxation and social benefits' (EC, 2019a: 4). In this regard, it is more realistic about the myriad of sectors that will need to participate in the transition. The discourse aligns, at least in principle, with that of the UN Agenda for 2030 of 'leaving no-one behind', by aiming for the transition to be 'just and inclusive' (EC, 2019a: 2), which has been further reaffirmed with the inclusion of a Just Transition Mechanism as part of the Sustainable Europe Investment Plan (EC, 2020b). In fact, there is explicit mention of the UN SDGs, with the EGD being part of the Commission's strategy to implement them. There is not much change related to the estimation of investments necessary to achieve the 2030 climate targets, with the figure of €260 billion being only €10 billion less than the estimate given in 2011, but it is admitted that said figure does not include the investment needs for environmental challenges such as biodiversity conservation, nor those for climate adaptation or the public investment required to address the social costs of the transition and the costs of inaction (EC, 2019a: 15), which indicates a much larger amount being required. The EGD does not in itself modify the targets for 2030, but it outlines the intention to revise the necessary policies to increase the target of GHG emissions reduction to at least 50% over the levels of 1990, and move towards a 55% reduction (EC, 2019a: 4). The first step in that direction came in 2020, in the middle of the Covid-19 pandemic, with the proposal of a 55% reduction target justified on the grounds of longer lead times required for the transformations necessary in certain sectors, particularly transport, but also based on the perceived risks of carbon locks-in, which require, in order to prevent them, 'clearer and stronger investment signals' so that planning decisions are coherent with the aim to achieve climate neutrality by 2050 (EC, 2020c). Once again, investment and innovation seem to be at the forefront of the narrative. The difference between the EGD and previous programmes is the attempt to bring more balance between the three key elements of sustainable development: economic, social and environmental. An example of this is the requirement, put forward through the Sustainable Europe Investment Plan (EC, 2020b), of a method for 'sustainability proofing', through which there will be a requirement for promoters of large projects to assess the 'environmental, climate and social impact of those projects' (EC, 2020b: 8).

The change in the GHG emission reduction target for 2030 to 55% was made official with the approval of the European Climate Law (Official Journal of the European Union [OJEU], 2021a), effectively reaffirming the aforementioned commitment to climate neutrality by 2050. From the resources point of view, it establishes that at least 30% of the total expenditure of the EU budget and the EU Recovery Instrument (created to deal with the extraordinary need for resources caused by the Covid-19 pandemic) will be dedicated to support climate objectives (OJEU, 2021a: 6). However, activists (Climate Action Network [CAN] Europe, 2020) criticise the Sustainable Europe Investment Plan on its climate neutrality credentials, remarking that most of the funding allocated already existed so there is hardly any additional resource and what has been done is to re-name them. It is also pointed out that investment on gas is eligible for funding, which would be contrary to the climate neutrality objective. Important recommendations are the conditionality of the funding to the phase-out and closure of coal-related activities and the application of the 'polluter pays' principle to State Aid rules (CAN Europe, 2020). From a multi-stakeholder participation point of view, the EGD has also been criticised as a step backwards in comparison with the Energy Union and the Clean Energy for All Packages (Fernandez, 2021), as citizens, but particularly communities, are included in a secondary role as part of a 'dialogue' but not as active participants in projects. This is not a new occurrence though, and it is typical that even at the local and national levels the involvement of citizens and communities gets reduced to the initial planning process (Carpenter and Brownhill, 2008; Shandas and Messer, 2008).

When it comes to the participation of the private sector and the financial institutions in the sustainability transition, the EGD describes their role as key (EC,

2019a: 16) since private finance (i.e. investment) is inherently required. But the EU has been criticised in the past for allowing the continuation of heavily polluting activities such as coal mining and even allowing national subsidies to keep financing those activities (Nowag et al., 2021), in contradiction with what is supposed to be an ambitious climate policy. It is no coincidence then that the EGD aims to introduce clarity with regard to what can be classified as an environmentally sustainable activity and what would constitute a sustainable or green investment. It set not only the requirement for the European Parliament and the Council to adopt a taxonomy, which should help with the clarification of concepts (EC, 2019a: 17), but also the scene for companies and financial institutions to disclose their climate and environmental data, so that potential and existing investors can have full information about the sustainability of their investments (and move their investments elsewhere if they are not happy with what they see). With a similar intention it suggests the creation of an EU green bond standard, so that investment can be done in a convenient way. The taxonomy regulation entered into force in July 2020 (OJEU, 2020) and outlines six environmental objectives to be covered:

- Climate change mitigation
- Climate change adaptation
- Sustainable use and protection of water and marine resources
- Transition to a circular economy
- Pollution prevention and control
- Protection and restoration of biodiversity and ecosystems

Uniform criteria need to be established to determine if certain economic activities contribute significantly to any of those objectives, and among those criteria the avoidance of significant harm to any of the environmental objectives should be included but should not be the only one, as some previous regulations had established (OJEU, 2020). The specific criteria are to be laid out in subsequent delegated regulations, and at the time of writing only a couple have been published, one of them with the technical criteria to qualify an economic activity as contributing to climate change mitigation or adaptation (OJEU, 2021b). This is applicable since January 2022 and is the result of intense discussions, consultations and negotiations, and still not free from controversy. Not everything related to one of the most important sectors, energy, has been clarified, with a proposal from the Commission in February 2022, finally published in July (OJEU, 2022) and in force since January 1st 2023, including specific nuclear and gas energy activities as part of the EU taxonomy, that is, as sustainable activities. Even if with strict conditions, the inclusion of nuclear energy is likely to continue under review as the text mentions the need to consider the possible technological advances in this sector. In the case of gas, its inclusion as sustainable goes against the opinion of activist groups (CAN Europe, 2020). But this reflects the complexity of the situation created by the scarcity of fuel supply since the conflict in Ukraine started. The first analyses on the effectiveness of the EU taxonomy to promote investments into more sustainable activities are not particularly positive. For instance, there seems to be a different approach taken for pumped hydro-storage in the draft delegated act to that of the technical expert group on taxonomy, including one form of storage and excluding another (Piebalgs and Jones, 2021). The taxonomy includes technical performance thresholds for economic activities to be considered green/sustainable, but questions emerge about the stringency with which those thresholds are going to be applied particularly in transition sectors, with calls (Schütze and Stede, 2021) for differentiated treatment of current versus new activities in emission-intensive sectors, as well as differentiation between low- and high-emission activities for those sectors not covered by the taxonomy. On the positive side, researchers (Dumrose et al., 2022) find that the EU taxonomy can help reducing the divergence between environmental, social and governance (ESG) ratings in use by different providers to rank a company's sustainability performance, though given the short period of time since the taxonomy has been approved, its positive effect has not reached its full potential. There are more developments expected in this area in the next couple of years.

Discussion questions

1. With which of the terms presented in this chapter do you feel more identified or connected to (weak or strong sustainability, low-carbon economy, net zero or carbon neutrality …)? Is there any term you hear in your particular circle more often than other?
2. Are the efforts to bring clarity about sustainable investments with an EU taxonomy actually helping or creating more confusion?
3. Bearing in mind the traditionally slow policy change process in the EU, do you think that the EGD is moving at a slow or a quick pace?
4. Are climate neutrality or net zero sufficiently ambitious goals? Should we aim to become 'carbon negative'?
5. Are the measures outlined by the EGD enough to reach the international goals committed for 2030 (SDGs and the Paris Agreement)?

Further readings

Blewitt, J. (2018) *Understanding Sustainable Development* (third edition). Earthscan from Routledge: This book will introduce the reader to many of the current debates about economic, social and environmental aspects of sustainable development across the world, from policy aspects to different actors, and the trade-offs that we face in the decision-making process towards sustainability, contrasting developed vs developing countries' approaches.

Hodson, D., Puetter, U., Saurugger, S. and Peterson, J. (eds) (2021) *The Institutions of the European Union* (fifth edition). Oxford University Press: If you are unfamiliar with the day-to-day activities of the EU, this book will provide a helpful introduction to each of its institutions, with their functions but also with a historical overview of their evolution, and the barriers they face to fulfil their mission.

Hoerber, T. and Weber, G. (eds) (2022) *The European Environmental Conscience in EU Politics. A Developing Ideology*. Routledge: With a focus on environmental and energy policy areas, this book will embark the reader onto the journey that the EU has experienced towards higher integration, with the growing environmental conscience as the driver for the current path.

Note

1 The Kyoto Protocol (UN, 1997) listed six greenhouse gases: carbon dioxide, methane, nitrous oxide, hydrofluorocarbons, perfluorocarbons and sulphur hexafluoride. Carbon dioxide is considered the biggest contributor to climate change (Reilly et al., 2003), so most measures use 'carbon' or 'carbon equivalence' as their unit (US EPA, n.d.), but it is important to try and address the issues associated with all greenhouse gases.

References

Baker, S. (2016) *Sustainable Development* (second edition). Abingdon and New York: Routledge.

Bernoville, T. (2021) What is the difference between carbon-neutral, net-zero and climate positive? *PlanA Academy* [Viewed 12 May 2022]. Available from: https://plana.earth/academy/what-is-difference-between-carbon-neutral-net-zero-climate-positive/

Cambridge Dictionary (2022a) Sustained [Viewed 1 March 2022]. Available from: https://dictionary.cambridge.org/dictionary/english/sustained

Cambridge Dictionary (2022b) Sustainable [Viewed 1 March 2022]. Available from: https://dictionary.cambridge.org/dictionary/english/sustainable

Capo McCormick, L., Torres, C., Benhamou, M. and Pogkas, D. (2021) The Covid-19 pandemic has added €19.5 trillion to global debt. Here are reasons to be grateful-and worried. *Bloomberg*, 27 January 2021 [Viewed 25 February 2022]. Available from: https://www.bloomberg.com/graphics/2021-coronavirus-global-debt/

Carpenter, J. and Brownhill, S. (2008) Approaches to democratic involvement: Widening community engagement in the English planning system, *Planning Theory & Practice,* 9 (2): 227–248.

Chen, J. M. (2021) Carbon neutrality: Toward a sustainable future, *The Innovation*, 2 (3): 100127.

Climate Action Network Europe (2020) *Sustainable Europe Investment Plan and a Just Transition Mechanism: Short on Climate Neutrality*. Briefing Paper. Climate Action Network Europe.

Creswell, J. W. (2013) *Qualitative Inquiry and Research Design: Choosing among Five Approaches* (3rd edition). Los Angeles and London: Sage.

Dalsgaard, S. (2022) Tales of carbon offsets: Between experiments and indulgences? *Journal of Cultural Economy*, 15 (1): 52–66.

Dumrose, M., Rink, S. and Eckert, J. (2022) Disaggregating confusion? The EU Taxonomy and its relation to ESG rating, *Finance Research Letters,* 48 (2022): 102928.

European Commission (2008) Communication from the commission to the European parliament, the council, the European economic and social committee and the committee of the regions: *2020 for 2020. Europe's Climate Change Opportunity*. COM (2008) 30 final. Brussels, 23.01.2008.

European Commission (2011) Communication from the commission to the European parliament, the council, the European economic and social committee and the committee of the regions. *A Roadmap for Moving to a Competitive Low Carbon Economy in 2050.* COM (2011) 112 final. Brussels, 08.03.2011.

European Commission (2014) Communication from the commission to the European parliament, the council, the European economic and social committee and the committee of the regions. *A Policy Framework for Climate and Energy in the Period from 2020 to 2030.* COM (2014) 15 final. Brussels, 22.01.2014.

European Commission (2015) *Energy Union Package.* Communication from the commission to the European parliament, the council, the European economic and social committee, the committee of the regions and the European Investment Bank. A framework strategy for a resilient energy union with a forward-looking climate change policy. COM (2015) 80 final. Brussels, 25.02.2015.

European Commission (2016a) Communication from the commission to the European parliament, the council, the European economic and social committee, the committee of the regions and the European Investment Bank. *Clean Energy for All Europeans.* COM (2016) 860 final. Brussels, 30.11.2016.

European Commission (2016b) Proposal for a regulation of the European parliament and of the council on the governance of the energy union. COM (2016) 759 final. Brussels, 30.11.2016.

European Commission (2018) Communication from the commission to the European Parliament, the council, the European economic and social committee, the committee of the regions and the European Investment Bank. *A* Clean Planet for All. *A European Strategic Long-Term Vision for a Prosperous, Modern, Competitive and Climate Neutral Economy.* COM (2018) 773 final. Brussels, 28.11.2018.

European Commission (2019a) Communication from the commission to the European parliament, the European council, the council, the European economic and social committee and the committee of the regions: The European Green Deal. COM (2019) 640 final. Brussels, 11.12.2019.

European Commission (2019b) *Clean Energy for all Europeans.* Directorate-General for Energy, Publications Office.

European Commission (2020a) *The EU in 2019: General Report on the Activities of the European Union.* Directorate-General for Communication, Publications Office.

European Commission (2020b) Communication from the commission to the European parliament, the council, the European economic and social committee and the committee of the regions. Sustainable Europe Investment Plan. European Green Deal Investment Plan. COM (2020) 21 final. Brussels, 14.01.2020.

European Commission (2020c) Communication from the commission to the European parliament, the council, the European economic and social committee and the committee of the regions. Stepping up Europe's 2030 climate ambition. *Investing in a climate-neutral future for the benefit of our people.* COM (2020) 562 final. Brussels, 17.09.2020.

European Commission (2021) Communication from the commission to the European parliament, the council, the European economic and social committee and the committee of the regions. *'Fit for 55': delivering the EU's 2030 Climate Target on the way to climate neutrality.* COM (2021) 550 final. Brussels, 14.7.2021.

European Council (2014) European Council 23 and 24 October 2014. Conclusions. EUCO 169/14. Brussels, 29.10.2014.

European Environment Agency (2021) *Trends and projections in Europe 2021.* EEA Report No 13/2021. Copenhagen.

European Parliament (2018) Energy: New target of 32% from renewables by 2030 agreed by MEPs and ministers. Press Release, 14.06.2018. Reference No. 20180614IPR05810.

Fagerberg, J. (2017) Mission (im)possible? The role of innovation (and innovation policy) in supporting structural change & sustainability transitions. *TIK Working Papers on*

Innovation Studies, no. 20180216. Version 27.12.2017. [Viewed 11 May 2022]. Available from: https://www.sv.uio.no/tik/InnoWP/tik_working_paper_20180216.pdf

Fernandez, R. M. (2018) Conflicting energy policy priorities in EU energy governance, *Journal of Environmental Studies and Sciences*, 8 (2018): 239–248.

Fernandez, R. M. (2021) Community renewable energy projects: The future of the sustainable energy transition? *The International Spectator*, 56 (2021): 87–104.

Fernandez Alvarez, C. and Molnar, G. (2021) What is behind soaring energy prices and what happens next? *International Energy Agency*, Commentary, 12 October 2021 [Viewed 25 February 2022]. Available from: https://www.iea.org/commentaries/what-is-behind-soaring-energy-prices-and-what-happens-next

Foxon, T. J. (2011) A coevolutionary framework for analysing a transition to a sustainable low carbon economy, *Ecological Economics,* 70 (2011): 2258–2267.

Giddings, B., Hopwood, B. and O'Brien, G. (2002) Environment, economy and society: Fitting them together into sustainable development, *Sustainable Development*, 10 (2002): 187–196.

Grin, J., Rotmans, J. and Schot, J. (eds) (2010) *Transitions to Sustainable Development. New Directions in the Study of Long-Term Transformative Change.* New York/London: Routedge.

The Guardian (2022) From New Zealand to Nigeria: The global toll of the cost of living crisis. June 20. Available from: https://www.theguardian.com/world/2022/jun/20/global-toll-cost-of-living-crisis

Han, H. and Ahn, S. W. (2020) Youth mobilization to stop global climate change: Narratives and impact, *Sustainability*, 12 (2020): 4127.

Hess, D. J. (2014) Sustainability transitions: A political coalition perspective, *Research Policy,* 43 (2014): 278–283.

Hickson, H. (2016) Becoming a critical narrativist: Using critical reflection and narrative inquiry as research methodology, *Qualitative Social Work,* 15 (3): 380–391.

Jordan, A., Gravey, V. and Adelle, C. (2021) EU environmental policy at 50: Retrospect and prospect. In Jordan, A. and Gravey, V. (eds) *Environmental Policy in the EU. Actors, Institutions and Processes* (4th edition). London: Routledge 357–374.

Köhler, J., Geels, F. W., Kern, F. et al. (2019) An agenda for sustainability transitions research: State of the art and future directions, *Environmental Innovation and Societal Transitions,* 31 (2019): 1–32.

Kraemer, D. (2021) Greta Thunberg: Who is the climate campaigner and what are her aims? *BBC News*, 5 November 2021 [Viewed 7 June 2022]. Available from: https://www.bbc.co.uk/news/world-europe-49918719

Laakso, S., Aro, R., Heiskanen, E. and Kaljonen, M. (2021) Reconfigurations in sustainability transitions: A systematic and critical review, *Sustainability: Science, Practice and Policy,* 17 (1): 15–31.

MCC (2022) Remaining carbon budget [Viewed 13 October 2022]. Available from: https://www.mcc-berlin.net/en/research/co2-budget.html

Morandin-Ahuerma, I., Contreras-Hernandez, A., Ayala-Ortiz, D. A. and Perez-Maqueo, O. (2019) Socio-ecosystemic sustainability, *Sustainability*, 11: 3354. https://doi.org/10.3390/su11123354

Niemann, A. and Zaun, N. (2018) EU refugee policies and politics in times of crisis: Theoretical and empirical perspectives, *Journal of Common Market Studies,* 56 (1): 3–22.

Nowag, J., Mundaca, L. and Åhman, M. (2021) Phasing out fossil fuel subsidies in the EU? Exploring the role of state aid rules, *Climate Policy*, 21 (8): 1037–1052.

Official Journal of the European Union (2020) Regulation (EU) 2020/852 of the European Parliament and of the Council of 18 June 2020 on the establishment of a framework to facilitate sustainable investment, and amending Regulation (EU) 2019/2088. L198, 22.06.2020.

Official Journal of the European Union (2021a) Regulation (EU) 2021/1119 of the European Parliament and of the Council of 30 June 2021 establishing the framework for achieving climate neutrality and amending Regulations (EC) No 401/2009 and (EU) 2018/1999 (European Climate Law). L243, 09.07.2021.

Official Journal of the European Union (2021b) Commission Delegated Regulation (EU) 2021/2139 of 4 June 2021 of the European Parliament and of the Council by establishing the technical screening criteria for determining the conditions under which an economic activity qualifies as contributing substantially to climate change mitigation or climate change adaptation and for determining whether that economic activity causes no significant harm to any of the other environmental objectives. L442, 09.12.2021.

Official Journal of the European Union (2022) Commission Delegated Regulation (EU) 2022/1214 of 9 March 2022 amending Delegated Regulation (EU) 2021/2139 as regards economic activities in certain energy sectors and Delegated Regulation (EU) 2021/2178 as regards specific public disclosures for those economic activities. L188, 15.07.2022.

Piebalgs, A. and Jones, C. (2021) The importance of the EU taxonomy: The example of electricity storage. Policy Brief. Florence School of Regulation. European University Institute. Issue 2021/11, March 2021.

Reilly, J. M., Jacoby, H. D. and Prinn, R. G. (2003) *Multi-Gas Contributors to Global Climate Change. Climate Impacts and Mitigation Costs of Non-CO_2 Gases*. Massachusetts Institute of Technology. Pew Center on Global Climate Change.

Ripple, W. J., Wolf, C., Newsome, T. M., Barnard, P. and Moomaw, W. R. (2020) World scientists' warning of a climate emergency. *BioScience*, 70 (1): 8–12. https://doi.org/10.1093/biosci/biz088

Rogelj, J., Schaeffer, M., Meinshausen, M. et al. (2015) Zero emission targets as long-term global goals for climate protection. *Environmental Research Letters,* 10 (2015): 105007.

Schütze, F. and Stede, J. (2021) The EU sustainable finance taxonomy and its contribution to climate neutrality, *Journal of Sustainable Finance & Investment.* https://doi.org/10.1080/20430795.2021.2006129

Shandas, V. and Messer, W. B. (2008) Fostering green communities through civic engagement: Community-based environmental stewardship in the Portland area, *Journal of the American Planning Association*, 74 (4): 4080418.

Turnheim, B., Brekhout, F., Geels, F. W. et al. (2015) Evaluating sustainability transitions pathways: Bridging analytical approaches to address governance challenges, *Global Environmental Change,* 35 (2015): 239–253.

UN (1997) Kyoto Protocol to the United Nations Framework Convention on Climate Change, 10 December 1997. FCCC/CP/1997/L.7/Add.1.

UN (2015a) Resolution adopted by the General Assembly on 25 September 2015. Transforming our world: the 2030 Agenda for Sustainable Development. A/RES/70/1.

UN (2015b) Paris Agreement. Adopted on 12 December 2015 (Paris, France).

UNDP (2011) *Human Development Report* 2011. *Sustainability and Equity: A Better Future for All.* New York: United Nations Development Programme.

UNESCO (n.d.) Sustainable development [Viewed 25 April 2022]. Available from: https://en.unesco.org/themes/education-sustainable-development/what-is-esd/sd#:~:text=Sustainability%20is%20often%20thought%20of,research%20and%20technology%20transfer%2C%20education

US EPA (n.d.) Overview of greenhouse gases [Viewed 13 May 2022]. Available from: https://www.epa.gov/ghgemissions/overview-greenhouse-gases#CO2-references

Van den Broek, O. (2021) Soft law engagements and hard law preferences: Comparing EU lobbying positions between UN global compact signatory firms and other interest group types, *Business and Politics,* 23 (2021): 383–405.

Webster, L. and Mertova, P. (2007) *Using Narrative Inquiry as a Research Method: An Introduction to Using Critical Event Narrative Analysis in Research on Learning and Teaching*. London and New York: Routledge.

World Commission on Environment and Development (1987) *Our Common Future*. Oxford University Press.

Part I

Policies and programmes

2 The EU budget and the Multiannual Financial Framework

Introduction

The EU defines itself not only as an economic and political union but also as an organisation, dedicated to coordinate actions in a number of policy areas (EC, 2020) for the common well-being of its Members. It is widely seen as a supranational organisation (University of Cincinnati, 2021) because it has characteristics of both an international organisation and a nation. In order to perform its functions, it makes use of financial resources (money); thus, similarly to countries and organisations, it uses a budgetary procedure to keep track of both the resources at its disposal and the expenditures it undertakes. It is important to distinguish though, between the annual budget and the so-called long-term budget, the Multiannual Financial Framework (MFF), which sets the ceiling for expenditures over a period of five to seven years (Mrak, 2018) and is the product of intense political negotiations.

As a procedure, the way in which annual budgets are approved could appear as a simple one (Calatozzolo, 2022), similarly to how an individual country's budget is approved: the different EU institutions prepare the priorities for the budget of the following year in the first half of the current year, with informal negotiations starting in July (DeHavilland, 2021). They send these priorities to the Commission, which drafts a proposal for submission to the Council and the Parliament before September 1st. The Council adopts its position over the proposed budget and forwards it to the Parliament before October 1st. Simultaneously, different parliamentary committees have been discussing the draft budget and have been sending their opinions to the Budgets Committee, which is, within the European Parliament, responsible to prepare the Parliament's position. The Parliament has then 42 days to decide: approve the Council's position, adopt amendments or decline to make a decision. In the latter case, the budget is deemed adopted (Calatozzolo, 2022). If amendments are approved (by majority of its members), the amended draft is sent back to the Council and Commission, and the Conciliation Committee needs to be convened immediately. Said Committee has 21 days to agree on a text. If agreement is not reached, the Commission will need to submit a new draft budget. If agreement is reached, the Parliament and Council will have 14 days to approve the joint text, and if this happens, the President of the Parliament will declare the

DOI: 10.4324/9781003224785-3

budget as definitively adopted. In this case, for the decision to be valid, it will require qualified majority[1] of members of the Council, and majority of members of Parliament. If agreement is not reached on time, one twelfth of the budget of the current year will be the maximum amount that can be spent per month in the following year (Mazur, 2019). This is a provisional system until a full new budget is approved. The procedure, where it is evident that all the main EU institutions have a say, has not always been like this, and the following sections will depict the changes that have occurred over time.

In the case of the MFF, the negotiations are much more time consuming, and they begin halfway through one multiannual period, to be ready at the beginning of the following one. The process begins with the presentation of the whole package by the Commission, which includes a MFF regulation, outlining how much the EU can spend, and an 'own resources decision', which says where the revenue, and thus, the resources, will come from (European Council, 2020). The approval process is special (special legislative procedure) and the MFF regulation requires unanimity in the Council and consent of the European Parliament (it can approve or reject but not make amendments). For the 'own resources decision' unanimity of the Council is also required, with only an 'opinion' from the Parliament needed, but in addition every Member State needs to ratify it following their own constitutional requirements (European Council, 2020).

From the point of view of the purpose of this book, the relevance of the EU budget relates to how much of said budget is dedicated to environmental protection, sustainable development and, in general, 'greening' European economies. This is not an easy question to answer, as this chapter will show, but it is important, bearing in mind that the European Court of Auditors, the body in charge of monitoring EU finances, has published a report related to the last MFF (2014–2020), stating that what had been previously reported by the Commission in terms of climate expenditure was not correct (European Court of Auditors, 2022) and in reality the amount spent was lower than what was reported, and also lower than what was initially committed for the fight against climate change.

The European Green Deal (EGD) hints at higher level of funding commitment for the current MFF (EC, 2019a): it starts with the proposed commitment of 25% as target across all EU programmes to be dedicated to climate mainstreaming. With regard to the revenue, it includes also proposals for new 'own resources' such as taxing non-recycled plastic packaging waste; or allocating 20% of the revenue coming from the auctioning of allowances through the EU Emissions Trading System (ETS) to the EU budget. Other commitments include that at least 30% of the InvestEU Fund (part of the new InvestEU programme) will contribute to the fight against climate change (EC, 2019a: 15), and at least 35% of the budget of Horizon Europe (the programme for Research and Development) will be dedicated to fund solutions for climate, relevant for the implementation of the EGD (EC, 2019a: 18). The actions are not limited to the internal frontiers of the EU, with a proposal for a Neighbourhood, Development and International Cooperation Instrument including a target of 25% of its budget to be allocated to climate-related purposes (EC, 2019a: 22). At least in paper, it appears that the EU budget is increasing its climate ambition, but verification will be necessary to ascertain that, unlike in the previous financial period, actions do not fall short from what is expected. It is worth noting that the EGD does not only propose actions for the EU and its budget as a whole, but it expects changes in each of the Member States, marking as one of its objectives the greening of national budgets (EC, 2019a: 17), with the Commission expected to screen and benchmark the green budgeting practices of individual countries. In this regard, green budgeting is understood as the use of 'tools of budgetary policymaking to help achieve climate and environmental goals' (EC et al., 2021).

The following sections will review how the EU budget has been allocated over time to different policy areas and among EU Member States, to then look at the budget for the current period (2021–2027) in the context of the EGD and the pandemic.

Evolution of the EU budget

The institutions involved

It has been previously stated that the budgetary decision-making process has not always been as participatory as it is nowadays. Among scholars there are two main views about the evolution of the budgetary procedure: Those who consider a before and after the reforms of the 1980s (Mrak, 2018), and those who focus on the differences brought by the Treaty of Lisbon from 2009 onwards (Bauer et al., 2015; Crombez and Høyland, 2015). But it could be argued that everything in between has had a role in the development of the budget functioning as it has been described in the previous section. Its legal basis is covered by articles 312–324 of the Treaty on the Functioning of the EU (TFEU), though there are some specific clauses applied to the EURATOM budget that are still ruled by the EURATOM Treaty (Mazur, 2019).

These statements call for some clarification: Since the original treaties were signed at different points in time and with different policy purposes, it made sense to have separated budgets. This meant that since 1952, we have the European Coal and Steel Community (ECSC), which did not run through traditional annual budgets but through a levy of 1% of the turnover of coal and steel industries, tariffs on imports of steel and coal and revenues from fines imposed over the affected companies, up to a maximum of 5% of their turnover (Benedetto, 2019). Procedurally speaking though, the ECSC Treaty allocated the resources through two budgets: an operating budget and an administrative budget (Mrak, 2018). The EURATOM Treaty and the European Economic Community (EEC) Treaty of 1957 also made provisions for their respective budgets, but while EURATOM established an administrative and a research and investment budget, the EEC worked with a single budget (Mrak, 2018). Additionally, while the EURATOM and EEC budgets had to be in balance (i.e. they could not run deficits), this was not the case for the ECSC (Benedetto, 2019). Different treaties and different communities for different policy areas had different governing institutions, but this changed with the merger of the institutions in 1965 through the Merger Treaty (Weil, 1967), resulting in a change of the financial provisions and the budgetary procedures. However the main changes on budgetary procedures came in 1970 and 1975, with the so-called 'Budget Treaties' (Knudsen, 2012). The first of these treaties introduced the concept of 'own resources' with the idea to replace national financial contributions. Those own resources would come from custom duties, agricultural levies, and certain percentage of the Value Added Tax (VAT) collected in the Member States. This modification would remove control of the budget by national parliaments and allow the European Parliament (then Assembly) to have some budgetary powers (Laursen, 2019). The second treaty not only increased the powers of the Parliament over budget by allowing it to reject the draft budget (similarly to what we have now) but also very importantly, created the institution now known as the European Court of Auditors, with the aim to solve accountability problems that the original Audit Board could not cope with, namely to control the management of expenditures by the Common Agricultural Policy (CAP) and the European Development Fund (EDF), and address the allegations of manipulation of agricultural levies and other mismanagement issues (Knudsen, 2012).

The enlargements of the 1980s, with Greece, Portugal and Spain joining – the latter as a big new Member State (geographically and in population terms), and the increase in the number of policy areas where the EU had competencies, demanded additional changes on the budget, particularly due to its insufficiency (Crowe, 2017) to take care of all the issues where common action was deemed required. The governance structure of the budget proved inadequate even earlier on, making impossible to approve the annual budget on several occasions and resulting in open conflict between Member States and EU institutions (Mrak, 2018). It is in this context that the Single European Act was ratified in 1987, creating the EU Internal Market, and bringing forward the proposal of the Commission for a new agreement on a long-term budget, then called 'financial perspective' (Benedetto, 2019) and renamed 'financial framework' by the Treaty of Lisbon in 2007. Said agreement involved the participation of the three main EU institutions (Commission, Council and Parliament) on a more equal footing in the budget approval process. The agreement also contributed to appease the disputes between Council and Parliament over power of approval of compulsory and non-compulsory expenditures. In an attempt to solve the insufficiency of resources, it was also at this point (1988) when a fourth 'own resource' was introduced, as a percentage of the Gross National Income (GNI) of the Member States, though initially the base was the Gross National Product (GNP) (Mrak, 2018). Its role as a resource increased rapidly, amounting to 74% of the total own resources in 2011, from a 10% in 1988. This change was the result of two Council decisions in the 1990s to shift the weight of the resources from the VAT-based resource to be more GNI-based, with two main purposes: to widen the financial scope of the EU budget, and to ease the financial burden that weaker Member States experienced, in the understanding that VAT presented more regressive features, and GNI would better reflect a country's economic capabilities (Schratzenstaller, 2013). Chronologically speaking, in 2002 the ECSC Treaty expired, which made its operating budget disappear. Since then, the EU has worked with a single EU budget (Mrak, 2018).

The Treaty of Lisbon (Official Journal of the European Union [OJEU], 2007) brought more changes, mainly with the purpose of making the budgetary procedure understandable by the EU citizens, but some (Crowe, 2017) argue that the reforms were modest in scope, codifying or simplifying pre-existing procedures without addressing the fundamental issues that had been affecting the EU public finances. While some literature tends to view the Treaty of Lisbon as positive to strengthen the powers of the European Parliament, for many the opposite is true with regard to the budgetary procedure, considering it poorly designed and with the potential to cause a breakdown in the negotiation process (Crombez and Høyland, 2015). In fact, some (Benedetto, 2013) not only conclude that the Treaty reduces the powers of the Parliament (Bauer et al., 2015), but also that it makes the budget more inflexible and reduces how much can be spent, due to how national governments can use the procedure.

As it has been mentioned in the Introduction, the EGD included some proposals to modify where the revenue would come from to constitute the resources for the EU budget, and the Commission has started working on the particulars for the new resources. Details will be provided later in this chapter, together with the resources being used for the current MFF (2021–2027).

The policy priorities: How is the budget spent?

The annual budget is organised in sections dedicated to each of the institutions of the EU (Mazur, 2019), while the MFF presents the ceilings on expenditure by programme, and as the name indicates, it covers several years. The programmes are associated to, or part of, specific policies and may create their own specific instruments. It is not surprising that one of the first instruments implemented was the European Agricultural Guidance and Guarantee Fund (EAGGF), created in 1962 as part of the CAP (Mrak, 2018). The CAP is one of the most criticised EU policies, not just because of the historical mismanagement of resources, as it was posited in the previous section, but precisely because of the amount of budget it has historically absorbed (around 70%) and continues absorbing (38%) (Heinemann and Weiss, 2018), which results on other policy areas having less funding allocated. Despite numerous reforms, the latest of them trying to address environmental degradation related to farming practices and aiming to connect payments to farmers to more sustainable practices, the results are not positive (Alons, 2017). Many believe that the design of the policy is fundamentally wrong (Hristov et al., 2020). More details on this will be provided in Chapter 4.

The other two instruments that have been at the forefront of the EU budget expenditure are linked to the implementation of the Cohesion Policy: The European Social Fund (ESF), established in 1971, and the European Regional Development Fund (ERDF), created in 1975. Together with the EAGGF (or its equivalent programme for the latest financial framework), they still amount to almost 80% of the EU budget (Mrak, 2018). The European Cohesion Policy aims to correct imbalances between EU countries and regions (EC, 2021a). It is based on the principle of inter-regional financial solidarity and as such it has redistributive effects among the

EU regions (Ahner, 2018). In plain terms, this means that EU countries with higher levels of economic development and income would help those with lower levels of income to improve their economic situation, with the purpose to reduce (and hopefully eliminate) the development and income gap. These differences between Member States became more visible with the accession of Greece, Spain and Portugal in the 1980s (Inforegio, 2008) and again with the enlargement to Eastern Europe in the early 2000s (Lima and Cardenete, 2008). It is then no surprise that even if policy instruments exist from very early on, it is considered that the main elements of the EU Cohesion Policy emerge from the Single European Act, and it could be argued that a more systematic allocation of funds can be found since 1988 (Inforegio, 2008), concurring with this increase in the visibility of income gaps between EU countries.

Funds can also be classified into two major categories: Structural Funds and Cohesion Funds. Interestingly, they have been re-labelled to add ‘Investment’ to their overall title, coinciding with the recently finished MFF (2014–2020), which aligned them with the Europe 2020 Strategy (EC, 2010). The emphasis on investment fits the situation of the EU at the time, with most Member States suffering from the effects of the economic crisis of 2007–2008, reflected on lower availability of funds and thus the expectation that the limited budget would be dedicated to those projects that would produce the highest return. The Europe 2020 Strategy fundamentally is a strategy for economic growth, and even if the title includes ‘sustainable’ and ‘inclusive’ as characteristics of said growth, its main purpose was to make the EU the most competitive economy in the world, by becoming a knowledge-based economy (Stec and Grzebyk, 2018).

Within the European Structural and Investment Funds, which are the main recipients of EU budget, we currently find:

- The ERDF, whose main goals are to strengthen labour markets and regional economies through investment in jobs, and to strengthen cross-border transnational and inter-regional cooperation. The overall objective is to correct regional imbalances (as it is for any regional policy instrument), and there is a focus on the conversion of declining industrial regions and developing those laggard regions through structural adjustment (Kołodziejski, 2022).
- The ESF, now called ESF+, with a very specific focus on the support of projects that enable the creation of jobs, and particularly addresses unemployment among young people (EC, 2007a).
- The Cohesion Fund (CF) was set up in 1994 with the purpose of strengthening economic, social and territorial cohesion, in this case with the explicit mention of promoting sustainable development. Once more, its regulation is focusing on establishing ‘investment’ priorities (OJEU, 2013), in alignment with the Europe 2020 Strategy, but some modifications are expected for the current financial period. As a difference with other structural funds (ERDF and ESF), accessible to all Member States, only countries whose GNI per capita is less than 90% of the EU average can access these funds (EC, n.d.a). The projects it supports are those investing on environment and trans-European networks of transport infrastructure (TENT-T).

- The European Agricultural Fund for Rural Development (EAFRD) replaces the EAGGF and the LEADER+. The latter was a special financial instrument initially designed for disadvantaged rural regions but then expanded to all rural areas (European Network for Rural Development, 2021). This is an instrument connected to one of the pillars of the CAP, which is rural development, and in order to promote sustainability, it is now a requirement that 30% of the funding for rural development programmes (RDPs) is to be spent in measures relevant for environment and climate change (Andersson et al., 2017).
- The European Maritime and Fisheries Fund (EMFF) replaced the European Fisheries Fund (EFF) in the MFF 2014–2020 and has been renamed as European Maritime, Fisheries and Aquaculture Fund (EMFAF) for the current MFF 2021–2027. One of the reasons why this funding has been criticised is that despite its goals to promote sustainable fishing practices, it has contributed to increase the fishing capacity of the EU, which, it is argued, has contributed to overexploitation of fisheries (Skerritt et al., 2020).

Apart from the above-mentioned instruments, the EU also allocates budget to the European Union Solidarity Fund, which covers eventualities such as major natural disasters, and the Instrument for Pre-Accession Assistance (IPA) to help potential candidate countries in their adaptation to EU functioning rules. The current IPA replaces a myriad of instruments created over time: PHARE, ISPA, Sapard, CARDS and the Financial Instrument for Turkey.

The origin of the resources: Where does the money come from?

This section will pay attention to the composition of the so-called 'own resources' over time and the rationale for their reform, particularly in the current financial period. It needs to be clarified first that though they are EU resources they are collected by each of the Member States, which retain a percentage (currently 25%) as a compensation for the costs of collection (Schwarcz, 2021).

The 'traditional own resources' are the ones established by the Budget Treaty of 1970, as introduced earlier in this chapter, and included the customs duties, agricultural duties and sugar levies. The sugar levies basically disappeared when the system of sugar quotas was eliminated in 2017, as part of the negotiations to modify the CAP and introduce fairer competition between EU sugar producers and international ones (with contentious negotiations taking place through the World Trade Organisation (WTO) rounds. The initial proposals intended to finish with the sugar quota regime in 2015, while the EU producers wanted the system to remain until 2020 (Matthews, 2012), so 2017 was a half-way solution. Currently, the customs duties on imports entering the EU are the main source of traditional own resources. It is not the purpose of this book to go into the detail of how import duties work, but as a summary it is worth noting that since the EU works as a customs union, products from third countries will be subject to a common external tariff, so in theory, it would be indifferent through which Member State the products enter EU territory. In practice though, there are significant differences between the products that each Member State imports, and the common external tariff for each product is moulded depending on the interests and preferences of each country, specific lobby groups, and the economic conditions at the time (Ehrlich, 2009). None of these resources account for a great proportion of the EU revenue side of the budget nowadays, totalling between 10% and 15% (Schwarcz, 2021).

The VAT-based own resource was approved in the first Budget Treaty but it took longer to be introduced, mostly because each Member State has different VAT rates and some have more than one VAT rate. There have been numerous modifications on the percentage of VAT that countries need to submit to the EU to become part of the budget in each of the MFFs, beginning with 1% in the 1970s and increasing up to 1.4% with the possibility to go up to 1.6% in the 1980s, coinciding with the need for more funding with the accession of Spain and Portugal (Benedetto, 2019). Since then, the move has gone in the opposite direction, standing at 0.3% for the current MFF, which makes this resource once more relatively small (10–15%) in the total EU revenue (Schwarcz, 2021). There are doubts about the efficiency of VAT as part of any fiscal system, with studies (Kowal and Przekota, 2021) suggesting that its efficiency in terms of preventing fraud and tax evasion (hence producing the desired revenue) are linked to those VAT systems where the basic VAT rate and the number of preferential rates are lower. Other studies (Alavuotunki et al., 2019) show evidence that the introduction of VAT has caused an increase in income inequality, while consumption inequality has not been affected. In the current cost of living crisis (linked to high energy and food prices, with record levels of inflation in some countries), reductions in the VAT rates are one of the first measures that many European countries are adopting in an attempt to alleviate the pressure on consumers (Witham, 2022).

The main source of revenue for the EU budget is the GNI-based own resource. When it was introduced in 1988, the idea was that it would cover the difference between the funding needs and the revenue collected through the traditional own resources and VAT, but since the needs were larger with more Member States, it was necessary to set a ceiling on how much money would be spent and how much money would be collected from Member States' GNIs. The ceilings were set up at different levels for commitments (expenditure) and payments (resources/Member States contributions). Initially the ceilings followed an upward trend, from 1.15% of GNP in 1988 to 1.20% in 1992, and then to 1.27% in 1999 for payments, the latter kept in the following MFF (Benedetto, 2019). From 2007 onwards the calculations are made over GNI instead of GNP, with the establishment of lower spending ceilings for the subsequent periods (Hudetz et al., 2017). This meant that the ceiling was set to 1.24% of GNI for payments between 2007 and 2013, and to 1.23% for 2014–2020 (Benedetto, 2019). The GNI-based own resource currently represents around 70% of the EU budget revenue (EC, 2021c).

The 2021–2027 MFF was initially going to follow a similar austerity approach, bearing in mind that the Brexit process left the EU without one of its net contributors (more on this in the next section). There were multiple proposals to address the gap in funding created by this situation, also considered in the context of wider reform proposals for the EU budget. Among those proposals we find the creation of a European nuclear power tax, on sustainability grounds (Dellinger and Schratzenstaller, 2017). Other proposals to modify the budgetary procedure include limiting the power of the Council to setting the budget ceiling, while the structure of the expenditure is determined by the Parliament; an inclusion of the share of VAT that goes to the EU in receipts, so that citizens are informed of the real contribution; a simplification of the system of rebates (Rebates will be referred to in the next section); or the abolition of the VAT-based resource altogether (Fuest et al., 2015). Specific proposals to increase the availability of resources for the EU budget have concentrated on taxation, that is, which type of taxes would be adequate and to which extent an EU tax is feasible, with the options of a carbon tax, a flight ticket tax, or a financial transaction tax among the possibilities under consideration (Hudetz et al., 2017). In the end, for the current MFF what has so far been approved as a new resource, in place since January 2021, is a national contribution of €0.80 per kilogram of plastic packaging waste that is not recycled, with a correction mechanism applicable to less prosperous Member States (European Commission, 2021b). The expectation is that this measure will provide a revenue of around €6 billion per year (European Commission, 2021c). At the end of the year 2021, the Commission also proposed to create the 'Next Generation of EU own resources', consisting on a 25% of the revenues from emissions trading (up from the 20% initially proposed by the EGD), a 75% of the revenues generated by a Carbon Border Adjustment Mechanism (CBAM) and a new own resource based on the reallocated profits of very large multinational companies, by which Member States would contribute 15% of the share of reallocated profits to the EU budget (European Commission, 2021d). Something else under consideration is the implementation of a digital levy, to ensure that digital business pay a fair amount of tax (EC, 2021c), after widespread criticism of existing practices, aiming to pay the lowest fare possible.

The unprecedented situation created by the Covid-19 pandemic required expedient action, which involved the approval of a MFF with €1,074.3 billion (European Council, 2022), a lower figure than the initially proposed in 2018 [€1,135 billion] (Dobreva, 2018), but with the addition of €750 billion in the form of an extraordinary recovery instrument (Next Generation EU) that the Commission will be authorised to borrow from capital markets (increasing the existing level of debt). This extraordinary instrument is temporary, with the expectation that the funding will be used between 2021 and 2023 (EC, 2021c). For a summary of the figures allocated to the 2021–2027 MFF, see Table 2.1. The full package aims to support the EGD, the digital transformation (a need exacerbated by the pandemic), and an enhancement of the EU resilience (European Council, 2022). The budget also counts with a 'Brexit Adjustment Reserve', aiming at counteracting any adverse consequences created by the UK leaving the EU in the worst affected sectors and Member States (EC, 2021c). With all these extraordinary adjustments, it is no surprise to see an approval of higher ceilings for expenditure and payments, with the ceiling for commitments since January 2021 set at 1.46% of the GNI of all Member States, and the ceiling for payments set at 1.40% of GNI, with an additional temporary buffer of 0.6% to cover the borrowing liabilities of the Next Generation EU instrument until all the borrowed funds are repaid (European Council, 2022).

Table 2.1 Multiannual Financial Framework 2021–2027 and NextGenerationEU (NGEU) (commitments – in million EUR, 2018 prices)

	2021	*2022*	*2023*	*2024*	*2025*	*2026*	*2027*	*Total*
1 Single market, innovation and digital (total)	19,712	19,666	19,133	18,633	18,518	18,646	18,473	132,781
+ NGEU	3,380	3,330	3,890	–	–	–	–	10,600
2 Cohesion, resilience and values (total)	49,741	51,101	52,194	53,954	55,182	56,787	58,809	377,768
+ NGEU	327,521	300,002	94,377	–	–	–	–	721,900
3 Natural resources and environment	55,242	52,214	51,489	50,617	49,719	48,932	48,161	356,374
+ NGEU	4,250	9,250	4,000	–	–	–	–	17,500
4 Migration and border management	2,324	2,811	3,164	3,282	3,672	3,682	3,736	22,671
5 Security and defence	1,700	1,725	1,737	1,754	1,928	2,078	2,263	13,185
6 Neighbourhood and the world	15,309	15,522	14,789	14,056	13,323	12,592	12,828	98,419
7 European public administration	10,021	10,215	10,342	10,454	10,554	10,673	10,843	73,102
Total	154,049	153,254	152,848	152,750	152,896	153,390	155,113	1,074,300
+ NGEU	335,151	312,582	102,267	–	–	–	–	750,000

Source: European Commission (2021c) The EU's 2021–2027 long-term budget and NextGenerationEU. Facts and Figures.

The distribution of the budget among Member States

It could be expected that once the budget is set and amounts are allocated to different categories it would be the end of the negotiating process, but that is not exactly the case. Member States contribute to the EU budget according to their own economic situation (GNI) and the structure of their economy in general (sectors, activities, and the design of their individual fiscal systems), as that will determine how many resources they collect and which proportion of those end up being part of the budget. Individual Member State's characteristics will also determine from which EU policies and programmes they can benefit and receive funding, as explained in the previous section. But some countries may perceive that they are contributing too much or that they are not benefitting as much as others (which bares questions about what has happened with the application of the principle of inter-regional solidarity), and conflicts may appear if they do not receive what they consider a fair compensation. This is why the EU budget allows for 'corrections' to be applied for different countries. The main correction of this type has been the UK correction or rebate, agreed in 1984 and applied since 1985, by which there was a reduction of two-thirds on the UK net contribution to the budget, financed by other Member States (Benedetto, 2019). The biggest contributors to pay for the UK rebate are France, Italy and Spain (EC, 2019b). After the enlargement of the early 2000s, some countries asked for the elimination of the UK rebate, but this did not happen. Other Member States gained their own corrections through reductions in the VAT call rate for Austria, Germany, Netherlands and Sweden, and lump-sum corrections paid to Netherlands and Sweden (Benedetto, 2019). The UK rebate has finally disappeared, but only as a result of Brexit.

All these corrections are the product of a change on Member States' behaviour with regard to the EU budget, using their position as net contributor or net beneficiary to advertise their negotiation capabilities in their respective national arenas, making the EU budget compete with national expenditure and eroding the concept and function of the own resources (European Parliament, 2013). The disputes between net contributors and net beneficiaries have affected the size and structure of the EU budget over time, with each country trying to minimise the net contributions or maximise the net benefits from an individual perspective instead of thinking of value added from a whole EU perspective (Hudetz et al., 2017). The latest initiatives to reform the EU budget, both on the side of the revenue and the expenditure, are attempts to put an end to this conflict of interests, but it will not be easy to find a definitive solution.

It has been previously outlined that countries and regions receive funding from the different EU programmes. With the establishment of multiannual planning and budgeting in 1988, regions in the EU were classified according to how their situation fitted with regard to the five priorities for the allocation of Structural and Cohesion Funds (Inforegio, 2008):

- Objective 1: promoting the development and structural adjustment of regions whose development is lagging behind

- Objective 2: converting regions seriously affected by industrial decline
- Objective 3: combating long-term unemployment
- Objective 4: facilitating the occupational integration of young people
- Objective 5: (a) speeding up the adjustment of agricultural structures and (b) promoting the development of rural areas

Reforms in 1993 brought the creation of the CF to help the then poorest Member States (Spain, Ireland, Portugal and Greece); a new Objective (6) was introduced to deal with issues associated to sparsely populated areas and some of the prior thematic objectives were slightly modified, particularly Objectives 2 and 5b, to give a greater role to Member States in the geographic area selection process (Manzella and Mendez, 2009). For the following financial period (2000–2006), there was a simplification of thematic objectives, grouping them in three (Inforegio, 2008):

- Objective 1: promoting the development and structural adjustment of regions whose development is lagging behind
- Objective 2: supporting the economic and social conversion of areas facing structural difficulties
- Objective 3: supporting the adaptation and modernisation of policies and systems of education, training and employment

This is a period that witnessed the enlargement of the EU to Eastern Europe, and as such, the redistribution of funds from the then 15 Member States to the newcomers (Breuss et al., 2010). Since the countries joining in 2004, and then Bulgaria and Romania in 2007 (with Croatia joining in 2013), had much lower-income per capita levels compared to the EU15 average, there were some Member States with regions that had not experienced the necessary level of development to achieve convergence with the EU average, but compared favourably with the new Member States (effectively the accession of the new countries made the EU GNI average to go down, so without any specific action some regions were closer to said average). This would have made those regions lose access to some of the structural funds, following the EU rules on 'phasing out' support as countries make progress, but this would only have been due to a 'statistical effect' and as such, temporary mechanisms were put in place to assist these regions (EC, 2007b). An example of one of those countries affected by the statistical effect can be found in Box 2.1.

Box 2.1 Case study: Spain and the effects of the EU enlargement to Eastern Europe

Since it joined the EU in 1986, Spain has been one of the main recipients of EU funding, both Structural Funds and Cohesion Funds (one of its first beneficiaries, together with Ireland, Portugal and Greece). During the first MFFs from 1988 onwards, most of the country's territory was classified as Objective 1 (Inforegio, 2008), with a GDP lower than 75% of the EU average at the time. This is the case of Andalucia, the region that has received the biggest amount of funding, due to its economic profile, geographical size and population (Lima and Cardenete, 2008). The main part of the EU funding in Spain was dedicated to infrastructure investment, as a difference with countries such as Ireland, where there was more focus on human capital (Farrel, 2004). With the enlargement of the EU to Eastern Europe, for the financial period 2000–2006, there were a number of territories that would have been Objective 1 in the past but no longer fell in that category, entering what was called 'phasing out' support. For the following financial period (2007–2013), the transitional support continued, as they would have remained below the 75% threshold for an EU with 15 Member States, but they were not in the EU25. The territories affected were Asturias, Murcia, and the autonomous cities of Ceuta and Melilla (EC, 2007b). In that same period, and very much affected by the international economic crisis of 2007–2008, there were four regions entitled to what was then called the 'convergence objective' support: Galicia, Castilla-La Mancha, Extremadura and Andalucia, and the country as a whole was the only Member State entitled to CF transitional support (EC, 2007b). In 2012, as a result of the transition support mechanisms, Spain was the second main recipient of EU budget after Poland (EC, 2014a). Between improvements in the economic situation in general and the statistical lowering of the EU average income due to the enlargement, Spain has passed from being one of the main net beneficiaries of the EU budget [with a positive operating budgetary balance of €5,263.6 million in the year 2000] to almost becoming a net contributor [with an operating budgetary balance of €729.4 million in 2017] (EC, n.d.b). That figure was reduced to €430 million in 2020 (Statista, 2022). In the current financial period, Spain is the biggest recipient of funds through the Recovery and Resilience Facility (to help with the crisis created by the Covid-19 pandemic) but is no longer recipient (since 2014) of the CF (EC, 2021c).

The simplification of thematic objectives continued in the 2007–2013 financial period, grouping Objective 1 and CF cover into one 'Convergence Objective'; Objectives 2 and 3 became the new 'Regional competitiveness and employment Objective', and a series of programmes funded by the ERDF and the ESF (Interreg III, URBAN II and EQUAL) became the 'European territorial cooperation Objective', funded by the ERDF (EC, 2007b).

The Cohesion Policy for the MFF 2014–2020 went back to more specific areas of action, setting 11 thematic objectives. For the first time we find sustainability-related objectives having headlines of their own, instead of being subsumed as part of bigger goals. Specific sustainability objectives are (EC, 2014b):

4 Supporting the shift towards a low-carbon economy
5 Promoting climate change adaptation, risk prevention and management

6 Preserving and protecting the environment and promoting resource efficiency
7 Promoting sustainable transport and improving network infrastructures
8 Promoting sustainable and quality employment and supporting labour mobility
9 Promoting social inclusion, combating poverty and any discrimination

It can be observed that Objectives 8 and 9 (and the others too) are in alignment with the UN SDGs that were approved in 2015.

The current MFF goes back to more generic thematic objectives, reducing the number to five, and focusing on growth, though there is some specific mention of sustainability-related topics (EC, n.d.c):

1 A more competitive and smarter Europe
2 A greener, low-carbon transitioning towards a net-zero carbon economy
3 A more connected Europe by enhancing mobility
4 A more social and inclusive Europe
5 Europe closer to citizens by fostering the sustainable and integrated development of all types of territories

While in the previous financial period, the ERDF, the ESF and the CF were the main financing instruments, for the current period we also have the Just Transition Fund for specific purposes, in particular to mitigate negative consequences of the sustainability transition on employment in certain sectors of the economy, financing the diversification and modernisation of local economies (OJEU, 2021a). Countries with access to CF resources are: Poland, Romania, Portugal, Hungary, Greece, Czechia, Slovakia, Bulgaria, Croatia, Lithuania, Latvia, Estonia, Slovenia, Cyprus and Malta. It is worth noticing that among the first beneficiaries of the CF, Portugal and Greece still require the extra support. It is also interesting that its first four beneficiaries were the first Member States to be bailed out in the aftermath of the international economic crisis of 2007–2008. This begs the questions of: to which extent there is an ex-post evaluation of the effectiveness of the EU funding, or to which extent there is a need for more specific guidelines or requirements for accountability of individual Member States. Importantly, even if we are talking about EU funding, the management of said funding is a shared responsibility between the EU and the Member States, and it is the latter who allocate most of the funding to their specific priorities and projects. It is no surprise then to find calls for more accountability on the EU budget implementation (Cipriani, 2021), rethinking the priorities of the European Court of Auditors to focus more on the Commission's internal control framework and the value for money, so that from a management level we can see the emergence of a performance culture, and the Court of Auditors as its performance assurance assessor.

The current Multiannual Financial Framework 2021–2027: Is it green or has it been derailed by the pandemic and the cost of living crisis?

It is necessary to understand the context in which the current MFF was decided (EC, 2018). It covers the period 2021–2027, and it was discussed once the Brexit vote had taken place, in the middle of the negotiations for the future relationship between the EU and the UK, so it is a budget that looks at an EU with 27 instead of 28 Member States. This is important because the UK was a net contributor to the budget, which indicates a limitation or reduction of the resources available for any policy. If this is coupled with the then recent commitments of the EU towards a low-carbon economy: through the Europe 2020 Strategy, the goals on energy and climate change set up for 2030 and through the Energy Union Package, the adherence to the Paris Summit Agreement and to the UN 2030 Agenda for SDGs, it becomes apparent that (additional?) resources would be necessary for this transition to sustainability, but in the absence of additional resources, the only option is the reorganisation of the available ones. So what does the current MFF tell us?

The total budget is slightly reduced, as expected, but from the outside, no major changes can be perceived. However, despite being described as a 'driver of sustainability' (EC, 2018: 12), the funds for the CAP and Fisheries, the main areas of resources for the environment, are reduced. There is a new element called 'Climate Mainstreaming' with increased budget, and the LIFE Climate & Environment area also increases, but other policies, namely Migration & Borders, Youth and Security, receive the biggest increases, as a reflection of the new reality the EU was experiencing at the time (refugee crisis), which could be interpreted as lowering the priority for environmental concerns. The differences between the current MFF and the previous one in terms of budget allocation to policy areas can be observed in Figure 2.1. Overall, the rubric 'Natural Resources & Environment' experienced a decrease in funding over the seven-year period (EC, 2018), and though it may be the case that part of it comes from restructuring and making the CAP more efficient, it does not speak well of the current structure of the budget, and this chapter has already noted the numerous calls for its reform. The budget in its initial conception was also a reflection of the overall trend at the time of the budget approval: other areas were replacing environment in the level of policy priority. This can be said not only for the expenditure side of the budget but also for the revenue side, since Member States environmental tax revenue collection had been following a downward trend for some time (Eurostat, 2021).

By the time the MFF entered into force in 2021, circumstances had changed significantly. On the one hand, civil society mobilisation in favour of effective actions to tackle climate change brought environment back to the forefront of policy priority. This is the context in which the EGD is presented, using the momentum created by bottom-up movements. A proof of the Commission's portraying of the EDG as a response to young people's demands for action is Von der Leyen's EGD introduction as Commission's President candidate:

> The message from Europe's voters – and those too young to vote – is loud and clear: they want real action on climate change and they want Europe to lead the way. I have been inspired by the [...] energy of the millions of our young people making their voice heard on our streets [...] it is our generational duty to deliver for them.
>
> (European Commission and von der Leyen, 2019)

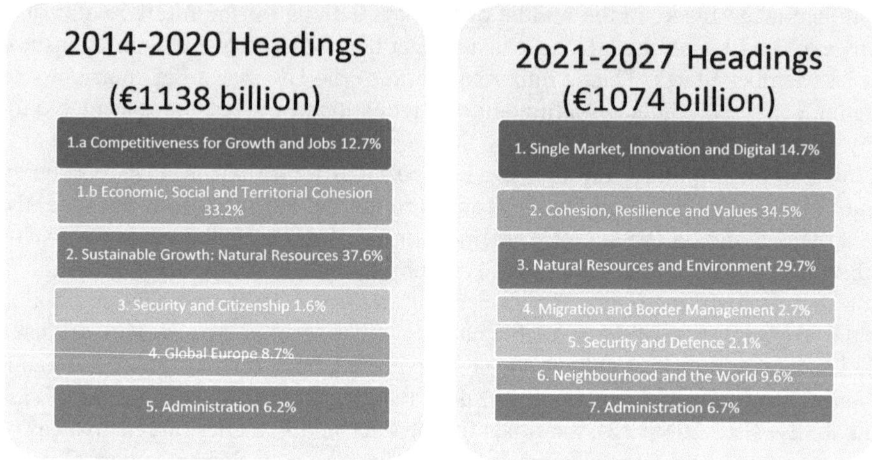

Figure 2.1 Comparison of budget distribution between MFFs 2014–2020 and 2021–2027 (%)

Source: Dobreva (2018) [European Parliament Research Service] and EC (2021c).

On the other hand, the whole world had been (and still is) affected by a global health pandemic that brought economic activity to a halt, with extraordinary financial support measures implemented in an attempt to cushion its negative effects, particularly in terms of unemployment. Levels of public (and private) debt increased beyond what may be considered safe or reasonable, with many countries recording debt rations about 100% of annual GDP (Wieland, 2022). The financial restrain shown in the initial approval of the MFF was toned down with the additional funding provided by Next Generation EU, in particular the Recovery and Resilient Facility. The latter works under six pillars, one of which is the 'Green transition', with expected reforms and investments in green technologies and capacities, while contributing to the EU climate targets (OJEU, 2021b). To these measures we can now add the REPowerEU initiative, which will benefit from the Recovery and Resilient Facility and argues for more funding to be allocated through its lines of grants and loans, with the purpose of reducing the reliance on Russian gas after Ukraine's invasion, and fast forward the clean transition (EC, 2022). It is true that most of the measures approved regarding funding available have included some conditionality related to the need to promote, facilitate or contribute to the sustainability transition of the EU economies. Thus, on the side of the budget expenditure it could be argued that the balance leans towards a greener approach, but not by much. On the revenue side, however, the new own resources, approved or proposed, have clear connection with the aim to make the EU and its Member States more sustainable, with the new national contributions based on plastic packaging not recycled, the proposal to increase the revenue coming from the EU ETS, or the Carbon Border Adjustment Mechanism. More on this will be discussed in Chapters 5 and 7. All these measures aim to become clear incentives for Member States to change behaviour in the right direction, so it would be fair to say that even if there is a long way to go to see the desired results, and there is a predominant economic rationale behind all the measures, the EU budget for the current financial period may be the greenest yet. However, the continuation of the cost of living crisis with inflationary pressures still running high through 2023, and only starting to signal a reduction in 2024, may force European and national authorities to take actions which may compromise or delay sustainability transition efforts. Time will tell.

Discussion questions

1 Would you agree with those who think that an opportunity has been lost with the current MFF to reform the EU budget in a way that is more efficient and sufficient to fulfil the EU goals?
2 To which extent is there room for a bigger role of the EU on taxation?
3 Has the principle of inter-regional solidarity been lost in the allocation of funding to the Member States?
4 What is your view of the budgetary powers of the European Parliament after the Treaty of Lisbon?
5 Can the EU realistically achieve its targets for higher climate spending in the current 'cost of living' crisis?

Further readings

Cipriani, G. (2014) *Financing the EU Budget. Moving Forward or Backwards?* Center for European Policy Studies: Rowman & Littlefield Publishers: This book will introduce the reader not only to some of the issues encountered in the reform of the EU budget but also to the reasons that justify the need for change, particularly to ensure transparency in the functioning of the system.

Majocchi, A. (2018) *European Budget and Sustainable Growth. The Role of a Carbon Tax,* Federalism Series, Volume 10. Peter Lang Publishing: This book uses the Economic and Monetary Union as a framework to call, once more, for a reform of the structure of the budget, with a focus on new own resources and in particular the imposition of a carbon tax, a controversial topic in EU politics, but which is gaining momentum through the Carbon Border Adjustment Mechanism.

Zamparini, L. and Villani-Lubelli, U. (eds) (2019) *Features and Challenges of the EU Budget. A Multidisciplinary Analysis*. Edward Elgar Publishing: If you are interested in different perspectives about the EU budget by different stakeholders and for different policy aspects such as competitiveness or further European integration, this book provides a good sample of topics to make the reader think about the challenges ahead.

Note

1 Qualified majority requires two conditions: that 55% of the EU Member States vote in favour (15 out of 27), and that the proposal is supported by Member States who represent at least 65% of the total EU population. This is also known as the 'double majority' rule, and for some special cases there are reinforced majorities that require 72% of Council members voting in favour (European Council, 2021).

References

Ahner, D. (2018) What do you really know about European cohesion policy? *Institute Delors.* [Viewed 10 July 2022]. Available from: https://institutdelors.eu/wp-content/uploads/2018/01/ecp_rational_and_objectives.pdf

Alavuotunki, K., Haapanen, M. and Pirttilä, J. (2019) The effects of the value-added tax on revenue and inequality, *The Journal of Development Studies*, 55 (4): 490–508.

Alons, G. (2017) Environmental policy integration in the EU's common agricultural policy: Greening or greenwashing? *Journal of European Public Policy*, 24 (11): 1604–1622.

Andersson, A., Höjgård, S. and Rabinowicz, E. (2017) Evaluation of results and adaptation of EU rural development programmes, *Land Use Policy*, 67 (2017): 298–314.

Bauer, M. W., Graham, J. D. and Becker, S. (2015) The EU budget system after Lisbon: How the European Parliament lost power and how it may compensate (somewhat) for it, *Journal for Comparative Government and European Policy*, 13 (4): 479–496.

Benedetto, G. (2013) The EU budget after Lisbon: Rigidity and reduced spending? *Journal of Public Policy*, 33 (3): 345–369.

Benedetto, G. (2019) *The History of the EU Budget. In-Depth Analysis.* Directorate General for Internal Policies. Policy Department D: Budgetary Affairs. PE 636.475 – May 2019.

Breuss, F., Egger, P. and Pfaffermayr, M. (2010) Structural funds, EU enlargement, and the redistribution of FDI in Europe, *Review of World Economics,* 146 (3): 469–494.

Calatozzolo, R. (2022) The Budgetary Procedure. Fact Sheets on the European Union-2022. 06/2022. European Parliament.

Cipriani, G. (2021) Improving the accountability of the EU budget's multi-level implementation: Strengthening the contribution of the European Court of auditors, *German Law Journal*, 22 (2021): 466–489.

Crombez, C. and Høyland, B. (2015) The budgetary procedure in the European Union and the implications of the Treaty of Lisbon, *European Union Politics*, 16 (1): 67–89.

Crowe, R. (2017) The European budgetary galaxy, *European Constitutional Law Review*, 13 (2017): 428–452.

DeHavilland (2021) EU budget procedure. *Briefing* [Viewed 2 July 2022]. Available from: https://www.dehavilland.co.uk/politicaluploads/DHEU/Briefing/EUBudgetProcedure.pdf

Dellinger, F. and Schratzenstaller, M. (2017) Sustainability-oriented future EU funding: A European nuclear power tax, *FairTax* Working Paper Series No. 09, H2020-EURO-SOCIETY-2-14, May 2017.

Ehrlich, S. D. (2009) How common is the common external tariff? Domestic influences on European Union trade policy, *European Union Politics*, 10 (1): 115–141.

European Commission (2007a) *European Social Fund. 50 Years Investing in People.* Luxembourg: Office for Official Publications of the European Communities.

European Commission (2007b) *Cohesion Policy 2007–13. Commentaries and Official Texts.* European Union Regional Policy. Guide. January 2007.

European Commission (2010) Communication from the Commission: Europe 2020, A strategy for smart, sustainable and inclusive growth. COM (2010) 2020. Brussels, 3.3.2010.

European Commission (2014a) *The EU Budget in My Country: Spain.* Luxembourg: Publications Office of the European Union.

European Commission (2014b) *An Introduction to EU Cohesion Policy 2014–2020,* June 2014. Luxembourg: Publications Office of the European Union.

European Commission (2018) Communication from the commission to the European parliament, the European council, the council, the European economic and social committee and the committee of the regions. *A Modern Budget for a Union that Protects, Empowers and Defends. The Multiannual Financial Framework for 2021–2027*. COM (2018) 321 final. Brussels, 2.5.2018.

European Commission (2019a) Communication from the commission to the European parliament, the European council, the council, the European economic and social committee and the committee of the regions: The European Green Deal. COM (2019) 640 final. Brussels, 11.12.2019.

European Commission (2019b) *EU Budget 2018. Financial Report*. Luxembourg: Publications Office of the European Union.

European Commission (2020) *The European Union. What It Is and What It Does*. Luxembourg: Publications Office of the European Union.

European Commission (2021a) Cohesion policy 2021–2027 [Viewed 30 June 2022]. Available from https://ec.europa.eu/regional_policy/en/2021_2027/#:~:text=EU%20Cohesion%20Policy%20contributes%20to,the%20green%20and%20digital%20transition.

European Commission (2021b) The next generation of EU own resources: Questions and Answers. Brussels, 22 December 2021.

European Commission (2021c) *The EU's 2021–2027 Long-Term Budget and NextGenerationEU. Facts and Figures*. Luxembourg: Publications Office of the European Union.

European Commission (2021d) The commission proposes next generation of EU own resources. Press Release. Brussels, 22 December 2021.

European Commission (2022) Communication from the commission to the European parliament, the European council, the council, the European economic and social committee and the committee of the regions. REPowerEU Plan. COM (2022) 230 final. Brussels, 18.5.2022.

European Commission (n.d.a) Cohesion fund. [Viewed 10 July 2022]. Available from https://ec.europa.eu/regional_policy/en/funding/cohesion-fund/

European Commission (n.d.b) Operating budgetary balance (%GNI) [Viewed 20 July 2022]. Available from https://ec.europa.eu/info/publications/operating-budgetary-balance-gni_en

European Commission (n.d.c) Priorities for 2021–2027 [Viewed 21 July 2022]. Available from https://ec.europa.eu/regional_policy/en/policy/how/priorities

European Commission, OECD and IMF (2021) *Green Budgeting: Towards Common Principles*. November 2021. Luxembourg: Publications Office of the European Union.

European Commission and von der Leyen, U. (2019) *A Union That Strives for More: My Agenda for Europe: Political Guidelines for the Next European Commission 2019–2024*. Publications Office. Directorate-General for Communication.

European Council (2020) Negotiating the EU long-term budget [Viewed 2 July 2022]. Available from: https://www.consilium.europa.eu/en/policies/the-eu-budget/negotiating-the-long-term-eu-budget/

European Council (2021) Qualified majority [Viewed 4 July 2022]. Available from: https://www.consilium.europa.eu/en/council-eu/voting-system/qualified-majority/

European Council (2022) Long-term EU budget 2021–2027 and recovery package. Available from: https://www.consilium.europa.eu/en/policies/the-eu-budget/long-term-eu-budget-2021-2027/

European Court of Auditors (2022) *Climate Spending in the 2014–2020 EU Budget. Not as High as Reported*. Special Report 09/2022. Luxembourg.

European Environment Agency (2021) *Trends and Projections in Europe* 2021. EEA Report No 13/2021. Copenhagen.

European Network for Rural Development (2021) LEADER/CLLD explained. LEADER Toolkit. European Commission.

European Parliament (2013) History of own-resources system. *EU Affairs* [Viewed 14 July 2022]. Available from: https://www.europarl.europa.eu/news/en/headlines/eu-affairs/20130723STO17551/history-of-own-resources-system

Eurostat (2021) Environmental tax revenues [Viewed 27 August 2021]. Available from: https://ec.europa.eu/eurostat/databrowser/view/ENV_AC_TAX__custom_1251537/default/table?lang=en

Farrel, M. (2004) Regional integration and cohesion – Lessons from Spain and Ireland in the EU, *Journal of Asian Economics*, 14 (6): 927–946.

Fuest, C., Heinemann, F. and Ungerer, M. (2015) Reforming the financing of the European Union: A proposal, *Intereconomics,* EU Budget, ZBW-Leibniz Information Centre for Economics, 288–293.

Dobreva, A. (2018) Multiannual financial framework 2021–2027: Commission proposal. Initial comparison with the current MFF. European Parliament Research Service (EPRS). Briefing PE 621.864 – May 2018.

Heinemann, F. and Weiss, S. (2018) The EU budget and common agricultural policy beyond 2020: Seven more years of money for nothing? *EconPol*, Working Paper. September 2018. IFO Institute.

Hristov, J., Clough, Y., Sahlin, U. et al. (2020) Impacts of the EU's common agricultural policy "greening" reform on agricultural development, biodiversity, and ecosystem services, *Applied Economic Perspectives and Policy*, 42 (4): 716–738.

Hudetz, A., Mumberd, A., Nerudova′, D. and Schratzenstaller, M. (2017) Reform needs and options in the EU system of own resources, *Empirica*, 44 (2017): 609–613.

Inforegio (2008) *EU Cohesion Policy 1988–2008: Investing in Europe's Future.* Inforegio Panorama, No. 26, June 2008. European Union Regional Policy.

Knudsen, A.-C. L. (2012) Chapter 5. The 1970 and 1975 budget treaties: Enhancing the democratic architecture of the community. In Laursen, F. (ed) *Designing the European Union. From Paris to Lisbon.* London: Palgrave Macmillan: 98–123.

Kołodziejski, M. (2022) European Regional Development Fund. Fact Sheets of the European Union – 2022, 03/2022. European Parliament.

Kowal, A. and Przekota, G. (2021) VAT efficiency – A discussion on the VAT system in the European Union, *Sustainability*, 13 (2021): 4768.

Laursen, F. (2019) Budgetary treaties and European union politics [Viewed 6 July 2022]. Available from: https://oxfordre.com/view/10.1093/acrefore/9780190228637.001.0001/acrefore-9780190228637-e-1095

Lima, M. C. and Cardenete, M. A. (2008) The impact of European structural funds in the South of Spain, *European Planning Studies*, 16 (10): 1445–1457.

Manzella, G. P. and Mendez, C. (2009) The turning points of EU Cohesion policy, Report Working Paper, *In the Context of the Report 'An Agenda for a Reformed Cohesion Policy'*. Available from: https://strathprints.strath.ac.uk/38743/1/8_manzella_final_formatted.pdf

Matthews, A. (2012) The political economy of eliminating sugar quotas in 2015. *CAP Reform,* Available from: https://capreform.eu/the-political-economy-of-eliminating-sugar-quotas-in-2015/

Mazur, S. (2019) Annual EU budgetary procedure. An introduction to the steps in the EP. European Parliament Research Service (EPRS). Briefing. PE 640.129 – July 2019

Mrak, M. (2018) European Union Budget, in *The New Palgrave Dictionary of Economics* (third edition). London: Macmillan Publishers. https://doi.org/10.1057/978-1-349-95189-5

Official Journal of the European Union (2007) *Treaty of Lisbon,* amending the treaty on European union and the treaty establishing the European community. 2007/C 306/01. 17.12.2007.

Official Journal of the European Union (2013) Regulation (EU) No 1300/2013 of the European parliament and of the council of 17 December 2013 on the Cohesion Fund and repealing Council Regulation (EC) No 1084/2006.

Official Journal of the European Union (2021a) Regulation (EU) 2021/1056 of the European parliament and of the council of 24 June 2021 establishing the just transition fund. 30.6.2021.

Official Journal of the European Union (2021b) Regulation (EU) 2021/241 of the European parliament and of the council of 12 February 2021 establishing the recovery and resilience facility. 18.2.2021.

Schratzenstaller, M. (2013) The EU own resources system – Reform needs and options, *Intereconomics,* 48 (5): 303–313.

Schwarcz, A. (2012) *Reform of the EU Own Resources*, In-depth analysis requested by the BUDG committee, European Parliament. PE 690.963 – March 2021.

Skerritt, D. J., Arthur, R., Ebrahim, N. et al. (2020) A 20-year retrospective on the provision of fisheries subsidies in the European Union, *ICES Journal of Marine Science,* 77 (7–8): 2741–2752.

Statista (2022) European Union: Operating budgetary balances in 2020, by member state (in billion euros).

Stec, M. and Grzebyk, M. (2018) The implementation of the Strategy Europe 2020 objectives in European Union countries: The concept analysis and statistical evaluation, *Quality & Quantity*, 52 (2018): 119–133.

University of Cincinnati (2021) Intergovernmental Organisations (IGOs): The European Union [Viewed 2 July 2022]. Available from: https://guides.libraries.uc.edu/c.php?g=222419&p=1472111

Weil, G. L. (1967) The merger of the institutions of the European communities, *American Journal of International Law*, 61 (1): 57–65. https://doi.org/10.2307/2196831

Wieland, V. (2022) Overview of how major economies have responded to the Covid-19 pandemic. Growth trajectories, debt sustainability, best practices. European Parliament. Economic Governance Support Unit. Directorate-General for Internal Policies. PE 689.450 – February 2022.

Witham, T. (2022) How Europe is using VAT to tackle cost of living crisis. *Innovate Tax,* 14 July [Viewed 16 July 2022]. Available from: https://innovatetax.com/how-europe-is-using-vat-to-tackle-cost-of-living-crisis/

3 Specific EU programmes for environmental protection and sustainable transitions

Introduction

In the previous chapters it has been established that the European integration process has not been easy and that when it comes to matters of money there has been an evolution in the needs, size and source of funding required. Bearing in mind that none of the founding Treaties included environment as a policy priority, one could wonder how is it that environment is the only EU policy area that works through multiannual action programmes (Krämer, 2020) since 1973, much earlier than the Multiannual Financial Frameworks (MFFs) used to set up the expenditure ceilings in the EU budget, in place since 1988. A simple answer, corroborated by its mention in academic literature (Correljé et al., 2007; Halmaghi, 2016; Hey, 2007) would be the influence of the international context, after the celebration of the first UN Conference on the Human Environment in Stockholm in 1972. It brought as a result the Stockholm Declaration, with principles that highlighted environmental issues to become a major part of international concerns, and an 'Action Plan', which basically grouped the Declaration's recommendations in three components: a global environmental assessment programme, environmental management activities and supporting measures (UN, 1973). As the name indicates, recommendations are not binding, and the same can be said about the EU Environmental Action Programmes (EAPs), even if they contain sets of planned activities (Hey, 2007). They could be better classified as frameworks for action, setting priority areas, and since the launch of the first EU Sustainable Development Strategy in 2001, they became another element contributing to environmental policy integration and the achievement of the strategy goals (Sarti and St. John, 2019). Another difference with the MFFs is that these are considered long-term programmes, while the EAPs are considered medium-term plans (Holzinger et al., 2006), at least until 1993, since their duration was four to six years. Longer programmes have been approved from 1993 onwards, with the last ones attempting to run parallelly to the MFFs. One problem in this respect is that there is a mismatch between the MFF periods and the Commission mandates, so we do not have one EAP shaped by each new Commission, and nothing ensures that each Commission will feel compelled to support an EAP that has been developed by a predecessor (Trinomics, 2019).

DOI: 10.4324/9781003224785-4

When it comes to the funding of environment-related initiatives, Chapter 2 provided a summary of environmental aspects covered by a number of EU policies with specific budget allocations, including the Structural and Cohesion Funds, or the European Agricultural Fund for Rural Development (Farmer, 2012). However, since 1992 the EU has its own funding instrument for the environment, called L'Instrument Financier pour l'Environnement (LIFE), with a modest but increasing budget allocation, and with a pluriannual (multiannual) working framework.

The following sections will be dedicated to a historical overview of the EAPs, the LIFE funding instrument and other programmes with specific allocations for the protection of the environment and the fight against climate change in the EU, looking at the rationale behind them and their connection with other EU aims and targets, particularly those related to economic growth.

The EU Environmental Action Programmes

The early years

The first EAP was approved in 1973 and has been the shortest in duration, covering the period between 1973 and 1976 (Official Journal of the European Communities [OJEC], 1973). In previous years, there had been a few directives addressing specific issues related to pollution, but this programme is seen by many as the beginning of what we know today as the EU environmental policy (Deters, 2019). The awareness over emerging environmental issues related to pollution and the overexploitation of resources had permeated the international community, culminating in the Stockholm Declaration, but it cannot be ignored that the conference that resulted in said Declaration was framed as one on 'human' environment, and the language used revolved around the improvement of human environment as something that affects peoples' well-being and economic development (UN, 1973). It is easily arguable then that the justification of environmental protection has an anthropocentric rationale, with economic development being the underlying goal. Similarly, the first EAP established the argument that 'economic development, prosperity and the protection of the environment are mutually interdependent' (Hey, 2007), thus providing a justification for actions related to environmental protection on the basis of their contributions to the single market (Deters, 2019) or their connection to international trade issues (Knill et al., 2020). The reader may want to reflect on what type of sustainability, weak or strong, this approach is portraying (see Chapter 1).

This first EAP establishes a programme of action in three main areas: reduction of pollution and nuisances, improvement of the environment and community action and joint action by the Member States in international organisations (OJEC, 1973). As main objectives of this programme, we can name (Halmaghi, 2016):

- Preventing and reducing environmental degradation
- Maintenance of ecological balance
- Rational use of the non-renewable natural resources

- Inclusion of the environment component in decisions for the realisation of any activity
- Public awareness on environmental issues (education and information)
- Correlation of EU environmental policy objectives with the policies of the Member States.

It is worth noting that this EAP explicitly mentions the application of the 'polluter pays principle', but avoiding distortions to trade and investment (OJEC, 1973: 9), and it includes specific provisions for the production of energy, acknowledging the pollution emerging from the activity (OJEC, 1973: 22). Being the first programme, there was a lot of emphasis on research to establish a good knowledge base, and the determination of quality standards, to make a comprehensive assessment of the causes of pollution, the costs of addressing negative environmental consequences, and the impact of environmental objectives in other policies (Hey, 2007). It could be then concluded that this was a good starting point with a realistic and gradual approach, even if there was no mention of how actions were going to be financed, nor specific instructions for implementation.

While the first EAP highlighted the need for a Community Environmental Policy, the second EAP (1977–1981) distinguished between actions that require implementation at Community level and those that should be carried out by Member States. Member States would supervise the proper execution of the projects under their responsibility, but the Council would keep powers of coordination (OJEC, 1977). In essence, this EAP is a continuation of the first one with an extension of the areas of action from water, waste and air to nature protection, but it has also been criticised for the loose and generic approach to definitions, particularly with regard to preventive measures (Trinomics, 2019). An additional issue was the economic crisis situation at the time (the two oil crises of the 1970s and the economic crisis of 1981–1983, with their associated inflation and unemployment challenges), so the overall assessment of the two EAPs is that their achievements were very limited in terms of implementation of actions (Halmaghi, 2016; Hey, 2007). In spite of the limitations, this period saw a good deal of legislative initiatives, with a number of directives approved, including one on biological screening of the population for lead (77/312/EEC) and a Council Directive on waste (75/442/EEC). Some of these initiatives mentioned the EAPs as part of their motivation (Trinomics, 2019).

The third EAP (1982–1986) marks a step forward. It highlights the need for integration of environmental concerns in other policy areas; it puts more responsibility on implementation of actions by the Member States, reserving Community action only when it is more effective than the national level; and for the first time acknowledges the need for resources specifically set aside for the environment, with an introduction of a small symbolic figure in the Commission's draft budget proposal of 1982 (OJEC, 1983). Importantly, it establishes the introduction of environmental impact assessments as a policy instrument, particularly for planning, and introduces the regional dimension in EU environmental policymaking, as it mentions the need to account for the differences in the levels of development of

European regions (Correljé et al., 2007). While the previous EAPs had always remarked the need to account for economic, financial and social consequences of environmental measures, bringing together the three pillars of sustainability, the third EAP gives an added level of consideration to the socio-economic element, indicating the potential of environmental protection initiatives to contribute to employment creation in a situation of worsening economic conditions (OJEC, 1983: 4), but also carefully intending not to create an added financial burden for older companies, which would jeopardise jobs (OJEC, 1983: 7). This period saw the enlargement of the Community to Spain and Portugal, adding the protection of the Mediterranean as part of the Community's tasks (OJEC, 1983). Said protection was to be part of international efforts and the European strategy would aim to align with those of the United Nations Environment Programme (UNEP), the International Union for the Conservation of Nature (IUCN) and World Wide Fund for Nature (WWF) through their World Conservation Strategy, considered the first global strategy for sustainable development (Hey, 2007) before the term was actually used.

From the Single European Act to the Eastern Europe enlargements

The Single European Act, signed in 1986 and entering into force in 1987, constitutes a turning point for environmental action (Hey, 2007) as it provides legal basis to a Community environmental policy, introducing its own title (IV) in the European Economic Community (EEC) Treaty (Correljé et al., 2007; Deters, 2019). This period begins with the fourth EAP (1987–1992), calling for additional measures and the harmonisation of existing ones, as Member States kept enacting divergent regulations that distorted the movement of goods across borders, becoming a barrier for the correct functioning of the single (internal) market and effectively free trade (Hey, 2007; Trinomics, 2019). This is a period in which qualified majority voting instead of unanimity was introduced for some environmental regulations, as well as the use of the cooperation procedure for policy proposals. This created bargaining power between greener Member States and Commission and Council, also providing a role for the European Parliament. Initially there had been a ban to enact at country level more restrictive environmental protection regulations than those approved at Community level, but this was softened, and the mix ended up having situations in which more environmentally stringent regulations were allowed both on environmental and market grounds (Deters, 2019). While financing of projects could be done at Community level, through Structural and other funds, particularly for big infrastructure projects, it was expected that Member States would also dedicate their own funding to achieve the aims of the EAP (OJEC, 1987: 44). Importantly, the fourth EAP mentions for the first time the possibility of using market instruments in addition to regulations (and the environmental impact assessments introduced by the previous EAP) for the improvement or maintenance of environmental quality, including taxes and tradeable permits, both to be covered later in this book. This marked a change in governance from command-and-control regulation to economic instruments and 'context-oriented' governance (Holzinger et al., 2006). Interestingly, 1987 is declared the European Year of the Environment (OJEC, 1987: 40), coinciding with the publication of the Brundtland report that coined the worldwide known definition of sustainable development.

From 1992, the EAPs receive specific titles or names (Halmaghi, 2016), with the fifth EAP being called 'Towards Sustainability' (OJEC, 1993). Several significant changes can be observed: the programme does not refer only to action but also to policy, and for the first time sustainable development is included as part of the strategy (OJEC, 1993). This EAP was prepared in parallel to the Rio Conference (1992) and its subsequent launch of Agenda 21 (Trinomics, 2019). It is organised in themes: climate change, acidification and air quality, protection of nature and biodiversity, management of water resources, the urban environment, coastal zones and waste management (OJEC, 1993). Also, for the first time we see long-term objectives and performance targets (both indicative) as well as specific targeted economic sectors: Industry, Energy, Transport, Agriculture and Tourism (OJEC, 1993: 14), including mention of the need to reduce the consumption of non-renewable energy. With regard to finance, there is a mention of specific financial support mechanisms, and this is the period in which LIFE starts working, with its first iteration (LIFE I) covering 1992 to 1995 (EC, 2021a). This is another deviation from previous programmes, in which legislative instruments dominated the support for action. With LIFE arrangements however, we can see one of the mismatches previously mentioned with regard to timings, since the fifth EAP covers the period 1993–2000, so LIFE II (1996–1999) and part of LIFE III (2000–2006) (EC, 2021a) are necessarily covering the needs of a bigger framework for environmental protection action.

This is quite an active period for the EU, with a new Treaty on the European Union approved in 1992 and entering into force in 1993 (Maastricht Treaty), solidifying the competences of the EU on environmental policy. It makes sustainability one of the guiding principles of the EU and brings the precautionary principle to the forefront of policymaking (Correljé et al., 2007). Some (Holzinger et al., 2006) argue that this period also indicates a change in the governance approach used for EU policymaking, not only due to the diversification of policy instruments, but also through the involvement of more stakeholders, remarking the shared responsibility for action of both public and private actors, including citizens. This period also saw an enlargement of the EU that not many mention, with the accession of Austria, Finland and Sweden in 1995. On the one hand, this not only required an increase in the funding allocated for environmental protection (EC, 2021a) but also contributed to the production of more environmental legislation than ever before (Deters, 2019).

The sixth EAP took a long time to be approved, under the title 'Environment 2010: Our Future, Our Choice' (EC, 2001a). It was negotiated at the same time as the accession of the Eastern European countries and includes provisions for the adoption of policies to contribute to sustainable development in those countries, ensuring that their environmental assets (biodiversity) are both sustained and protected (OJEC, 2002). It is also longer in duration than previous programmes, as it covers ten years (2002–2012) despite the mention of 2010 as benchmark, and it has three important contextual background highlights:

- The Treaty of Amsterdam, signed in 1997 and entering into force in 1999, with more clear references to sustainable development and going a step further in terms of environmental policy goals, requiring 'high level' of protection and improvement of environmental quality, and explicitly including the integration of environmental protection requirements in the rest of policy areas (Correljé et al., 2007).
- The Kyoto Protocol, approved also in 1997 (though it did not enter into force until 2005), framing all actions of the EAP with regard to climate change (OJEC, 2002: 5–14) and reinforcing the international dimension of the actions required to achieve sustainable development.
- The first EU Sustainable Development Strategy, proposed in 2001 (EC, 2001b), even if not completely accepted by EU leaders and subject of subsequent revisions and multiple criticisms. It provided a new official step for environmental policy integration, linking its action to the Lisbon Strategy for jobs and growth (2000) and reinforcing the need to address the three pillars of sustainability hand in hand (Farmer, 2012), with the reduction of poverty as part of Cohesion Policy as the main goal from the social point of view. The monitoring of this Strategy however, focused more on the social and economic indicators set by the Lisbon Strategy, with environmental indicators seemingly appearing as an afterthought (Pallemaerts et al., 2007).

The sixth EAP in theory benefits from another initiative of the EU Commission at the time, the simplification in the regulatory procedures under the Better Regulation agenda, intended to contribute to improving the governance system under the principles of openness, participation, accountability, effectiveness and coherence (Hjerp et al., 2010). This is what informed the organisation under thematic strategies of the EAP (see Table 3.1 for details). The shortcomings identified through the evaluation of the sixth EAP provided the background for the development of the seventh EAP (OJEU, 2013a), with this programme running in parallel to the recently completed MFF (2014–2020). In this case, the organisation is a bit different but continuing with the use of themes. The seventh EAP has nine priority objectives, organised under three rubrics: thematic priorities, with objectives 1–3 (similar to the priority areas of the sixth EAP); the enabling framework, with objectives 4–7 (similar to the thematic strategies of the sixth EAP); and objectives 8 and 9 grouped under 'meeting local, regional and global challenges' (OJEU, 2013a). A comparison between the sixth and seventh EAPs can be found in Table 3.1.

These last two programmes, particularly the seventh, constitute a new milestone in EU environmental policy governance, since they explicitly refer to both ex-ante evaluation and ex-post evaluation of the measures implemented (Schoenefeld and Jordan, 2019), while the evaluation had been limited to the planning stage (i.e. ex-ante) in the past. This aligns with the accountability principle that has been embedded as part of the EAPs, which with time will hopefully contribute not just to

Table 3.1 Priorities and thematic strategies of the Sixth and Seventh EAPs

Sixth EAP (2002–2012)		*Seventh EAP (2013–2020)*	
Priority areas	*Thematic strategies*	*Priority areas (thematic priorities)*	*Thematic strategies (enabling framework)*
Climate change Nature and biodiversity Environment and health and quality of life Natural resources and wastes	Soil protection Protection and conservation of the marine environment Sustainable use of pesticides Strengthen a coherent and integrated policy on air pollution Integrated horizontal approach across Community policies and improvement of urban environment Sustainable use and management of resources Waste recycling	To protect, conserve and enhance the Union's natural capital Turning the Union into a resource-efficient, green and competitive low-carbon economy Safeguarding the Union's citizens from environment-related pressures and risks to health and well-being	Maximise the benefits of Union environment legislation by improving implementation Improve the knowledge and evidence base for Union environment policy Secure investment for environment and climate policy and address environmental externalities Improve environmental integration and policy coherence

Source: OJEC (2002) and OJEU (2013a).

make funding allocation more efficient, but also to ensure that implemented actions do not deviate from commitments. For the seventh EAP, there was a more comprehensive consultation process with other EU institutions (the Committee of the Regions and the European Economic and Social Committee) and its development could be qualified as a cooperative process (Trinomics, 2019). This did not prevent, as it was stated in Chapter 2, that a mismatch happened between the budget committed for environmental and climate purposes and what was actually spent.

The latest EAP (2021–2030)

Something that can be noticed with the latest EAPs is that they have been finally approved once the period they are supposed to cover has already started, which means the extension in the duration of some of the preceding programmes, and it gives an idea of how difficult it may become to reach agreement even in an area that in principle enjoys overarching support.

The eighth EAP is no different in that regard. It was proposed by the Commission in 2020, but it has only entered into force in May 2022 (OJEU, 2022). The evaluation of the seventh EAP was generally positive (EC, 2019) but it also reported shortcomings, including the still insufficient integration of environmental concerns in other policy areas, and the need for more consideration of social issues, linking environment with social policy and having regard for the impacts on vulnerable groups, jobs, social inclusion and inequality (EC, 2019: 8). Interestingly, it recognises that the expenditure on environmental protection has remained stagnant at around 2% of the GDP (of the EU25) and that failure to implement environmental legislation in the Member States costs the EU economy around €55 billion a year (EC, 2019: 7). This goes back to the economic aspect or pillar being put at the forefront of the argumentation to incentivise change in behaviour. The eighth EAP aims to overcome some of these shortcomings, using the term 'systemic' solutions (OJEU, 2022: 23) and embedding its framework for action within the European Green Deal (EGD). It establishes the creation of a new monitoring mechanism to measure the effectiveness of the EAP, with indicators and governance tools that will not only look at environmental aspects, but also at economic and social ones (OJEU, 2022: 28). Following the steps of the seventh EAP, the eighth one reinforces the long-term goal of achieving climate neutrality by 2050 (living well within planetary boundaries) and also aligns itself with the UN Agenda for 2030 and the SDGs (OJEU, 2022: 29). As in previous occasions, we find thematic priority objectives (OJEU, 2022: 30):

- Achieve the 2030 greenhouse gas (GHG) emission reduction target and climate neutrality by 2050
- Enhance adaptative capacity, strengthening resilience and reducing vulnerability to climate change
- Advance towards a well-being economy where growth is regenerative, decoupling economic growth from resource use and environmental degradation, accelerating the transition to a non-toxic circular economy
- Pursue zero pollution in order to achieve a toxic-free environment for air, water and soil, as well as in relation to light and noise pollution, protecting the health and well-being of people, animals and ecosystems [a nice addition that deviates from the typical anthropocentric focus]
- Protect, preserve and restore marine and terrestrial biodiversity and biodiversity of inland waters by halting and reversing biodiversity loss and improving the state of ecosystems (enhancing natural capital)
- Reduce environmental and climate pressures related to production and consumption, particularly in the areas of energy, industry, buildings and infrastructure, mobility, tourism, international trade and the food system [expanding the number of policy areas where action is required, in line with the systemic approach]

It can be observed that some of these priorities already existed in previous EAPs (see Table 3.1), so one would question to which extent the EAPs are fit for purpose if each of them reiterates the need for action in the same areas, indicating insufficient progress. It also bears the question of which mechanisms or tools the EAPs have to enforce measures' implementation, but this chapter has already pointed out that the EAPs have generally had an indicative purpose so it may be the case that Member States consider non-compliance or lack of implementation as having no consequence. This view is behind the thought of those who argue for the elimination of the EAPs or a substantial change in their design (Krämer, 2020). Interestingly, the eighth EAP has incorporated some of the proposals for change, including the need to establish infringement procedures in cases where EU environmental law implementation is lacking (OJEU, 2022: Art. 3). In anticipation of the UN resolution that recognises the right to a clean, healthy and sustainable environment as a human right (UN, 2022), the eighth EAP already recognises said right (OJEU, 2022), adopting a 'Think Sustainability First' approach and the 'do no significant harm' principle, as set out in the Taxonomy Regulation that was mentioned in Chapter 1. It could be argued then that this EAP becomes a new steppingstone, in which for the first time, at least in paper, economic principles and arguments lose some of their stellar role to let social and environmental principles move forward to enable a more balanced approach towards the achievement of a true sustainability transition, in which the three pillars sustain with equal footing the policy decision-making process. The key, however, for said transition, will be if the policy process is translated into action that triggers behavioural change in all stakeholders, and it is too early to assess if this will be the case.

Environmental action funding: 30 years of LIFE and more

It has already been mentioned that LIFE is the EU specific funding instrument for the environment. Before its appearance in 1992, the EU was providing very limited funding for environmental-related purposes, even if the approval of the Birds Directive in 1979 already called for the co-financing of the management of special protected areas to preserve birdlife (EC, 2021a). The 1980s saw the approval of two Regulations for the establishment of a specific financial instrument, Action Communautaire pour l'Environnement (ACE), which provided funding between 1984 and 1991, to support projects in three areas: the development of clean technologies, the development of new techniques for measuring and monitoring the natural environment, and the protection of habitats of endangered species of particular importance for the EU (EC, 2021a). When it was first launched in 1992, LIFE (I) had a budget of only ECU[1] 400 million, but this was only one-tenth of the estimated environment-related expenditure for the period 1988–1993, and the rest was 'mainstreamed' through the Structural Funds (Farmer, 2012). The second iteration (LIFE II), running between 1996 and 1999, saw an increase of the funding to ECU 450 million, to account for the enlargement to Austria, Finland and Sweden (EC, 2021a) and began an organisational structure for the projects into categories that still continue to these days. The initial categories were LIFE-Nature, LIFE-Environment and LIFE-Third countries, with most of the budget allocated to the first two (46% each), and with Romania being the first candidate country at the time to participate (National Fund for Environmental Protection and Water Management, n.d.). LIFE III was initially meant to cover between 2000 and 2004, but it was extended up to 2006 to avoid a gap between the end of the programme and the following MFF (2007–2013), adding €317 million to the €640 million originally allocated (EC, 2021a), and showing an important increase in funding dedicated exclusively to the environment. Similarly to the EAPs, the funding provided by

LIFE is expected to co-finance the projects, which means that budget from the Member States is necessary for successful implementation. On average the EU would cover around 50% of the cost of the projects (National Fund for Environmental Protection and Water Management, n.d.), and importantly, making use of economic jargon, the Commission expects the projects to have 'value added' for the EU (Farmer, 2012). An example is the conservation of natural habitats such as the Natura 2000 network, which continued through LIFE-Nature, or the encouragement of actions that involved more than one Member State (EC, 2021a).

The fourth phase of the LIFE instrument, called LIFE+, brought a few changes. It was the product of numerous discussions between the Commission and the Parliament, particularly with regard to the governance system for the projects: Originally the approval of projects was centralised in the Commission, who would have liked to see a decentralisation into the Member States, but the Parliament feared this would water down the EU value added of the projects, and in the end the compromise resulted on the programme being centrally managed by the Commission, with 78% of the budget available for co-funding of projects in the Member States (Farmer, 2012). The Commission also wanted to see LIFE-Nature disappear, with the funding for its purposes allocated through other means such as the Structural Funds, but the Parliament succeeded in its demands and in the end the three categories for funding allocation for the period 2007–2013 became (EC, 2021a):

- LIFE+ Nature and Biodiversity
- LIFE+ Environment Policy and Governance
- LIFE+ Information and Communication

The total budget allocated was €2.143 billion, with the novelty of establishing funding for educational and information campaigns under the third category (National Fund for Environmental Protection and Water Management, n.d.). The allocation per Member State is made based on a number of indicators: population size and density, area of Sites of Community Interest (SCIs) under the Habitats Directive, and the percentage of the Member State's territory occupied by SCIs. This makes for significant differences, with Spain being allocated €140 million during the period, in comparison with €14 million for Cyprus (Farmer, 2012). An example of the use of LIFE funding by one Member State can be found in Box 3.1.

Box 3.1 Case study: LIFE programme in Finland

Finland is geographically the sixth largest country in Europe (Country Reports, 2022) but its population size and density are not as large, with 5.5 million people and a density of 18.1 people per square km (Biodiversity. Europa, n.d.). As it has been mentioned in the main text, its accession to the EU took place in 1995, and since then it has been an active participant in LIFE consecutive phases. In fact it has benefited from LIFE since 1992

(COWI, 2009). The country has 16,668 protected areas, which account for 13.2% of the land and 9.83% of marine waters. Of this total, 21.23% is part of the Natura 2000 network, with 4.6% only protected by Finnish national laws, and an overwhelming 74.17% counting on both protective frameworks (Biodiversity.Europa, n.d.). With these characteristics one could think that the number of projects financed under LIFE instruments would be low, but this is not the case. Between 1996 and 2006, LIFE co-financed 92 projects in Finland (45 Nature projects and 47 Environment projects), contributing with €58.7 million (COWI, 2009). In total the most recent figures show that LIFE has funded 155 projects in Finland whose costs amount to €389 million, of which the EU has contributed with €197.6 million (CINEA, 2022). It would appear that there has been a higher concentration of projects in the first decades of the existence of the instrument but this should not be perceived as lack of commitment to environmental protection, since the accession of Austria, Finland and Sweden brought the approval of more environmental protection regulation than ever before (Deters, 2019). The proportion of protected territory is lower than in other EU countries, bearing in mind that 74% of the territory is composed of forest ecosystems, but then 53% of the protected area network covers said forest ecosystems (Biodiversity.Europa, n.d.). The overall evaluation of the projects that LIFE has contributed to is positive, since it has allowed the purchase of big plots of land to give them a protected status, which would not have been possible, or not in the same proportion, without LIFE support (COWI, 2009). The bulk of the projects would fall under two categories if the classification for the latest LIFE iteration is used: Nature & biodiversity, and Circular economy & quality of life (CINEA, 2022). One of the projects currently being developed is CANEMURE (Towards Carbon Neutral Municipalities), approved in 2018 and expected to last until 2024, with a budget of €15.3 million (Finnish Environment Institute, 2018). The project touches upon many of the EGD purposes, with the promotion of smart and low-carbon transport, the production of distributed renewable energy and the improvement of energy efficiency. In addition to practical measures the project will run courses and training, will create cooperation networks and disseminate good practices (Finnish Environment Institute, 2018).

The governance of this funding instrument includes a mid-term evaluation and then a final evaluation at the end of the funding period. LIFE+ was evaluated one year before it ended, as it included recommendations for the proposal of the subsequent programme (2014–2020). The overall evaluation was positive, with highlights such as the participation of Non-Governmental Organisations (NGOs), the preference for integrated projects across Member States and the increase in the weight of EU value added in the projects' selection process, with one of the main criticisms being the excessive administrative burden (Williams, 2012).

The period 2014–2020 was covered through a Regulation approved at the end of 2013 (OJEU, 2013b) which changed slightly the coverage to include climate change. The main categories for funding are precisely simplified into environment and climate action, each of them with their own priority areas. Interestingly, this period is subdivided into two multiannual work programmes, one for 2014–2017 and one for 2018–2020, with their own budget allocations per priority area (EC, 2021a):

- 2014–2017: Environment – €1.1 billion; Climate Action – €0.36 billion
- 2018–2020: Environment – €1,243.81 million; Climate Action – €413.25 million

While the main funding from the LIFE programme is allocated through grants, this period saw the piloting of a new financial instrument, the Natural Capital Financing Facility (NCFF), which is managed jointly by the Commission and the European Investment Bank (EIB). It supports projects related to biodiversity and climate adaptation through loans and investments backed by an EU guarantee, under the condition that the projects would generate revenues or contribute to cost savings (EC, n.d.). This instrument is now being replaced by InvestEU (EIB, 2022).

Another financial instrument launched during this period was the Private Finance for Energy Efficiency (PF4EE). Also managed by the EIB, in this case the purpose is to provide access to affordable commercial financing for energy efficiency investments (EIB, 2014), including but not limited to, the National Energy Efficiency Action Plans of the Member States (EC, n.d.). The PF4EE combines credit risk protection through what is called a cash-collateral (risk sharing facility), with long-term finance provided by the EIB (EIB, 2014). This instrument is also being replaced in the current MFF by InvestEU (to be covered later in this book).

The latest LIFE programme was approved in 2021 (OJEU, 2021a), with the largest ever allocation of funding, €5.4 billion for the period 2021–2027, running in parallel to the current MFF. Similarly to its predecessor, it also counts on a multiannual work programme covering a shorter period, 2021–2024. It keeps the two main division of priorities between environment and climate action, with four sub-categories: Nature and Biodiversity, and Circular Economy and Quality of Life (under the Environment category); and Climate Change Mitigation and Adaptation, and Clean Energy Transition (under the Climate Action category) (OJEU, 2021a). Some projects have already been approved, and in line with the previously dominant economic language, they are presented as investments (i.e. a return is expected). The package includes 132 projects mobilising €562 million, with a major transnational project involving Belgium, Germany, Ireland, the Netherlands and Poland, to restore degraded peatlands, being highlighted as an example (EC, 2021b).

The current LIFE programme is fully aligned with the goals of the EGD and this is visible already in its preamble (OJEU, 2021a). Importantly, it pays a lot of attention to its governance and the avoidance of funding duplication. With regard to said governance, even before the programme was approved it was decided that its management would be in charge of a new institution, the European Climate,

Infrastructure and Environment Executive Agency (CINEA), as part of the new set of executive agencies implementing the programmes included in the MFF 2021–2027 (OJEU, 2021b). The CINEA will absorb the management of actions related to environment, climate action and infrastructure that remain unfinished, as a legacy, and were part of the responsibility of the previous executive agencies (mainly the Innovation and Networks Executive Agency and the Executive Agency for SMEs). It will be in charge of the implementation of the following parts of the EU programmes (OJEU, 2021b):

- Innovation Fund
- Connecting Europe Facility: Transport and Energy
- Horizon Europe: Pillar II, cluster 5: Climate, Energy and Mobility
- LIFE: Nature and biodiversity; Circular economy and quality of life; Climate change mitigation and adaptation; Clean energy transition
- Renewable Energy Financing Mechanism
- Public sector loan facility, under the Just Transition Mechanism
- European Maritime, Fisheries and Aquaculture Fund and compulsory contributions to Regional Fisheries Management Organisations (RFMOs) and other international organisations

The delegation of these functions to an executive agency had been already used in the previous financial period, under the assumption that it would be more cost-effective and would allow the continuation of actions and synergies between programmes (OJEU, 2021b). As it can be observed, the programmes go beyond what could be initially understood as part of the remit of an environmental or climate agency.

Other options for the funding of environmental and climate actions

If environmental policy integration is fully embraced, it is possible to fund projects that contribute to the preservation of biodiversity and other environmental and climate objectives through actions out of the remit of environmental or climate policies. It has been already established that the EAPs call for action in a myriad of policies, including social policy, transport policy, industrial policy, agricultural policy or energy policy. Within those policies we can see the implementation of projects in the field, such as rail infrastructures, renewable energy parks, modernisation of farms, coordination of help in case of natural disasters, youth employment programmes, etc. All of them contribute to different sustainability pillars, economic, social and environmental. But one aspect mentioned by all the EAPs is education and research, to promote behavioural change and expand the knowledge base that helps fight pollution or other negative externalities, as well as increase the competitiveness of the EU economies. Education and research have been also part of the areas covered by the different LIFE funding streams, and the regulations of the last two programmes, 2014–2020 and 2021–2027, highlight research and one specific instrument connected to it, the Horizon programme (OJEU, 2013, 2021a).

The funding of research activities has been present in the EU from the outset, but in a programmatic way the first Framework Programme was established in the 1980s, covering 1984–1987 (Jeupiste, n.d.). Similarly to the EAPs and LIFE, the Research Framework Programmes have been working with thematic priorities, but in this case the environment was not the largest beneficiary of the research efforts, with energy absorbing the largest proportion of funding, at least during the first years (Secretariat for Education, Research and Innovation [SERI], n.d.). The last two Framework Programmes, Horizon 2020 (FP8) and the current Horizon Europe (FP9) are organised around pillars, with one of the pillars defining the thematic areas. In the case of Horizon 2020, these were identified as societal challenges (SC) and included (EC, 2017):

- SC1: health, demographic change and well-being
- SC2: food security, sustainable agriculture and forestry, marine and maritime and inland water research and the bioeconomy
- SC3: secure, clean and efficient energy
- SC4: smart, green and integrated transport
- SC5: climate action, environment, resource efficiency and raw materials
- SC6: Europe in a changing world – inclusive, innovative and reflective societies
- SC7: secure societies – protecting freedom and security of Europe and its citizens

For the current Framework Programme, the thematic priorities are grouped in six clusters, with what appears to be a merger of the societal challenges two and five into one cluster. These are (EC, 2021c): Health; Culture, Creativity & Inclusive Societies; Civil Security for Society; Digital, Industry & Space; Climate, Energy & Mobility and Food, Bioeconomy, Natural Resources, Agriculture & Environment. The LIFE Programmes Regulations aim for Horizon funding to be complementary to that of LIFE, being used to create synergies and avoid duplication, expecting that the results of the projects funded by Horizon will be made available to the projects funded by LIFE (OJEU, 2013b, 2021a). Even if supposedly 84% of investments in Horizon 2020 addressed Sustainable Development Goals (SDGs), with 30% dedicated to climate change (EC, 2021c), the headlines above listed indicate that a big focus of the EU research and innovation efforts continues being given to energy, which begs questions about the level of complementarity of the actions but more importantly, about the true priorities set by the Commission officials. One could argue that energy is such an important part of the fight against climate change that anything that contributes to improve energy efficiency and reduction of GHG emissions in the energy sector will ultimately benefit the environment and the sustainability transition. The counterargument would be that energy production and consumption is still making use of scarce natural resources (whether it is fossil fuels, uranium for nuclear energy, silica for solar panels, steel and others for wind turbines, water, etc.), and despite efforts in decoupling economic growth from energy consumption, it still holds true that economic growth results in increased energy consumption (Saidi and Hammami, 2015). There are not many voices though, arguing for a reduction in energy consumption, even amidst the current soaring prices (support for innovation that reduces energy use exists – see Abnett, 2021), which ultimately means that natural resources will continue being exploited or overexploited, with direct consequences for the environment, namely the depletion of said natural resources, and the generation of GHGs with their own set of consequences.

Energy policy for a sustainable transition

Under the circumstances depicted in the previous paragraphs it is necessary to ask what the connection between energy and environmental policies in the EU is. To cover all the aspects that energy policy deals with would be impossible even in a whole book, let alone one section in a book chapter, so the following lines will just provide an introduction to some key aspects that will be further developed in other parts of the text.

Energy is at the core of the EU's existence, as the foundational treaties attest (one on coal and steel, and one on nuclear energy), but being a sensitive national topic that most countries connect with national security, the journey towards a Union Energy Policy has not been easy. The environmental aspects related to the production and consumption of energy were not the main concern in the first years of EU Energy Policy. The principal goal was linked to the economic pillar of sustainability, that is, the correct functioning of the internal market, with the liberalisation of gas and electricity (Nowak, 2006) to boost competition and drive energy prices down. There have been gas and electricity directives since the 1990s, and it would be fair to say that none of them have really managed to achieve that full market liberalisation. Some Member States began a transformation of their energy sector early on, with the promotion of renewable energy aided by specific support instruments. However the Commission Communication on An Energy Policy for Europe did not come until 2007 (Mengolini and Masera, 2021), which gives an idea of the complications that common policy in this sector involve. Since the EU adhesion to the Kyoto Protocol, there are more steps towards the environmental aspects of energy policy, with a commitment to reduce the GHG gas emissions coming from the energy sector. This is one of the reasons why the energy sector is one of those originally included as participant in the EU Emissions Trading System (ETS), though the effectiveness of the system is questioned (Canal Vieira et al., 2021). But sometimes contradictions appear in the way sustainability aspects are included in the policy initiatives, like in the Energy Union Package, where energy security and sustainability seem to compete, and the requirement to keep minimum reserves of crude oil or petroleum seems to be at odds with the targets to increase the use of renewable energies (Fernandez, 2018). Social aspects seem to have gained momentum with the EGD (Mengolini and Masera, 2021) in an attempt to build a just transition, with specific aims to fight against energy poverty and empower citizens and communities. In the current cost of living crisis, which has a huge cost of energy component, this becomes even more relevant, but so far it is the prerogative of each individual Member State to exert their national competences in the energy area and approve their own measures (Twindale, 2022). There is not a unified message coming from the EU, though it allows countries to implement emergency measures and already approved a toolkit in October 2021 to help with the increase in energy prices observed at the time.

Most of the market instruments that Part II of this book covers are related to the energy sector, including the feed-in-tariffs, green certificates and the ETS, as market incentives to change behaviour towards a more sustainable one. A question that remains unanswered is if the discourse for energy policy is really aligned with that of environment and climate action, or if due to the inherently economic components of this sector, the discourse needs to have the economic connotation, as only economic benefits highlighted act as sufficient incentive to change behaviour. A possible way forward is likely to be related to the social pillar of sustainability, as unless high policy level decision-making happens, we will see high levels of energy poverty (and food poverty) across Europe in a not so distant future.

Discussion questions

1. To which extent do you think environmental policy integration has been achieved at Member State level? Would that be an indicator of policy implementation success at EU level?
2. Do you agree with those who argue that EAPs are not necessary?
3. Should there be a different set of priorities for the funding of environmental-related actions (i.e. research and development or education before practical development projects)?
4. When it comes about environment, climate and sustainable development action, is it all about funding?
5. What is your view about the multi-level governance of environmental policy in Europe? Where do you think the balance of power sits? Are there stakeholders missing?

Note

1 The ECU (European Currency Unit) was the predecessor of the Euro and was adopted in 1979, as a basket of currencies of the then European Economic Community. It was in use until 1999, only in electronic format, and it was replaced by the Euro at a 1:1 ratio (Eurostat, 2021).

Further readings

Jordan, A. and Gravey, V. (eds) (2021) *Environmental Policy in the EU. Actors, Institutions and Processes*. Earthscan from Routledge. This book provides a nice up-to-date overview of the evolution of EU environmental policies across 50 years of existence, focusing on policy dynamics and the interaction between different actors and institutions, the response to evolving challenges, and the different stages of policymaking.

Langlet, D. and Mahmoudi, S. (2016) *EU Environmental Law and Policy*. Oxford University Press: This book presents the connection between policymaking and the enactment of such policy through specific regulations. With specific consideration to elements of environmental policy, including a summary of the Environmental Action Plans, this book also covers the trade-offs between environmental protection and market functioning.

Burns, C., Tobin, P. and Sewerin, S. (eds) (2019) *The Impact of the Economic Crisis on European Environmental Policy*. Oxford University Press: This book offers an innovative approach to the evaluation of environmental policy through the use of an index that combines the measurement of policy density and intensity. It does so looking into how the economic crisis of 2007–2008 affected environmental policies in a number of EU Member States presented as case studies.

References

Abnett, K. (2021) Factbox: How is the EU responding to record-high energy prices? *Reuters*, 13 October [Viewed 25 July 2021]. Available from: https://www.reuters.com/business/energy/how-is-eu-responding-record-high-energy-prices-2021-10-13/

Biodiversity.Europa (n.d.) Finland. Biodiversity information system for Europe. Partnership between European commission and European environment agency. Available from: https://biodiversity.europa.eu/countries/finland

Canal Vieira, L., Longo, M. and Mura, M. (2021) Are the European manufacturing and energy sectors on track for achieving net-zero emissions in 2050? An empirical analysis, *Energy Policy*, 156 (2021): 112464. https://doi.org/10.1016/j.enpol.2021.112464

CINEA (2022) *LIFE Programme in Finland. Facts and Figures*. European Commission. Last updated 28.03.2022.

Correljé, A., François, D. and Verbeke, T. (2007) Integrating water management and principles of policy: Towards an EU framework? *Journal of Cleaner Production*, 15 (2007): 1499–1506.

Country Reports (2022) Finland. Available from: https://www.countryreports.org/country/Finland/facts.htm

COWI (2009) Ex-post evaluation of projects and activities financed under the LIFE programme. Country-By-Country analysis. Finland. July 2009.

Deters, H. (2019) European environmental policy at 50: Five decades of escaping decision traps? *Environmental Policy and Governance*, 29 (2019): 315–325.

European Commission (2001a) *Commission Proposes New Action Programme for the Environment*. Brussels: Press Release, 24 January 2001, IP/01/102.

European Commission (2001b) Communication from the commission, a sustainable Europe for a better world: A European union strategy for sustainable development (commission's proposal to the Gothenburg European Council). COM (2001) 264 final, Brussels, 15.5.2001.

European Commission (2017) Interim evaluation of horizon 2020. *Commission Staff Working Document*. DG-Research and Innovation.

European Commission (2019) Report from the commission to the European parliament, the council, the European economic and social committee and the committee of the regions on the evaluation of the 7th environment action programme. COM (2019) 233 final, Brussels, 15.5.2019.

European Commission (2021a) The LIFE programme. *Archives*. Available from: https://ec.europa.eu/environment/archives/life/about/index.htm#background

European Commission (2021b) LIFE programme: More than €290 million in EU funding for nature, environment and climate action projects. Press Release IP/21/6178. Brussels, 25.11.2021.

European Commission (2021c) Horizon Europe. The EU research & innovation programme 2021–27. Presentation 19 March 2021.

European Commission (n.d.) LIFE financial instruments. Available from: https://ec.europa.eu/clima/eu-action/funding-climate-action/life-financial-instruments_en

European Investment Bank (2014) Announcement of the new EIB product under the programme for environment and climate action (LIFE) dedicated to energy efficiency investments. December 9th 2014.

European Investment Bank (2022) NCFF-natural capital financing facility. Available from: https://www.eib.org/en/products/mandates-partnerships/ncff/index.htm

Eurostat (2021) Glossary: European currency unit (ECU). Statistics Explained.

Farmer, A. M. (ed) (2012) *Manual of European Environmental Policy*, Institute for European Environmental Policy (IEEP). London: Routledge.

Fernandez, R. M. (2018) Conflicting energy policy priorities in EU energy governance, *Journal of Environmental Studies and Sciences*, 8 (2018): 239–248. https://doi.org/10.1007/s13412-018-0499-0

Finnish Environment Institute (2018) Large EU Life project for Finland to mitigate climate change. Press Release, 21.12.2018. Available from: https://www.syke.fi/en-US/Current/Large_EU_Life_project_for_Finland_to_mit(48905)

Halmaghi, E.-E. (2016) Environmental action programmes of the European Union – Programmes supporting the sustainable development strategy of the European Union, *De Gruyter Open Scientific Bulletin*, XXI, 2 (42): 87–90.

Hey, C. (2007) EU environmental policies: A short history of the policy strategies. European Commission working paper *EU Environmental Policy Handbook.* Archive of European Integration.

Hjerp, P., Homeyer, I., Pallemaerts, M. and Farmer, A. (2010), *The Impact of Better Regulation on EU Environmental Policy under the Sixth Environment Action Programme*, Report for the Brussels Institute for Environmental Management, IEEP, London.

Holzinger, K., Knill, C. and Schäfer, A. (2006) Rhetoric or reality? 'New governance' in EU environmental policy, *European Law Journal*, 12 (3): 403–420.

Jeupiste (n.d.) Historical timeline of the framework programme. EU-Japan Centre for Industrial Cooperation. Available from: https://www.jeupiste.eu/horizon-2020-and-around/historical-timeline-framework-programme

Knill, C., Steinebach, Y. and Fernández-i-Marín, X. (2020) Hypocrisy as a crisis response? Assessing changes in talk, decisions, and actions of the European Commission in EU environmental policy, *Public Administration,* 98 (2020): 363–377.

Krämer, L. (2020) Come on, let's make a plan – Towards an 8th EU environmental action programme, *ERA Forum*, 20 (2020): 659–681.

Mengolini, A. and Masera, M. (2021). EU energy policy: A socio-energy perspective for an inclusive energy transition. In Weijnen, M. P. C., Lukszo, Z. and Farahani, S. (eds) *Shaping an Inclusive Energy Transition*. Cham: Springer: 141–161. https://doi.org/10.1007/978-3-030-74586-8_7

National Fund for Environmental Protection and Water Management (n.d.) History of LIFE. Government of Poland. Available from: https://www.gov.pl/web/nfosigw-en/history-of-life

Nowak, B. (2006) Electricity and gas market liberalization in the EU as a part of the internal energy market strategy – Chosen aspects. The lesson for Poland, *The Journal of Interdisciplinary Economics,* 17(4):465–480. https://doi.org/10.1177/02601079X06001700406

Official Journal of the European Communities (1973) Declaration of the council of the European communities and of the representatives of the governments of the member states meeting in the council of 22 November 1973 on the Programme of Action of the European Communities on the Environment, No C112, 20.12.1973.

Official Journal of the European Communities (1977) Resolution of the council of the European communities and of the representatives of the governments of the member states meeting within the council of 17 May 1977 on the continuation and implementation of a European Community policy and action programme on the environment, No C139, 13.6.1977.

Official Journal of the European Communities (1983) Resolution of the council of the European communities and of the representatives of the governments of the member states meeting within the council, of 7 February 1983 on the continuation and implementation of a European community policy and action programme on the environment (1982 to 1986). No C46, 17.2.1983.

Official Journal of the European Communities (1987) Resolution of the council of the European communities and of the representatives of the governments of the member states meeting within the council, of 19 October 1987 on the continuation and implementation of a European Community policy and action programme on the environment (1987 to 1992). No C328, 7.12.1987.

Official Journal of the European Communities (1993) Towards sustainability, a European community programme of policy and action in relation to the environment and sustainable development. No C138/5, 17.5.1993.

Official Journal of the European Communities (2002) Decision No 1600/2002/EC of the European parliament and of the council of 22 July 2002 laying down the sixth community environment action programme. L242, 10.9.2002.

Official Journal of the European Union (2013a) Decision No 1386/2013/EU of the European parliament and of the council of 20 November 2013 on a general union environment action programme to 2020 'Living well, within the limits of our planet'. L354/171, 28.12.2013.

Official Journal of the European Union (2013b) Regulation (EU) No 1293/2013 of the European parliament and of the council of 11 December 2013 on the establishment of a programme for the environment and climate action (LIFE) and repealing Regulation (EC) No 614/2007. L347/185, 20.12.2013.

Official Journal of the European Union (2021a) Regulation (EU) No 2021/783 of the European parliament and of the council of 29 April 2021 establishing a programme for the environment and climate action (LIFE), and repealing Regulation (EU) No 1293/2013. L172/53, 17.5.2021.

Official Journal of the European Union (2021b) Commission implementing decision (EU) 2021/173 of 12 February 2021 establishing the European climate, infrastructure and environment executive agency, the European health and digital executive agency, the European innovation council and SMEs executive agency, the European research council executive agency, and the European education and culture executive agency and repealing implementing decisions 2013/801/EU, 2013/771/EU, 2013/778/EU, 2013/779/EU, 2013/776/EU and 2013/770/EU. L50/9, 15.2.2021.

Official Journal of the European Union (2022) Decision (EU) 2022/591 of the European parliament and of the council of 6 April 2022 on a general union environment action programme to 2030. L114/22, 12.4.2022.

Pallemaerts, M., Herodes, M. and Adelle, C. (2007) *Does the EU Sustainable Development Strategy Contribute to Environmental Policy Integration?* EPIGOV Paper No. 9. DG Research.

Saidi, K. and Hammami, S. (2015) The impact of CO2 emissions and economic growth on energy consumption in 58 countries, *Energy Reports*, 1 (2015): 62–70.

Sarti, M. and St. John, S. K. (2019) Raising long-term awareness: EU environmental policy and education. In St. John, S. K. and Murphy, M. (eds) *Education and Public Policy in the European Union. Crossing Boundaries.* Zurich, Switzerland: Palgrave Macmillan, 165–181.

Schoenefeld, J. J. and Jordan, A. J. (2019) Environmental policy evaluation in the EU: Between learning, accountability, and political opportunities? *Environmental Politics,* 28 (2): 365–384.

Secretariat for Education, Research and Innovation (n.d.) EU framework programmes for research and innovation. Switzerland. Available from: https://www.sbfi.admin.ch/sbfi/en/home/research-and-innovation/international-cooperation-r-and-i/eu-framework-programmes-for-research.html#:~:text=The%20European%20Framework%20Programmes%20for,of%20around%20EUR%2095.5%20billion

Trinomics (2019) The evolution of the EU environment and climate policy framework: From the 6th to the 7th EAP. Service contract to support the Evaluation of the 7th Environment Action Programme, Issue Specific Paper Number 2, June 2019.

Twindale, S. (2022) Factbox: Europe's efforts to shield households from soaring energy costs. *Reuters,* 26 May [Viewed 28 July]. Available from: https://www.reuters.com/business/energy/europes-efforts-shield-households-energy-cost-spike-2022-03-21/

UN (1973) *Report of the United Nations Conference on the Human Environment.* Stockholm, 5–16 June 1972. New York, 1973.

UN (2022) *The Human Right to a Clean, Healthy and Sustainable Environment,* Draft resolution of the UN General Assembly, A/76/L/75, 26 July 2022.

Williams, R. (2012) *Final Evaluation of LIFE+. Summary of Conclusions and Recommendations.* December 14, 2012. Triple E Consulting.

4 The changing role of the common agricultural policy

Introduction

The Common Agricultural Policy (CAP) has been in place since 1962, being one of the first common policies developed by the EU institutions, with its rationale emerging from the Treaty of Rome (EC, 2022a). From those lines it is easy to discern that the purpose of the policy was not related to any kind of environmental concern, and EU institutions recognise that those objectives remain practically unchanged to these days, as they appear in Art. 39 of the Treaty of Functioning of the EU (Nègre, 2022): *to increase agricultural productivity by promoting technical progress and ensuring the optimum use of the factors of production, in particular labour; to ensure a fair standard of living for farmers; to stabilise markets; to ensure the availability of supplies; and to ensure reasonable prices for consumers*. If the previous lines are read trying to uncover their connection with sustainability objectives, it could be inferred that the focus of the CAP has been to deal with the social and economic pillars of sustainable development. The use of economic terminology (productivity, factors of production, markets, supply, prices, consumers) reinforces this assertion. The main focus has changed, however, with subsequent policy reforms attempting to address the negative impact of agricultural policy and practices on environment and biodiversity (Daugbjerg and Swinbank, 2011; Hristov et al., 2020). It is in fact now accepted that the CAP is multidimensional (Alons, 2017) and multifunctional (Swinbank, 2011). However, the policy is often criticised for falling short on environmental and biodiversity protection credentials (Gravey in Burns et al., 2016), climate justice (Friends of the Earth Europe, 2022), and alignment with the Sustainable Development Goals (Scown and Nicholas, 2020; Pe'er et al., 2019).

In this context it is important to acknowledge that the CAP is grounded in two main pillars: scholars mention Pillar I with a focus on the direct payments to farmers (Cardwell, 2004), which took time to be implemented as the following section will attest. However, Pillar I also refers to the common organisation of the markets (CMO) for agricultural products, which includes the regulations on market interventions, the trade with third countries, and a new reserve fund for periods of crisis in the agricultural sector, established in 2013 (Nègre, 2022). Pillar II covers rural development policy, funded through the European Agricultural Fund for Rural

DOI: 10.4324/9781003224785-5

Development (EAFDR), with specific support programmes for the development of rural areas and 'environmentally sound farming' (Salhofer and Feichtinger, 2021). Some argue (Cardwell, 2004) that it is direct payments what allowed for a wider consideration of environmental aspects in agricultural policy, though with limitations in the scope of the actions and the need to account for exemptions in the application of environmental requirements.

As it has been mentioned in previous chapters, one of the main criticisms that the CAP has traditionally received is the large proportion of the EU budget it absorbed, which reached 75% in the 1970s (Greer, 2013). Even if since then that proportion has decreased considerably, it still requires around one third of the EU's resources (Nègre, 2022). To all those critiques, academics add the reluctance or difficulty to achieve change in the CAP (Grant, 2010), despite the many reforms experienced over the years. One could conclude that the CAP should be considered as a failure, however the opposite seems to be true if one reads the Commission's positive assessment (ex-ante) of the new CAP, which will operate from 2023 onwards (EC, 2022b).

This chapter will review the reforms the CAP has experienced over time with a focus on the latest changes, the CAP connections with the European Green Deal and its Farm to Fork Strategy, the instruments used to assess and monitor its performance, and its links with other policies and institutions, particularly in light of the current food crisis. This will serve to enlighten the debate about the role of the CAP as part of the sustainability transition in the EU.

The reforms of the Common Agricultural Policy

From the 1970s to 2013

The first reform of the CAP took place in 1970, through what was called the Mansholt Plan (European Council, 2022). It came up after observing that farmers' income remained stagnant despite the support received through the policy, due to what was thought to be an imbalance between over-production and price support. The purpose of this first reform was then the optimisation of the land area under cultivation and the merging of farms to create larger units of production (European Council, 2022). In the 1980s the support system of the CAP managed to create more over-production problems, with milk being the ultimate example of the system's malfunction. A reform in 1984 introduced a quota system, in an attempt to reduce dairy stocks, but it cannot be said that it provided a solution for the problem and it caused unintended consequences (Grant, 2010). Quotas favoured existing farmers, creating barriers for new entrants unless Member States established measures to facilitate entry. The result was a slow down in the reform of a market that was already non-competitive compared to international suppliers (Grant, 2010).

Some argue (Swinbank, 2011) that international pressures played a determinant role in the reform of the CAP in the early 1990s, with negotiations in the Uruguay Round of the World Trade Organisation (WTO) paying specific attention to agricultural subsidies that distorted market functioning. It was in this context that the so-called 'MacSharry reform' took place in 1992. Instead of market support through fixed prices for agricultural products, the system passed to direct income support for farmers, adding obligations with regard to the protection of the environment and incentives for the improvement of food quality (European Council, 2022). The change introduced 'compensatory coupled payments', determined through the combination of indicators related to levels of past production and market-price support (Erjavec and Erjavec, 2021). Further modifications of the support system were implemented later in the same decade, aiming for more liberalisation of the market, particularly regarding dairy products. The levels of price intervention were lowered, with grains reaching world market-prices, while the scope for direct support was widened (Erjavec and Erjavec, 2021). It was not until the reform of 2003, called 'Fischler Reform', that totally decoupled direct payments were introduced, based on historical averages of areas and heads of livestock (Sinabell et al., 2013), without the need to actually plant crops or requirements about operating inputs. This new 'Single Payment Scheme' (SPS) kept, however, the coupling with land, since it included the requirement of having (ownership or rental) one hectare of eligible land for the entitlement to payment to be activated (Salhofer and Feichtinger, 2021). Reading this requirement, it is easily argued that the policy is biased towards big producers and land owners, with the current Commissioner for Agriculture (Janusz Wojciechowski) agreeing and blaming errors and mistakes of the CAP for the disappearance of four million farms in the EU between 2005 and 2014, many of them small farms (Foote, 2021). The reform of 2003 was based on the Agenda 2000 agreed in the 1997 European Council in Luxembourg, which declared that agriculture should be 'multifunctional, sustainable, competitive and spread throughout European territory' (Nègre, 2022). The objectives of the reform were later agreed in Berlin in 1999, with the introduction of environmental cross-compliance as condition to receive aid and establishing the then new rural development policy that became the Second Pillar of the CAP (Nègre, 2022).

Given the shortcomings observed through the period it is no surprise to find a new major attempt of CAP reform in 2013, in alignment with the Europe 2020 Strategy, to have a better functioning CAP for the 2014–2020 financial period (Nazzaro and Marotta, 2016). Debates for the reform had started earlier, with interest on greening the policy and a reorientation towards environmental objectives. This was aided by the inclusion of a wider group of stakeholders in the decision-making process, with more involvement of environmental NGOs and a co-legislator role for the European Parliament (Erjavec and Erjavec, 2021). Through this reform single farm payments were replaced by a system of staged payments with seven components: basic payment; greening payment for environmental public goods; additional payment for young farmers; redistributive payment with additional support for the first hectares of farmland; income support for areas subjected to natural constraints; aid coupled to production (going back partly to the previous system); and a simplified system for small farmers (Nègre, 2022). One of the aims of the changes implemented through this reform was to ensure that the support measures reached 'active' farmers (Nazzaro and Marotta, 2016), as opposed to the simple availability of the land. The evaluation of the policy does not show much progress on this aim though, with additional questions over fairness since it became apparent that 20% of CAP beneficiaries received 80% of the direct payments (EC, 2021a). It reveals some improvement over the previous period, with an increase in payments to small farmers by 18% between 2017 and 2019 compared to 2011–2013, but it also shows room for improvement in relation to the support that should target those who need it most, as well as limited effects on the reduction of disparities between regions within Member States (EC, 2021a). An example of the implementation and effects of the CAP in a Member State can be found in Box 4.1. Detractors of the CAP (Heinemann, 2017) claim that the EU budget could be more efficiently spent elsewhere and advocate for a progressive elimination of the direct payment system and the introduction of co-financing with the Member States. In this light, the reform of 2013 is seen as a failure (continuation of the status-quo) compared with the 2003 one, on the basis of a conglomerate of factors leading to the 2003 reform which did not materialise in 2013. These refer to the confluence of a strong individual as agriculture commissioner, the external pressures coming from the WTO, the then upcoming Eastern enlargement, and food crises such as the mad cow disease which damaged the CAP reputation (Heinemann, 2017). Given the long history of the CAP, the lack of effectiveness of each attempt of reform, and the added complexity to food supplies created by the conflict in Ukraine, one can but wonder if the latest changes brought for the current financial period will result in an optimal functioning of the agricultural sector across Europe with sustainability credentials at heart.

Box 4.1 Case study: The Common Agricultural Policy in Italy

Italy is one of the main agricultural producers in the EU. The Common Agricultural Policy provided €41.5 billions to Italy between 2014 and 2020, through a mix of direct payments (€27 billions), Common Organisation of Markets for wine, fruit and vegetables (€4 billions) and funds for rural development (€10.5 billions) (Sarvia et al., 2021). However, and similarly to Germany, Italy is a net contributor to the CAP funding, since its share of national contributions is larger than the CAP payments it receives (Heinemann, 2017). The financial support received has been decreasing overtime, which became more visible after the EU enlargement to Eastern Europe (Cagliero and Henke, 2005). Within the total funding, the part dedicated to rural development is organised through a National Rural Development Programme (RDP) that outlines the country's priorities, and then 21 Regional RDPs that classify regions as 'less developed', 'transition' and 'more developed' (EC, 2021b). Academic research has been trying to analyse the effectiveness of the CAP in Italy looking into different aspects of the implementation of policies. One such analysis (Mantino et al., 2022) focuses on how funding that attracts investment in rural areas, which is deemed to have longer lasting effects, is allocated – instead of direct subsidies. This was done using calls for tenders in all the Italian regions as the unit of analysis, concluding that the distributive effects of investment through RDPs are uneven, with projects concentrating in areas that are already dynamic and strongly competitive. Closing development gaps is better achieved if instead of open competition approaches a modulation of territorial criteria is used in the implementation phase of the projects (Mantino et al., 2022). This goes to show that 'one size fits all' approaches tend to result in disappointing outcomes. Other scholars have tried to assess opportunities for the agricultural sector in Italy related to the type of crops that can potentially reach higher yields. Some (Santucci et al., 2021) conclude that there is room for further development of organic olive oil, while others (De Boni et al., 2022) posit that crop diversification is the way to go in areas where availability of water is problematic, highlighting the financial viability of almond farming and the environmental suitability of pomegranate cultivation. It is worth noting that most of the funding received in the area of rural development (around 78%) has been dedicated to risk management (EC, 2021b), which is not surprising given the uncertainties provoked by extreme weather events and natural disasters (earthquakes).

In the context of the new CAP for the financial period 2023–2027, Italy received at the end of March 2022 the observations of the European Commission on its proposed national strategic plan for rural development, but of course this proposal was submitted before the war in Ukraine began. The conflict is the main reason alluded by the Italian government to reorient its plan and ask for more flexibility, including a delay of the new CAP entry into force (Lettig, 2022). As it will be seen later in the text, this is not the only country asking for this flexibility, and the Commission has given some steps in this direction.

The CAP in the current Multiannual Financial Framework

It cannot be forgotten that before the interruption of foodstuff movement caused by the war in Ukraine, Europe and the rest of the world were affected (still are) by the lockdowns that halted international trade due to the Covid-19 pandemic. The extraordinary situation was responded with emergency measures in most countries, and within the EU a similar approach was taken. The CAP regulation was amended in 2020 to provide temporary emergency assistance to farmers and small and medium enterprises (SMEs) dedicated to activities linked to agricultural products (Eur-lex, 2022). The pandemic also affected the general EU budget, as explained in Chapter 2, and has caused delays in the implementation of measures scheduled through the EGD. The context of the new CAP is much wider though, if we bear in mind that negotiations started in 2016 during the Dutch Presidency of the Council. It had to consider the effects of Brexit, which materialised in January 2020, and the uncertainty in EU-US relationships after the election of Donald Trump (Nègre, 2022). The Commission put forward proposals in 2018, for the strategic plans that Member States should draw for the new CAP (EC, 2018a), for the general financing, management and monitoring of the CAP (EC, 2018b), and for the CMOs (EC, 2018c). A final agreement for a new CAP was reached at the end of 2021 and its regulations are applied from the beginning of 2023 (EC, 2022c), even if as it has been mentioned (Box 4.1) some Member States asked for a rethink of the CAP and some of its flagship initiatives: the Farm to Fork Strategy (that we will look at later in this chapter) and the Biodiversity Strategy, in light of the threats to food security posed by the war in Ukraine (Fortuna et al., 2022). These flagship initiatives were approved with the purpose of contributing to the achievement of targets set up by the EGD for 2030, with the overall goal of creating a greener and fairer CAP (EC, 2022b). The new CAP establishes ten specific objectives linked to the three pillars of sustainability – economic, social and environmental (EC, 2022c):

- to ensure a fair income for farmers;
- to increase competitiveness;
- to improve the position of farmers in the food chain;
- climate change action;
- environmental care;
- to preserve landscapes and biodiversity;
- to support generational renewal;
- vibrant rural areas;
- to protect food and health quality;
- fostering knowledge and innovation (this one being a cross-cutting instead of specific objective).

These objectives are to be achieved through the strategic plans that each Member State has been submitting to the Commission for consideration, which signals the wider role aimed for Member States going forward with regard to policy implementation. It can be considered a step in the direction called for those who argue that the funding for the CAP should be reduced (Heinemann, 2017) and that co-financing and renationalisation of the CAP would contribute to higher efficiency and flexibility (Kengyel, 2022). The reduction of the funding is also confirmed, since even if agricultural funding is still 28.5% of the MFF for 2021–2027, real cuts of around 15% are embedded in the proposal, with a decrease of 10% on the first pillar (the EAGF), but a 19% decrease in the second pillar (the EAFRD), accounting for the loss of the UK as a net contributor to the budget but also for new policy priorities such as migration, external borders, the digital economy or transport (Nègre, 2022). Parallel to the approval of the new system from 2023 onwards, a transition period for 2021–2022 was established so that farmers could continue receiving payments after the conclusion of the previous financial period (2014–2020). The budget for these two years comes from the corresponding funding of the MFF 2021–2027 with additional €8 billion from the NextGenerationEU Recovery Instrument (EURI), assigned to the EAFRD (EC, 2022d).

One characteristic of the new CAP is the enhanced conditionality, that is, a strong set of mandatory requirements that beneficiaries will need to fulfil to receive any payment. These requirements are linked to the attempts to make the CAP greener, with conditions such as farms dedicating at least 3% of arable land to biodiversity and non-productive activities, with access to eco-schemes (25% of the budget) to incentivise climate and environment-friendly farming practices (EC, 2022c). There are also those who argue (Fortuna, 2021) that the new CAP is laying the foundations for a third pillar on agricultural policy, a social pillar, given the social conditionality added for the first time to the allocation of payments. The requirements include the transparency and predictability of working conditions, which should be provided in writing, as well as ensuring the health and safety of workers in farms (EC, 2022c).

On paper, it appears that this new CAP is trying to address many of the shortcomings of existing policies, but we are yet to see if it will provide the desired results. It is worth then having a look at the mechanisms and tools currently used to evaluate the performance of the CAP.

Assessing the performance of the CAP

Each time a new CAP (and most EU policies) is approved, it is presented as the product of a learning exercise, by which the issues detected in previous iterations would be corrected. Said issues are detected through different evaluation processes and instruments. There are many indicators that could be used to assess if the CAP has been performing adequately. It could be measured against its overarching objectives as established by the Treaty of Functioning of the EU, which were mentioned in the introduction of this chapter. It could also be assessed against the specific objectives set for each financial period, at the end of said period, though given the relatively long duration of each iteration, mid-term evaluations are frequent. Ex-ante evaluations can also take place, but this would be to assess individual elements of the programme. For the current CAP, a meticulous process for ex-ante evaluation of the CAP Strategic Plans has been established (European Network for Rural Development [ENRD], 2020), which needs to be completed by independent evaluators, jointly or separately from the Strategic Environmental Assessment that also needs to be completed. Implicitly this indicates that the CAP performance is measured (or at least it should be) against the three pillars of sustainability: the economic, the social and the environmental. Some criticisms about the economic aspect have already been outlined, with calls for more efficiency in the allocation of funding. The social element has also been highlighted in terms of inequalities not being corrected. Some figures that exemplify the issues include the fact that while 74.9% of CAP beneficiaries in 2019 received less than €5,000 per year, there was a 1.93% of farms that received more than €50,000 each. The Member States with more abundance of big farms, recipients of these larger amounts are Denmark, United Kingdom (before Brexit), Czech Republic, Slovakia and France (Nègre, 2022).

The Commission established a Common Monitoring and Evaluation Framework (CMEF) for the 2014–2020 CAP (EC, 2015), which has been extended to cover the new transitional period until the end of 2022. The purpose of the framework is to provide information on the implementation of the CAP, its results and impacts, with quantification of the actions of each Member State, and assessment of the efficiency of the different policy instruments used. A first report following this framework was published in 2018 (EC, 2018d), with a second report at the end of 2021 (EC, 2021a). The framework aims to assess the performance of the CAP against ten specific objectives (similar to the ones established for the current period) and three long-term objectives, using a series of indicators: contextual, impact, result, and output (EC, 2015). The two performance reports cover progress related to pillar I of the CAP, while for pillar II a series of annual implementation reports (AIRs) need to be completed (EC, 2015). The first report, which according to the framework would cover pillar I, provided information on pillar II also, already highlighting the inadequacy of the framework, given the excessive number of indicators (more than 200, with more than 900 sub-indicators) not all of them fit for purpose, and with insufficient or incomparable data between Member States (EC, 2018d). The information of the report includes data up to 2016, so it can be considered a mid-term evaluation exercise, where it is remarked (as a negative point) the low uptake of risk management tools by farmers, with insurance being the preferred method, when in use (EC, 2018d). The report published at the end of 2021 confirmed that some data were not produced with enough frequency (lags of four or six years), and that targets were only quantified for rural development expenditure, so in that sense, it is not possible to assess the contribution of the CAP to impact indicators (EC, 2021a).

What has been described in the previous paragraphs refers to internal monitoring and evaluation tools used by European institutions that could also inform future public policies in this area. But it is important to look at what external independent research can add to policy evaluation, such as that undertaken by academic researchers or independent bodies. The complexity of the elements that may be part of evaluation exercises can be observed in Figure 4.1. Examples of results provided by academic research with regard to CAP effects include: improvement in the environmental impact of agricultural activities in Portugal, but with the continuation of spatial differences, the confirmation of a reduction in arable cropping and increase in pastures and livestock, and a reduction in competitiveness particularly after the 1992 CAP reform, with a need for better links of the support provided to specific local conditions (Pereira Domingues Martinho, 2017); uneven redistributional effects of Rural Development Programmes funding in Italy, with increase of inequalities when funding is allocated using open competition processes (Mantino et al., 2022); decrease in the number of farmers in Greece but with a higher proportion of environmentally conscious new younger farmers compared to non-environmentally conscious ones (Kontogeorgos et al., 2015); positive contribution of CAP programmes to the creation of employment in rural areas, correlated with positive GDP growth in the Baltic countries – Estonia, Latvia and Lithuania (Grodzicki and Jankiewicz, 2022). These are only a few examples. More detail about the economic analysis techniques used in this type of studies and others to assess the performance of the CAP can be found in Annex 4.1 at the end of this chapter. Information on the specific economic instruments used as policy tools will be covered by Part II of this book.

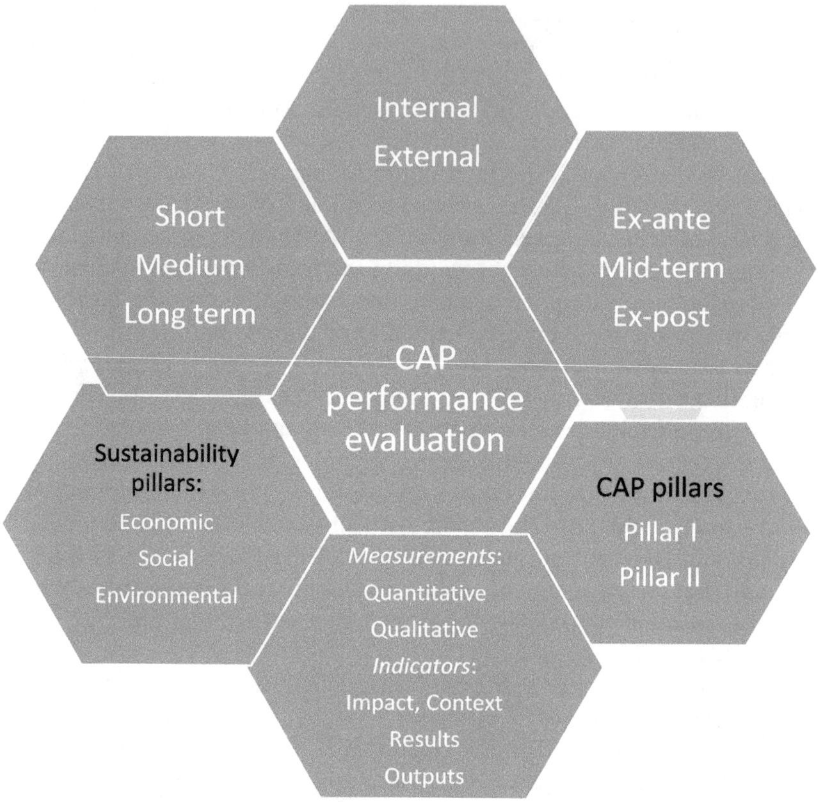

Figure 4.1 Elements to consider when evaluating CAP performance

Source: Author's elaboration.

An added problem when assessing performance is interpreting the wording of reports of academic papers. In its assessment of the CAP 2014–2020, the Commission builds on the positive reading from a World Bank report (2018) where it is indicated that the CAP has contributed to the improvement of farmers' income and to a reduction in the income gap between the agricultural sector and other sectors of the EU economies. However, the progress achieved in the EU has been clearly uneven, and the problems detected by the report with regard to a worsening of absolute poverty in Southern Europe (World Bank, 2018) are not addressed (EC, 2021a).

For the current financial period a new evaluation framework has been approved, under the name of Performance Monitoring and Evaluation Framework (PMEF), applicable from 2023 onwards (Official Journal of the European Union [OJEU], 2021). In the spirit of a learning exercise between one period and the next one, several differences can be observed between the new framework and its predecessor. There is a shift in the focus from compliance with specific rules to performance and results, which seems to be linked to the need to demonstrate 'value for money'. The set of common performance indicators, however, keeps the classification of the previous period, with distinction between output, results, context and impact. Member States are given flexibility for the design of the strategic plans according to their specific circumstances and the working of their labour markets, particularly with regard to the social conditionality element (OJEU, 2021: 8). There is a reinforced emphasis on food security (which the conflict in Ukraine has made more prominent as it will be seen in the following sections) and very importantly, on the role of the agricultural sector to promote healthier nutrition, animal welfare and reduction of food waste (OJEU, 2021: 6). It is for this reason that instead of the previous cross-compliance, new conditionality for the receipt of support includes specific compliance with newly determined basic standards on 'environment, climate change, public health, plant health and animal welfare' that become Statutory Management Requirements (SMRs) (OJEU, 2021: 7). This speaks of the multifunctionality of the CAP and its attempt to respond to new societal demands. The question is if that many requirements, targets, indicators and functions will result in added complexity for farmers, when in theory the new system should simplify processes and reduce said complexity.

The EGD and the Farm to Fork Strategy

The Farm to Fork Strategy approved in 2020 (EC, 2020) is one of the flagship initiatives of the EGD (EC, 2019a), which stated as purpose for European food to become a global standard for sustainability, and for the CAP (and the Fisheries policy) to be a supporting tool for farmers to 'tackle climate change, protect the environment and preserve biodiversity' (EC, 2019a: 12) as part of that overarching purpose. The three pillars of sustainability are present in the Farm to Fork (F2F) Strategy, and the reader is left to decide if they are addressed in a balanced manner. For this author it becomes apparent that the economic pillar is very much dominant, with language that uses frequent economic terminology: 'value', 'investments', 'circular bio-based economy', 'price', 'affordability', 'competition rules', 'business', 'competitive advantage, productivity gains and reduced costs' (EC, 2020), are just but a few examples. It is true that there has been a big push to include proposals that help with the aim to reverse biodiversity loss, but reality has shown that they have faced fierce opposition. The beginning of 2023 saw how discourses shifted in some policymakers (DG AGRI), governments (France, Italy), and lobby groups (farmers) in light of the crisis created by the conflict in Ukraine (Wax, 2023), while civil society organisations called on the Commission to continue with the roadmap for a sustainable food system regulation (Askew, 2023). The Nature Restoration Law, connected to both the Farm to Fork and Biodiversity strategies, was only approved with a narrow margin by the European Parliament in July 2023, in what is considered a watered-down version of the original proposal, after agitated debates (Niranjan, 2023) and even street protests. This confirms the fears of those who pointed out (Schebesta and Candel, 2020) that the potential of the Farm to Fork Strategy to create change in the existing food system is conditional to the willingness of the Parliament and the Council to support the Commission's ambition, and the capacity to reconcile opposing interests of the relevant stakeholders.

The justification of many of the measures proposed in the F2F Strategy is made on health grounds, and this has put at odds DG AGRI with DG SANTE. Objectives for 2030 include (EC, 2020):

Achieve a minimum of 25% of agricultural land dedicated to organic farming.
Reduce the use of pesticides by 50% and the use of fertilisers by 20%.
Reduce the EU sales of antimicrobials for farmed animals and in aquaculture by 50%.
Reduce soil nutrient losses by at least 50% while ensuring that there is no deterioration in soil fertility.

As it can be seen, these goals directly impact current farming practices, hence the connection between F2F and the CAP and the calls from the farming sector for the necessary funding to accomplish the required changes. But how funding is going to flow becomes a bit blurry. The F2F Strategy mentions both national governments funding allocations through their CAP Strategic Plans, and the focus on investments in areas such as digitalisation of the food systems facilitated not so much by direct funding but by EU budget guarantees through the InvestEU fund (EC, 2020). Researchers (Triantafyllidis et al., 2023) highlight the challenges in the reduction of pesticides and particularly herbicides, concluding that there is a need for integrated policy approaches that involve not only farmers but also consumers. They also make a point of the need to take criticisms of the F2F Strategy into account and be able to adjust it accordingly. In a similar way, other researchers point at the dichotomy between protection of natural value areas and financial viability (Wiśniewski et al., 2021), with farmers choosing to participate in schemes with the lowest financial cost for them and/or the ones with the highest financial return, with environmental objectives taking a secondary role. This is why some argue in favour of a carrot and stick approach to incentivise farmers to take action, using both taxes and subsidies as policy instruments (Triantafyllidis et al., 2023). Some (Heyl et al., 2023), however, present evidence of the limited impact that subsidies have so far in the area of precision fertilisation (using digital innovations), signalling a limited role of the CAP in its current design to contribute to the F2F and generally the EGD. The 'green architecture', as it has been called, that defines the conditional allocation of funding in the current CAP needs to recognise the role of farmers as managers of ecosystem services (Boix-Fayos and de Vente, 2023; Guyomard et al., 2023). Otherwise, the issues that currently act as barriers for more sustainable practices (maintenance of crop yields and nitrogen needs, land demand, need for change in people's diets, food waste and externalisation of problems to third countries [Boix-Fayos and de Vente, 2023]), will remain unsolved. Despite the protests against the demands that the new strategies have brought for farmers, there are also those (Guyomard et al., 2023) who think that they could have gone further and there is potential for the green architecture to be greener. It is a difficult balance that EU institutions are trying to strike, particularly when the starting point for each stakeholder and each member State is different. An added level of complexity comes from the area that the F2F is aiming to transform: food systems.

The understanding of the concept and the multiplicity of factors that affect and get affected by food systems cannot be underestimated, and even countries who want to position themselves as frontrunners in the sustainable transformation of their food systems (Sweden) face challenges created by the high level of carbon emissions of their food systems linked to trade (processing occurring out of Sweden and food being imported) so the required level of transformation and change would necessitate interventions in multiple areas (Eliasson et al., 2022). Interestingly the F2F Strategy presents these transformations as business opportunities with potential to create economic growth (EC, 2020; Eliasson et al., 2022) so the message portrayed is that of a food system that is economically sustainable, in line with the EGD as a strategy for economic growth.

The external dimensions of the CAP

Traditionally, the CAP has received criticism in international fora on the grounds that protection of EU farmers constitutes a competitive disadvantage for non-EU countries. This criticism has not been limited to developing countries, and developed countries like the US and Australia, which are also exporters of agricultural products, often complain about the EU's subsidisation of its agricultural sector (Seidel, 2020). It is these views that influenced some of the CAP reforms under the GATT and then WTO negotiations, as it has been mentioned in previous sections of this chapter. Assessments of the impact that the latest CAP reform would have on markets and trade affected by WTO rules (Matthews, 2018) suggest that the EU trade balance on agricultural products would decrease under most scenarios considered, particularly in those where greater environmental focus is given to the final policy implementation. It is also stated, however, that it is difficult to predict what the effects of the CAP would be, given the greater flexibility allowed for Member States and their country strategies. A decrease in production in EU soil could bring opportunities for third country producers to enter the internal market, but this would pose questions about the environmental effects of an increase in imports.

The crisis created by the conflict in Ukraine and the initial softening of environmental credentials of the CAP to address potential product shortages has been criticised given the long-term impacts on biodiversity loss, with suggestions of alternative measures based on the ecological functionalities of farmland and long-term perspectives (Morales et al., 2022). This is notwithstanding that most of the calls for increasing production are connected to the need of crops for livestock feeding (Morales et al., 2022), which ultimately speaks of a high dependency of our diets on animal products, seemingly contradicting the health objectives outlined for the CAP and the F2F Strategy.

With regard to the effects of the CAP on developing countries, the negative impacts have been extensively documented (Cantore, 2012), and recognised by European institutions. They include impacts on international food prices, given the EU role as large importer and exporter of agricultural products, but also influences on land-use change, biodiversity loss and migration, as a result of both EU policies and increased demand for international agricultural products to cover EU consumer needs (European Parliament, 2018). The latest CAP includes arrangements to evaluate its impact on third countries, as part of its 'Policy Coherence for Development' (PCD) but bearing in mind that the evaluation of the 2014–2020 CAP revealed a lack of a systematic and consistent approach to the evaluation of external impacts (European Parliament, 2018) and that the latest PCD report covers the years 2016–2019 (European Commission, 2019b) but only appeared as available in the Commission's website as of 2022, there is considerable delay in the implementation of necessary corrective measures. Meanwhile, research shows that a decrease or elimination of support for EU agriculture could have a positive impact (even if not that significant) for the economy and poverty indicators of less developed countries (Boysen et al., 2016). It is unlikely though to see a full elimination of support instruments given the sensitive nature of farming for a considerable proportion of EU Member States. Other studies (Kornher and von Braun, 2020) suggest that the new CAP would decrease exports of EU agricultural products to African countries, but they will be replaced by other exporters instead of fostering the development of the agricultural industry in Africa. They call for more transparency in the EU rules of origin, social and hygiene standards for food imports, and support for the improvement of standards in African producers so that they can have access to the EU market.

If support for agriculture is not going to disappear, it makes sense to explore if more efficient support instruments for this and other sectors could be implemented, so that market distortions are minimised while sustainability transition targets can be achieved. This will be the object of analysis of the next section in this book.

Discussion questions

1 Does the current Common Agricultural Policy have true sustainability credentials?
2 How does the Farm to Fork Strategy compare with other food strategies around the world?
3 To which extent food security may water down food sustainability plans in a climate of conflict (Ukraine-Russia) and high temperatures that decrease crop yields?
4 Should food poverty be addressed at EU level or should it be left for the national and local levels?
5 Which interactions between the CAP and other EU policies you think may dominate policy debates in the near future (trade, health, environment…)?

Further readings

McMahon, J. A. and Cardwell, M. N. (eds) (2015) *Research Handbook on EU Agriculture Law.* Edward Elgar: The comprehensive variety of topics that this book covers provides the reader with insightful views, from a legal and regulatory perspective, on many land and agriculture-related themes, but particularly welcomed are those that connect agriculture with other policies, such as food, biofuels, water resource management, trade or sustainability.

Sorrentino, A., Henke, R. and Severini, S. (eds) (2016) *The Common Agricultural Policy after the Fischler Reform. National Implementations, Impact Assessment and the Agenda for Future Reforms.* Routledge: This book presents a remarkable analysis of the CAP from a political economy point of view, but most importantly it provides numerous examples of the impacts of said policy through the use of case studies in different EU Member States and their regions, not only in terms of agricultural production, but also with regard to environmental impacts and rural development.

Meuwissen, M. P. M., Feindt, P. F., Garrido, A., Mathijs, E., Soriano, B., Urquhart, J. and Spiegel, A. (eds) (2022) *Resilient and Sustainable Farming Systems in Europe. Exploring Diversity and Pathways.* Cambridge University Press: From the title the reader can deduce that the latest themes and topics related to agriculture and farming have moved from policy to practice and this book is a good example of the use of modern concepts and methods to address the issues of different farming experiences across Europe.

References

Alons, G. (2017) Environmental policy integration in the EU's common agricultural policy: Greening or greenwashing? *Journal of European Public Policy*, 24 (11): 1604–1622.

Askew, K. (2023) Is Europe's farm to fork strategy in trouble? 'Political resistance is threatening to derail the process'. *Food Navigator,* 13 February [Viewed 31 July]. Available from: https://www.foodnavigator.com/Article/2023/02/13/Is-Europe-s-Farm-to-Fork-strategy-in-trouble-Political-resistance-is-threatening-to-derail-the-process?utm_source=copyright&utm_medium=OnSite&utm_campaign=copyright#

Boix-Fayos, C. and de Vente, J. (2023) Challenges and potential pathways towards sustainable agriculture within the European Green Deal, *Agricultural Systems,* 207 (2023): 103634. https://doi.org/10.1016/j.agsy.2023.103634

Boysen, O., Jensen, H. G. and Matthews, A. (2016) Impact of EU agricultural policy on developing countries: A Uganda case study, *The Journal of International Trade & Economic Development,* 25 (3): 377–402.

Burns, C., Jordan, A., Gravey, V. et al. (2016) *The EU Referendum and the UK Environment: An Expert Review.* Ixelles, Belgium: Vrije Universiteit Brussel.

Cagliero, R. and Henke, R. (2005) Evidence of CAP support in Italy between first and second pillar. *Presentation at 11th Congress of the EAAE (European Association of Agricultural Economists)*, Copenhagen, Denmark, August 24–27, 2005.

Cantore, N. (2012) *Impact of the Common Agricultural Policy on Food Price Volatility for Developing Countries.* London: Overseas Development Institute, November 2012.

Cardwell, M. (2004) Chapter 4. The two pillars of the common agricultural policy. In Cardwell, M. (ed) *The European Model of Agriculture.* Oxford, UK: Oxford University Press: 172–262.

Colen, L., Gomez y Paloma, S., Latacz-Lohmann, U., Lefebvre, M., Preget, R. and Thoyer, S. (2016) Economic experiments as a tool for agricultural policy evaluation: Insights from the European CAP, *Canadian Journal of Agricultural Economics*, 64 (2016): 667–694.

Daugbjerg, C. and Swinbank, A. (2011) Explaining the 'health check' of the common agricultural policy: Budgetary politics, globalisation and paradigm change revisited, *Policy Studies*, 32 (2): 127–141.

De Boni, A., D'Amico, A., Acciani, C. and Roma, R. (2022) Crop diversification and resilience of drought-resistant species in semi-arid areas: An economic and environmental analysis, *Sustainability*, 14 (2022): 9552. https://doi.org/10.3390/su14159552

Eliasson, K., Wiréhn, L., Neset, T.-S. and Linnér, B.-O. (2022) Transformations towards sustainable food systems: Contrasting Swedish practitioner perspectives with the European Commission's Farm to Fork Strategy, *Sustainability Science*, 17 (2022): 2411–2425. https://doi.org/10.1007/s11625-022-01174-3

Erjavec, K. and Erjavec, E. (2021) Framing agricultural policy through the EC's strategies on CAP reforms (1992–2017), *Agricultural and Food Economics* 9 (5). https://doi.org/10.1186/s40100-021-00178-4

Eur-lex (2022) European Agricultural Fund for Rural Development. Summary of Regulation (EU) No 1305/2013 – Support for rural development. Available from: https://eur-lex.europa.eu/EN/legal-content/summary/european-agricultural-fund-for-rural-development.html

European Commission (2015) *The Monitoring and Evaluation Framework for the Common Agricultural Policy 2014–2020.* Luxembourg: Publications Office of the European Union.

European Commission (2018a) Proposal for a regulation of the European parliament and of the council establishing rules on support for strategic plans to be drawn up by member states under the Common Agricultural Policy (CAP Strategic Plans) and financed by the European Agricultural Guarantee Fund (EAGF) and by the European Agricultural Fund for Rural Development (EAFRD) and repealing regulation (EU) No 1305/2013 of the European parliament and of the council and regulation (EU) No 1307/2013 of the European parliament and of the council. COM (2018) 392 final. Brussels, 1.6.2018.

European Commission (2018b) Proposal for a regulation of the European parliament and of the council on the financing, management and monitoring of the common agricultural policy and repealing Regulation (EU) No 1306/2013. COM (2018) 393 final. Brussels, 1.6.2018.

European Commission (2018c) Proposal for a regulation of the European parliament and of the council amending regulations (EU) No 1308/2013 establishing a common organisation of the markets in agricultural products, (EU) No 1151/2012 on quality schemes for agricultural products and foodstuffs, (EU) No 251/2014 on the definition, description, presentation, labelling and the protection of geographical indications of aromatised wine products, (EU) No 228/2013 laying down specific measures for agriculture in the outermost regions of the Union and (EU) No 229/2013 laying down specific measures for agriculture in favour of the smaller Aegean islands. COM (2018) 394 final. Brussels, 1.6.2018.

European Commission (2018d) Report from the commission to the European parliament and the council on the implementation of the common monitoring and evaluation framework and first results on the performance of the Common Agricultural Policy. COM (2018) 790 final. Brussels, 5.12.2018.

European Commission (2019a) Communication from the commission to the European parliament, the European council, the council, the European economic and social committee and the committee of the regions: The European Green Deal. COM (2019) 640 final. Brussels, 11.12.2019.

European Commission (2019b) Commission staff working document: 2019 EU report on policy coherence for development. SWD (2019) 20 final. Brussels, 28.1.2019.

European Commission (2020) Communication from the commission to the European parliament, the council, the European economic and social committee and the committee of the regions: *A Farm to Fork Strategy for a Fair, Healthy and Environmentally-Friendly Food System.* COM (2020) 381 final. Brussels, 20.5.2020.

European Commission (2021a) Report from the commission to the European parliament and the council on the implementation of the common monitoring and evaluation framework including an assessment of the performance of the common agricultural policy 2014–2020. COM (2021) 815 final. Brussels, 16.12.2021.

European Commission (2021b) Factsheet on the national rural development programme 2014–2022 for Italy. October 2021.

European Commission (2022a) *Feeding Europe. 60 Years of Common Agricultural Policy.* Available from: https://agriculture.ec.europa.eu/document/download/f783ebe8-8405-4e86-8646-354c758e274a_en?filename=60-years-cap_en.pdf

European Commission (2022b) *A Greener and Fairer CAP.* Available from: https://agriculture.ec.europa.eu/system/files/2022-02/factsheet-newcap-environment-fairness_en_0.pdf

European Commission (2022c) *The New Common Agricultural Policy: 2023–27 (online).* Available from: https://agriculture.ec.europa.eu/common-agricultural-policy/cap-overview/new-cap-2023-27_en

European Commission (2022d) *CAP Transitional Regulation: 2021–22 (online).* Available from: https://agriculture.ec.europa.eu/common-agricultural-policy/cap-overview/transitional-regulation_en

European Council (2022) *Timeline – History of the CAP.* Available from: https://www.consilium.europa.eu/en/policies/cap-introduction/timeline-history/

European Network for Rural Development (2020) Preparing the ex-ante evaluation. Tools to support preparing the ex-ante evaluation of the CAP Strategic Plan (online). Available from: https://enrd.ec.europa.eu/evaluation/preparing-ex-ante-evaluation-nutshell_en

European Parliament (2018) *The Impact of the Common Agricultural Policy on Developing Countries,* Directorate-General for External Policies. Policy Department. February 2018 – PE603.862.

Foote, N. (2021) Agriculture Commissioner Points finger at CAP for demise of small farms. *Euractiv,* 19 April [Viewed 15 September 2022]. Available from: https://www.euractiv.com/section/agriculture-food/news/agriculture-commissioner-points-finger-at-cap-for-demise-of-small-farms/

Fortuna, G. (2021) CAP deal lays ground for third 'social' pillar. *Euractive*, 30 August [Viewed 15 September 2022]. Available from: https://www.euractiv.com/section/agriculture-food/news/cap-deal-lays-ground-for-third-social-pillar/

Fortuna, G., Koreň, M. and Foote, N. (2022) Italy, Slovakia call to rethink CAP in light of Ukraine war. *Euractiv,* 14 March [Viewed 15 September 2022]. Available from: https://www.euractiv.com/section/agriculture-food/news/italy-slovakia-call-for-rethinking-cap-in-light-of-ukraine-war/

Friends of the Earth Europe (2022) *The Re-CAP: Does the EU's New Farming Policy Represent a Shift Towards Climate Justice?* Brussels: Friends of the Earth Europe.

Grant, W. (2010) Policy instruments in the common agricultural policy, *West European Politics,* 33 (1): 22–38.

Greer, A. (2013) The common agricultural policy and the EU budget: Stasis or change? *European Journal of Government and Economics,* 2 (2): 119–136.

Grodzicki, T. and Jankiewicz, M. (2022) The role of the common agricultural policy in contributing to jobs and growth in EU's rural areas and the impact of employment on shaping rural development: Evidence from the Baltic States, *PLoS ONE,* 17 (2): e0262673. https://doi.org/10.1371/journal.pone.0262673

Guyomard, H., Détang-Dessendre, C., Dupraz, P. et al. (2023) How the green architecture of the 2023–2027 common agricultural policy could have been greener, *Ambio,* 52 (2023): 1327–1338. https://doi.org/10.007/s13280-023-01861-0

Heinemann, F. (2017) The Case for Co-Financing the CAP. *EconPol,* Working Paper No. 04, ifo Institute – Leibniz Institute for Economic Research at the University of Munich, Munich. https://hdl.handle.net/10419/219466

Heyl, K., Ekardt, F., Roos, P. and Garske, B. (2023) Achieving the nutrient reduction objective of the farm to fork strategy. An assessment of CAP subsidies for precision fertilization and sustainable agricultural practices in Germany, *Frontiers in Sustainable Food Systems*, 7 (2021):1088640. https://doi.org/10.3389/fsufs.2023.1088640

Hristov, J., Clough, Y., Sahlin, U. et al. (2020) Impacts of the EU's common agricultural policy "greening" reform on agricultural development, biodiversity, and ecosystem services, *Applied Economic Perspectives and Policy,* 42 (4): 716–738.

Kengyel, Á. (2022) Would renationalisation and co-financing of the common agricultural policy be justified? *Intereconomics*, 57 (2): 113–119.

Kontogeorgos, A., Tsampra, M. and Chatzitheodoridis, F. (2015) Agricultural policy and environment protection through the eyes of new framers: Evidence from a country of Southeast Europe, *Procedia Economics and Finance,* 19 (2015): 296–303.

Kornher, L. and von Braun, J. (2020) EU common agricultural policy – Impacts on trade with Africa and African agricultural development, *ZEF-Discussion Papers on Development Policy* No. 294, Bonn, May 2020.

Lettig, D. (2022) Italy to review its CAP plan amid calls for 'reorientation' and flexibility, *Euractiv,* 29 April [Viewed 19 November]. Available from: https://www.euractiv.com/section/agriculture-food/news/italy-to-review-its-cap-plan-amid-calls-for-reorientation-and-flexibility/

Mantino, F., De Fano, G. and Asaro, G. (2022) Analysing the policy delivery system and effects on territorial disparities in Italy: The mecanisms of territorial targeting in the EU rural development programmes 2014–2020, *Land*, 11 (2022): 1883. https://doi.org/10.3390/land11111883

Matthews, A. (2018) The EU's common agricultural policy post 2020: Directions of change and potential trade and market effects, *International Centre for Trade and Sustainable Development,* Issue Paper: Agriculture, November 2018.

Morales, M. B., Diaz, M., Giralt, D. et al. (2022) Protect European green agricultural policies for future food security, *Communications Earth & Environment,* 3 (2022): 217. https://doi.org/10.1038/s43247-022-00550-2

Nazzaro, C. and Marotta, G. (2016) The common agricultural policy 2014–2020: Scenarios for the European agricultural and rural systems, *Agricultural and Food Economics,* 4 (16). https://doi.org/10.1186/s40100-016-0060-y

Nègre, F. (2022) *The Common Agricultural Policy (CAP).* Fact Sheets on the European Union – 2022. European Parliament, 04/2022.

Niranjan, A. (2023) EU passes nature restoration law in knife-edge vote, *The Guardian,* July 12th [Viewed July 14th]. Available from: https://www.theguardian.com/world/2023/jul/12/eu-passes-nature-restoration-law-vote-meps

Official Journal of the European Union (2021) Regulation (EU) 2021/2115 of the European parliament and of the council of 2 December 2021 establishing rules on support for strategic plans to be drawn up by member states under the Common Agricultural Policy (CAP Strategic Plans) and financed by the European Agricultural Guarantee Fund (EAGF) and by the European Agricultural Fund for Rural Development (EAFRD) and repealing Regulations (EU) No 1305/2013 and (EU) No 1307/2013.

Pe'er, G., Zinngrebe, Y., Moreira, F. et al. (2019) A greener path for the EU common agricultural policy. It's time for sustainable, environmental performance, *Science, Insights. Policy Forum,* 365 (6452): 449–451.

Pereira Domingues Martinho, V. J. (2017) Insights from over 30 years of common agricultural policy in Portugal, *Outlook on Agriculture,* 46 (3): 223–229.

Salhofer, K. and Feichtinger, P. (2021) Regional differences in the capitalisation of first and second pillar payments of the CAP into land rental prices, *European Review of Agricultural Economics,* 48 (1): 8–41

Santucci, F. M., Callieris, R. and del Bello, D. (2021) Organic olive oil in Italy: A missed opportunity? *Bulgarian Journal of Agricultural Science,* 27 (6): 1039–1050.

Sarvia, F., Xausa, E., Petris, S. D., Cantamessa, G. and Borgogno-Mondino, E. (2021) A possible role of copernicus sentinel-2 data to support common agricultural policy controls in agriculture, *Agronomy* 11 (110). https://doi.org/10.3390/agronomy11010110

Schebesta, H. and Candel, J. J. L. (2020) Game-changing potential of the EU's farm to fork strategy, *Nature Food,* 1 (2020): 586–588. https://doi.org/10.1038/s43016-020-00166-9

Scown, M. W. and Nicholas, K. A. (2020) European agricultural policy requires a stronger performance framework to achieve the sustainable development goals, *Global Sustainability,* 3 (2020). https://doi.org/10.1017/sus.2020.5

Seidel, K. (2020) The external dimensions of the common agricultural policy: From developed to developing countries. In Krotz, U., Patel, K. K. and Romero, F. (eds) *Europe's Cold War Relations: The EC Towards a Global Role'*. London: Bloomsbury Academic: 165–185.

Sinabell, F., Schmid, E. and Hofreither, M. F. (2013) Exploring the distribution of direct payments of the common agricultural policy, *Empirica,* 40 (2013): 325–341.

Swinbank, A. (2011) The European Union's common agricultural policy (CAP), *The New Palgrave Dictionary of Economics.* https://doi.org/10.1057/978-1-349-95121-5_2980-1

Triantafyllidis, V., Mavroeidis, A., Kosma, C. et al. (2023) Herbicide use in the era of farm to fork: Strengths, weaknesses, and future implications, *Water, Air, & Soil Pollution*, 234 (2023): 94. https://doi.org/10.1007/s11270-023-06125-x

Wax, E. (2023) From farm to flop? Political risks choke EU's green food plan. *Politico,* January 26 [Viewed July 31st]. Available from: https://www.politico.eu/article/blocked-and-delayed-political-risks-choke-eus-green-food-plan-farmers/

Wiśniewski, P., Rudnicki, R., Kistowski, M., Wiśniewski, Ł. ChodkowskaMiszczuk, J. and Niecikowski, K. (2021) Mapping of EU support for high nature value farmlands, from the perspective of natural and landscape regions, *Agriculture*, 11 (2021): 864. https://doi.org/10.3390/agriculture11090864

World Bank (2018) *Thinking CAP. Supporting Agricultural Jobs and Incomes in the EU.* EU Regular Economic Report 4. Washington DC: World Bank Report on the European Union.

Annex 4.1 Economic techniques for the evaluation of the CAP (and/or other policies)

The dominant orthodox Economics discipline focuses on the use of statistical and econometric techniques for the analysis of quantitative (and more often these days qualitative) data. As the introduction of this book stated, it is not its purpose to explain how these techniques work, but for those interested in or with a background in Economics, the following lines may be helpful. It is worth noting that there are many branches of Economics that can study different policies from a variety of perspectives, the same way that economic issues can be approached from other disciplines and perspectives such as sociology, geography, history, politics or international relations. We have environmental and climate economics, energy economics, agricultural and land economics, behavioural and experimental economics, or public economics, to name a few, which can provide insights on the performance of the CAP and other policies.

Within Chapter 4, the paper from Grodzicki and Jankiewicz (2022) uses data collected as indicators of Objective 8 of the CAP (employment and economic growth) between 2000 and 2006, to assess the situation of rural areas in Baltic States, with the conclusion that an improvement in income and employment in rural areas contributes to the overall economic growth of the countries under analysis. The research includes a literature review and a time series econometric analysis, with the purpose of identifying frequencies or trends in the characteristics of different time periods and distinguishing possible non-stationary features. The equations used for each of the models, with specific variables and coefficients, are neatly explained in the paper. Data are extracted from the information that Member States need to provide to the EU institutions and in the case of this paper are quantitative in nature.

Kontogeorgos et al. (2015) also use statistical modelling, but in this case the information is extracted from a survey that includes qualitative data, namely the perceptions and understanding of young farmers' behaviour and role as being environmentally conscious (environment protectors) or not. The analysis aims to investigate if there are behavioural differences based on a series of characteristics (demographic, awareness over Genetically Modified Organisms (GMOs), environmental practices and environmental perceptions). This initial work identifies two clusters of farmers (more and less environmentally conscious), which are then used in what is called a 'binary logistic regression' to determine the variables that influence farmers' behaviour. It concludes that the number of years of experience in farming, the consumption at home of agricultural produce, and the practices used for agrochemicals recycling can be used to determine young farmers' environmental consciousness.

Beyond the examples provided in this chapter, the work of Colen et al. (2016) suggests that experiments can also be used for agricultural policy evaluation, including lab and field experiments, randomised controlled trials (RCTs) and discrete choice experiments (DCE), which are more typical in other areas (for instance health economics).

Part II

Policy instruments

5 Market-based instruments for a sustainable transition

Introduction

In economics there is an essential assumption that economic agents (consumers and producers but also governments) respond to incentives (Sloman et al., 2022), and this is the basis for numerous policy interventions. It is acknowledged that prices act both as signals and incentives and as such, instruments that have an effect on prices tend to be considered as more efficient. When we are trying to change the behaviour of countries and their economic agents towards less pollutant and more sustainable ones, the thinking behind the approval of regulations, schemes and instruments follows – or at least it should follow – the same rationale.

There are two main types of instruments that policymakers have been using to improve environmental outcomes and incentivise behavioural change. *Command-and-control* instruments aim to force companies (and others) to adopt specific technologies or operating procedures, based on standards that have been previously defined (Callan and Thomas, 2013): ambient standards, technology-based standards or performance-based standards. In the context of pollution control measures, these standards usually make reference to desired levels for the quality of environmental elements (for instance, concentrations of pollutants in water), the obligation to use specific abatement technologies, or the limitation of emissions levels in regulated sectors without imposing a particular technology to achieve said levels. This type of measures does not take into account the costs that different actors would have to incur to implement them (marginal abatement costs) and focus instead on the social benefits expected from their success. In addition, they tend to carry high costs associated with monitoring and compliance mechanisms, sometimes international legislation, and very importantly, they do not encourage companies to go beyond compliance, limiting sustainable innovations. This is why all in all they are not considered cost-effective (Mazaheri et al., 2022). In spite of their relative inefficiency, command-and-control measures are widely used, since their alternative, *market-based-instruments* (MBIs), and in particular taxes, do not enjoy public support and may cause political backlash (Beiser-McGrath et al., 2023). However these instruments are classified, as the following paragraphs will summarise, they are part of the fiscal policies that governments can implement, with fiscal policy understood as 'the use of government spending and taxation to

DOI: 10.4324/9781003224785-7

influence the economy, typically to promote strong and sustainable growth and reduce poverty' (Horton and El-Hanainy, 2017).

An example of command-and-control (CaC) measures within the EU is, for instance, the regulation of smart meters, included in the latest Electricity Directive (OJEU, 2019). It regulates the characteristics that smart meters should have though it does not really force Member States to adopt them – even if the language used clearly encourages their takeout. Other problems associated with command-and-control measures relate to the availability of information or the existence of hidden information (Hanley et al., 2019), which make it almost impossible to ascertain the real benefits and costs of the measures proposed, or to calculate the gap between real and perceived costs and benefits, as well as the differences between social and private costs and benefits. On most occasions, CaC measures are imposed nationally, without accounting for regional differences (Callan and Thomas, 2013) in the values of marginal social benefits or costs, which may be linked to differences in levels of income, education or population. MBIs are not perfect either, insofar they do not reflect 'non-market' values for environmental projects, but they tend to be more cost-effective. Some researchers (Lamperti et al., 2016) favour CaC measures over MBIs arguing that they guarantee policy effectiveness irrespectively of the timing of their introduction and they always direct technical change towards greener technologies, while with MBIs, a delay in their introduction may lead to lack of effectiveness in promoting technical change and in avoiding, for instance, environmental catastrophes.

It is worth noting that MBIs could be divided into two main groups, those that affect prices by imposing an added cost (which could subsequently be passed to market participants increasing prices), such as taxes, fees and charges, or those that reduce the cost (subsidies) or guarantee a minimum return (such as feed-in-tariff systems). Textbooks tend to classify MBIs in four categories (Callan and Thomas, 2013): pollution charges, subsidies, deposit/refund systems and pollution permit trading systems. However, subsidies and deposit/refund systems do not receive much attention from the literature, and most analyses tend to distinguish two main instruments: green taxes and cap-and-trade systems (Hanley et al., 2019). Other authors include feed-in systems as a type of subsidy (Mazaheri et al., 2022). Chapter 6 of this book will pay attention to the most popular cap-and-trade system, the European ETS, while Chapter 7 will look at taxation and the limitations of its use at EU level. In this chapter we will cover a whole range of instruments, classified as MBIs, but specifically used across Europe to promote the penetration of renewable energy and reduce greenhouse gas emissions, hence contributing directly to the sustainable transition this book is analysing.

Overview of main market-based-instruments used in the EU

The instruments used to support the uptake of renewable energy across the EU have evolved overtime as policies, targets and market conditions have changed. The Renewables Directive of 2009 (OJEU, 2009) named as possible support schemes *investment aid, tax exemptions or reductions, tax refunds, renewable energy obligation support schemes including those using green certificates, and direct price support schemes including feed-in tariffs and premium payments*. The use of tendering processes, by which energy companies bid to gain contracts to supply energy services with specific technologies in specific locations once the government has established the capacity for renewables of the country's grid (Pablo-Romero et al., 2017), was hardly mentioned in 2009, but was given full attention in 2018, when the Directive was first amended (OJEU, 2018a – remember its mention in Chapter 1), being then known with the acronym RED II. It made sense, in a context where price support schemes had almost disappeared as a result of the budget constraints created by the international economic crisis of 2007–2008 (Fernandez, 2018), once the Commission had set up the scene for more market competition already in 2013 (European Commission [EC], 2013) with plans to move in 2016 from feed-in tariffs to feed-in premiums. The latest reform (November 2023) responds on one side to the ambitions of the European Green Deal (EC, 2019) of putting renewables at the centre of a green energy transition, and on the other side to the need of reducing external energy dependency in the context of high prices created by the war in Ukraine (which could be further worsened by the even more recent conflict in the Middle East). The revised Directive (known as RED III) EU/2023/2413 (OJEU, 2023) aims to accelerate the penetration of renewables and facilitate their integration in Member States' energy mix. It increases the target for renewables to 42.5% for 2030, as overall EU binding target, with a desire to reach 45%, and again with Member States setting only indicative targets (i.e. not binding). Additionally, there is a transition period for the transposition of the Directive to national legislations, so measures will not be implemented until 2024 or 2025, leaving little room for manoeuvre for a 2030s deadline. It is also worth noting that support instruments are addressing mostly the electricity aspect of the energy production and consumption mix even if these pieces of legislation make reference to heating, cooling and transport.

In terms of sustainability credentials of the support mechanisms and the changing regulatory frameworks, it could be argued that the environmental pillar is always present, insofar any increase in the penetration of renewables that leads to a reduction in the use of fossil fuels should contribute to the reduction of greenhouse gas emissions. But we cannot forget that we are talking about market-based mechanisms, which means that the economic component or pillar is at the heart of the rationale to implement them. In fact, both the recast of 2018 (OJEU, 2018a) and its recent review (OJEU, 2023) specifically instruct countries to carefully design support mechanisms in a way that market distortions are avoided, more generally in 2018, and with regard to biomass and biogas markets in 2023. The latter makes also reference to the social pillar, alluding to the possibility of employment creation and the fostering of local industries (OJEU, 2023: 1), but it could be argued that very limited consideration is given to this aspect.

Let's see in the following paragraphs what some of these instruments are and what their development has been across EU Member States.

Feed-in systems

The first example of a feed-in tariff (FiT) system was found in the United States in 1978, but after an analysis of its effectiveness it was implemented in several European countries (Ritzenhofen and Spinler, 2016). The basic features of a FiT system are a guaranteed price that is sufficient to cover the return on investment (ROI) – which means that it is higher than the market price, a guaranteed access to the grid and a contract sufficiently long to provide stability to the aforementioned investment (Yuliani, 2017). Germany is often mentioned as an example of a successful implementation of the FiT system, followed by Spain, though in the case of the latter the design was not as efficient and disproportionally benefitted solar photovoltaic installations, with economic support that more than doubled that of wind energy installations (Fernandez-Gonzalez et al., 2021). Both countries had some sort of feed-in system since the 1990s and initiated the 'International Feed-in Cooperation' agreement in 2004, with the purpose of sharing experiences to improve the design of said systems. Slovenia joined the agreement in 2007 (Klein et al., 2008), however, it cannot be said that penetration of renewables has enjoyed a great development in the country, with statistics indicating almost no change in the proportion of renewables in Slovenia's energy mix in the last decades (see Figure 5.1).

The main difference between the systems in these three countries is that Germany established a fixed tariff scheme while Spain and Slovenia followed a premium tariff system (Held et al., 2007), though properly speaking in Spain tariffs and premiums coexisted for a number of years (Schallenberg-Rodriguez and Haas, 2012). With a FiT system utility companies are obliged to purchase the energy generated by renewable energy producers paying a tariff determined by the government, which is guaranteed for a long number of years, usually between 15 and 25 (Campoccia et al., 2014). A feed-in premium (FiP) works

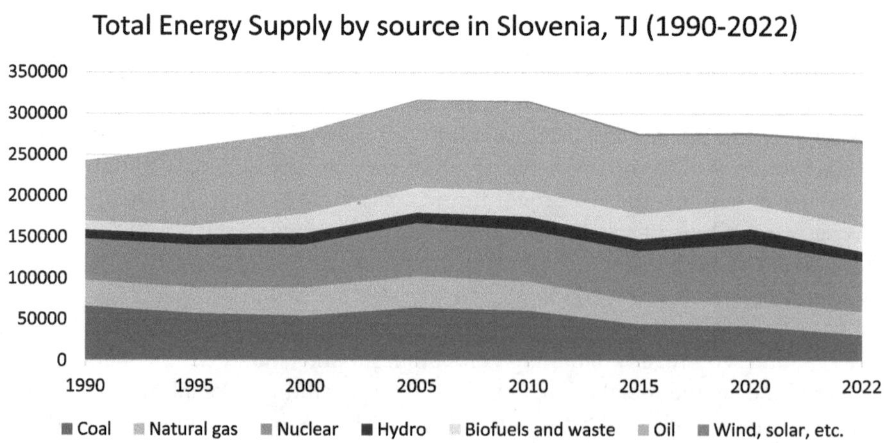

Figure 5.1 Total energy supply by source in Slovenia, TJ (1990–2022)

Source: IEA World Energy Balances, Extracted on 20/11/2023 from https://www.iea.org/countries/slovenia.

slightly different, and consists of an additional amount (premium) paid to renewable energy producers over the existing market price, which is variable, making this instrument more 'market integrated' (Xydis and Vlachakis, 2019). Similarly to variations in the type of FiTs for different types of renewable technologies, we can find three main types of FiPs: those with a fixed premium independent of the average power market price; those with a premium that has cap and floor prices, which limit the amount of revenue that can be obtained; and those with a sliding premium or contract for differences, where the premium depends on the average electricity price while the tariff (also called strike price) remains constant (Held et al., 2014). Variations of all these feed-in systems have been implemented in most EU Member States and across the world, but as it was previously mentioned, the budget constraints originated by the economic crisis of 2007–2008 caused the schemes to be severely reduced and in many cases completely eliminated (Fernandez, 2018). While functioning, most studies confirmed their positive contribution to the integration of renewable energies in the market, and their cost-effectiveness compared to other support instruments, with additional positive effects such as the promotion of technological innovation (Böhringer et al., 2017), even if this is punctualised and dependent on the design of the specific policy. In fact, some studies (Mazaheri et al., 2022) point at negative effects of subsidies (with feed-in tariffs being a subset) for sustainable innovation, arguing that companies that innovate are already ahead of the curve so subsidies do not influence their decision to innovate, or that some companies may use the subsidies for non-sustainable innovations if there is not enough transparency in the allocation process. Early studies confirmed feed-in tariffs contribution to research and development – boosting innovation, employment creation, reduction of greenhouse gas emissions, and contribution to GDP for both Germany and Spain (Garcia-Alvarez and Mariz-Perez, 2012). With the favourable regime created for specific technologies, it is no surprise that feed-in systems contribution to the economic profitability of photovoltaic companies is also highlighted by the literature (Milanes-Montero et al., 2018). This questions, though, if said companies could survive without the government support, which could not continue indefinitely. The limitation of the times over which the support is available, the size of the installations and the type of technology that could access the schemes have been factors introduced in many countries to reduce the financial burden on national budgets of feed-in systems, but that has originated frequent modifications of their regulatory frameworks, which created uncertainty for potential investors, and at times delayed or hindered the development of projects (Ritzenhofen and Spinler, 2016). In most jurisdictions feed-in systems are used in combination with other instruments, but there are countries where other instruments have progressively replaced them. It is worth noting though that 2021 saw for the first time an increase in the number of countries worldwide using feed-in systems, from 83 to 92, and countries like Ireland, which had eliminated them in 2015, reintroduced them (REN21, 2022), as explained in Box 5.1.

Box 5.1 Case study: Market-based instruments for the promotion of renewable energy in Ireland

Ireland began the implementation of a Feed-in Tariff system in 2006, after the unsuccessful use of a competitive tender system called Alternative Energy Requirement (AER), believed to have lower cost, but resulting in speculative bids that were uneconomic to enable the development of the projects (Doherty and O'Malley, 2011). The scheme aimed at boosting wind energy production in particular, but researchers (Clancy et al., 2012) pointed out the potential of the system to help the country reach other targets in connection with its obligations under the Renewables Directive of 2009. Ireland had set a target to replace 30% biomass for peat in its three co-firing power stations by 2015 (Clancy et al., 2012), but it was apparent that the price estimated for biomass crops would be insufficient to actually convince farmers to switch production, and a feed-in tariff system was suggested as a viable option to provide the necessary incentives. At the time, the Irish scheme was considered a novelty, insofar it included a floor price and a direct payment to cover the balancing costs of renewable energy generation, not used by many countries (Doherty and O'Malley, 2011). However, the FiT system was suspended in 2015, and only recently (2021) it has been reintroduced, with the aim to boost citizens and communities' participation in the energy transition (REN21, 2022), in line with the UN Sustainable Development Goals (leaving no one behind) and the European Green Deal. Ireland is a complex case study, given its geographical characteristics (an island, small size, Northern latitude and weather conditions), which limit the development potential of renewable technologies, and only recently has started exploring the solar photovoltaic possibilities (Ryan et al., 2023). It has been very active though in the policy side, with numerous supporting measures introduced during 2022 and 2023. Some of them were emergency ones and temporary in nature, to deal with the hike in energy prices created by the invasion of Ukraine (REN21, 2022), such as the reduction of energy taxes or VAT, and direct transfers to vulnerable groups. Other are more long-term focused, aiming at the transition of their energy system into a low-carbon one. These include (Ryan et al., 2023): enhanced support for businesses through a solar PV scheme, solar capital investment schemes, a so-called 'rooftop revolution' as strategy involving new planning permission exemptions for rooftop solar panels on homes and other buildings, clean export premiums and clean export guarantees (in the form of transfers and grants respectively). In 2021 Ireland had already introduced a strengthened carbon price system to balance the price of electricity in relation to gas (REN21, 2022). Geopolitically, the Irish case added complexity emerges from the market integration of its electricity system with the UK and France, in what was intended to facilitate the free movement of energy across the three countries (Wang et al., 2020) connecting all-island electricity markets with continental Europe, but this has been complicated by Brexit and the uncertainty in the decision-making process by legislators in the UK about future relationships. In the meantime, Ireland is well positioned to continue its decarbonisation process, having pledged in COP26 to stop using coal, and with wind already accounting for 31% of its electricity generation, higher than the EU average (REN21, 2022). The combination of fiscal instruments for the transition to renewable energies seems to go in the right direction, but more progress is required, for instance, in the transport sector.

Evidence seems to confirm that no one measure on its own is enough to provide sufficient incentives to accelerate the transition to low-carbon economies, hence the search for efficiency promoted by a combination of measures, including the ones explored in the following paragraphs. It is necessary to point out though, that efficiency is very much constrained by the design of the measure itself, and how well it fits with the rest of the fiscal system of the country or area where it is implemented, aiming at correcting or minimising social inequalities, given that it is widely argued that the energy transition will negatively affect those in the poorer segments of society. It is for the reader to decide if the elimination of systems like FiTs or FiPs, in the name of market competition, is having a negative impact on the most disadvantaged groups or sufficient safeguards are being implemented to prevent this from happening, both at the EU and national levels.

Green certificates

Green certificates, also known as renewable energy certificates (RECs) or tradable green certificates, are the most common alternative measure to feed-in-systems in the promotion of renewable energy generation and reduction of greenhouse gas emissions. However, their effectiveness in achieving this goal has been questioned by some (Bjørn et al., 2022; Hulshof et al., 2019). As the name indicates, a certificate supposedly offers a guarantee of origin, or in other words, proof that energy (mostly electricity) is generated from renewable sources (Chrysikopoulos et al., 2024). Early ideas on how a system of certificates would work were outlined in the 1990s, during the design phase of the ETS, and the first scheme in Europe was established in Belgium in 2002, in the Flanders region (Verbruggen and Laes, 2021). In the US, Iowa adopted the first scheme in 1999 and Texas followed in 2001 (Chrysikopoulos et al., 2024). The functioning is relatively simple, but with variations in each of the countries where it has been operating. In Romania, for instance, the green certificates are paired with a quota system, and energy suppliers are forced to buy certain amount of electricity produced by renewable sources and sell it to their customers (Atanasoae and Pentiuc, 2017). The regulator assigns one certificate for each MegaWatt hour (MWh) generated from a list of approved renewable energy sources (as then defined by the 2001/77/EC electricity directive).

Generators sell that energy with its accompanying certificates to retail energy suppliers, who sell directly to end-users. These suppliers will transmit the expenses associated with the certificates to the price that end-users pay, and they will have to submit at the end of the year the certificates back to the regulator to meet the renewable energy target agreed for the country in each year (Verbruggen and Laes, 2021). As adoption of renewable energy increased and the dynamics of energy markets changed overtime, so it changed the regulatory framework, with numerous modifications of the gas and electricity directives, which never achieved the market integration and liberalisation expected to, among other purposes, bring prices down for consumers. Importantly, modifications of the Renewables Directive of 2009 in 2018 (RED II) and 2023 (RED III) integrated the use of green certificates into wider energy strategies such as power purchase agreements (Chrysikopoulos et al., 2024), which will be discussed later in this chapter. Evidence confirms that there has been an increase in the certification rate of renewable electricity (Hulshof et al., 2019), which in theory has contributed to decreasing the problem of information asymmetry consumers face with regard to the origin of energy, particularly electricity, they purchase. However, the design of the certification systems may have created new inefficiencies, such as excess profits when there is no distinction in the treatment of different generation technologies (benefitting those whose costs of production are lower), or focus on reaching quotas and targets, stopping once they are reached instead of promoting further technological advancements (Verbruggen and Laes, 2021).

Differences in the performance of the markets for green certificates have also been identified to be influenced by the nature of the certification body as a public or private institution, in addition to the price volatility of the certificates (Hulshof et al., 2019). This leads to questions about the appropriateness of establishing 'markets' to 'trade' with these certificates. Is it necessary, and above all, ethical, to create markets over a document whose function is to guarantee the origin of the energy we consume? If suppliers, businesses in general, and countries can exchange these certificates for a price, do consumers really have a guarantee of where their energy is coming from? These questions will also become relevant when we speak about the EU ETS in the next chapter, but I invite the readers to reflect once more on what type of sustainability transition is being promoted here, where the economic incentive created by the potential profit that the sale of certificates can bring takes centre stage. Research provides evidence (Karakosta and Petropoulou, 2022) on the fact that the possibility of trading with certificates, particularly between countries that have established national targets for renewable energy generation (as it is the case of EU Member States) originates a misalignment with the EU targets – which supposedly aim at maximising welfare. When private certifiers are at play, such as in the US, their main interest becomes the maximisation of profits, which create incentives to provide dishonest certifications (i.e. certify grey electricity as green), erodes the trust that consumers can put into the certification system (Hulshof et al., 2019), and again hinders policy outcomes. This would be the opposite to the actions of a public certifier who should aim for the maximisation of social welfare (this should be a reminder of the role of the social pillar of sustainability and take us to question if the social aspect has been properly considered in the design of these instruments). The acquisition of certificates by companies affected by emission reduction targets has effectively meant that their real abatement efforts are no longer aligned with the 1.5 degrees Paris Agreement goal (Bjørn et al., 2022), so despite the claim that the increase in the use of green certificates contributes to bringing transparency to the energy system and incentivises the engagement of citizens in the energy transition (Chrysikopoulos et al., 2024), reality confirms that not all the certificates are used within a year and so they expire (Hulshof et al., 2019), which in economic terms signify an excess of supply and as such the inefficiency of this market. The question is then what instrument or combination of instruments could offer the optimal outcome?

Other market-based instruments

The previous sections made reference to a few instruments and policy options that frequently appear associated to feed-in systems and certificates, attesting that it would be highly unlikely to find one country using a single instrument as part of their attempts to boost the generation and use of renewable energy and/or the reduction of greenhouse gas emissions. One of said instruments are the *corporate power purchase agreements* (CPPAs). These are 'bilateral contracts between an electricity generator and a corporation to sell and purchase electricity outside the wholesale spot electricity market, with a typical duration of 10 to 15 years' (Gabrielli et al., 2022). As an instrument, it puts the onus of action in the private sector, which tends to lag behind and reduce commitments to more sustainable futures to the bare minimum (with some exceptions), and depending on the sector, lobby against more stringent regulatory measures. But businesses also need stability of the regulatory framework to plan for the medium and long term, and with so many changes in recent years, it is not easy to keep the pace, unless one has a true sense of corporate social responsibility and moves ahead of the curve. In any case, the Commission seems to agree on the need to reduce administrative burdens and its Recommendation issued in 2022 (EC, 2022a: 8) calls for the removal of both administrative and market barriers to CPPAs, with emphasis on their role to accelerate their uptake of renewable energy by SMEs. Regulatory barriers are also identified by the European Investment Bank (EIB) as an issue for the uptake of this type of contractual agreements, more common in the US but with uneven development by EU Member States (Ruderer, 2022), where large contracts in Spain and Scandinavian countries lead the way. The advantages of this instrument relate to the stability they offer to the price of electricity for customers (private companies in this case), in a market with high price volatility at the same time that they provide stability of the revenue streams for energy producers (Gabrielli et al., 2022; Ruderer, 2022). But it is this long-term commitment what also encounters reluctance among private companies, in the fear that more favourable prices may come in the future. In fact, long-term contracts, though helpful in reducing risk, may 'lock in' power generation that is not competitive, and has sometimes trapped customers into keeping the consumption of fossil fuels despite the existence of cheaper renewable options (Srivastav, 2023). This is why the Commission regulations specifically mention this instrument for agreements on renewable energy.

A similar instrument that has gained popularity is the *Contract-for-Differences* (CfD). While there are several types, the simplest understanding of the term tells us that through this contract energy generators can sell their electricity in the market and then pay or receive the difference between the 'strike price' and a 'reference price' multiplied by a 'reference quantity' (Fabra, 2023). The strike price is a predetermined contract price at which both buyers and sellers agree to settle the differences with the prevailing electricity spot price (Beiter et al., 2021). This strike price is also used in other instruments, including the aforementioned CPPAs and FiTs, and also in *auctions*. Auctions are part of the so-called *tenders* or *tendering process,* by which a government issues a 'call for tenders' to procure a certain capacity or generation of renewable-based electricity (IRENA and CEM, 2015). In general, there is a bidding process, and the successful bidder is decided based on the lowest price plus any other conditions that the government may have established. In the EU, the first auctions for renewable energy took place in Denmark in 2005, and Portugal in 2006, but most Member States are now using similar types of MBIs in the sense that they are 'premium-based' schemes (EC, 2022b), in a trend that follows the change from FiT to FiP that was covered in the previous section.

These instruments have in common their characteristic of being price-base policy instruments, which means that somehow they have the ability or the purpose of affecting energy prices. If they are effective, we should observe progressive reductions on energy prices for end-consumers, but as we know, this has not materialised. The exception among the instruments covered so far are the green certificates, which rely on a quota system. *Quotas* are quantity-based instruments, which usually require energy retailers to supply a minimum percentage of energy (mostly electricity) from renewable sources (Kilinc-Ata, 2016). A variation of the quota system is the *Renewable Portfolio Standards* (RPS), which directly mandate companies (instead of governments) to have a certain percentage of their electricity production or delivery (depending on the type of company) sourced from renewable sources (Grafstrom and Poudineh, 2023). The downside is that this alternative may encourage import of energy instead of developing domestic capacity. Similar quota systems can be found under the name of *Renewables Obligation*, used by the UK but now replaced by CfDs (House of Commons, 2016), or *Renewable Electricity* Standard (RES) (Kilinc-Ata, 2016).

One could continue listing instruments for a very long time, as they are modified or replaced relatively frequently. To some extent the variation is understandable given the progress achieved in the penetration of renewables as part of the energy mix across the EU and changing energy market dynamics. But some variation has happened also as part of the learning process that involves the realisation that some of these instruments have not been effective or efficient enough to reach their goals. The changing political and policy landscape may also justify variations in the instruments used, in the EU as a whole and in each Member State. This could be said, for instance, in the case of *Net Metering.* Effectively it is a variation of a FiT which allows both residential and commercial customers who generate power (prosumers) to sell the unused electricity back to the utility company at whole retail price (Ryan et al., 2023). In this light and in the context of the EGD, the instrument allows for wider citizen and community engagement in the energy transition. In the area of efficiency, research has consistently supported the idea that quota systems (quantity-based instruments) are less efficient than price-based instruments (Menanteau et al., 2003; Kilinc-Ata, 2016; Strunz et al., 2021), however, within the EU framework their use has become more common, including hybrid instruments that mix both price and quantity support mechanisms (Fabra, 2023), such as the ETS that will be covered in the next chapter. But such proliferation of instruments can also bring confusion to both private businesses and citizens. A table with a summary of instruments used by several Member States and their assessed efficiency (as per academic and/or official reporting evidence) is included in Table 5.1, to exemplify the observable puzzle that support for renewable energy has become across the EU.

This set of mixed results in the implementation of supporting instruments shows that the multiplicity of factors to take into consideration makes it very difficult to find the right balance in the design of the policy mix (through MBIs) that Member States can use. It is worth noting that 'efficiency' is being assessed through different variables and it can be seen in terms of cost-effectiveness, increase in the percentage of renewable energy installation, relative efficiency compared to other instruments, etc. Internal policy or political pressures, trust and distrust in schemes, treatment of different technologies, and design of the systems in general, demonstrate that overall the EU and its Member States are still in a trial and error phase, and when certain instruments reach a considerable level of maturity (i.e. they have been in place for more than a decade, such as the case of FiTs), there are always reasons found to modify or even eliminate said instrument altogether. While change sometimes is necessary, when it comes to finding the necessary resources to finance the transition to cleaner energies and modes of production in general, stability is always a welcome feature to promote investment, particularly if the private sector is to be involved, so an initial instrument design that includes flexibility and adaptation features, may be a recommendation that policymakers should consider.

The new Renewable Energy Financing Mechanism

We need to see the mix of supporting mechanisms for renewable energy in the context of the EGD but also the governance of the Energy Union package preceding it (OJEU, 2018b), as part of the 'Clean Energy for All Europeans' commitment. As it has been highlighted elsewhere in this book, one of the reasons for the increase in regulation coming from EU institutions is the perception that sufficient progress towards more sustainable economies is not being made at Member State level, and while energy policy instruments have been characterised as soft forms of governance, the developments of 2018 point at the 'hardening' of said soft governance (Knodt et al., 2020). The implementation of the governance regulation, particularly its article 33, is the basis for the approval in 2020 of the new Union Renewable Energy Financing Mechanism [REFM] (OJEU, 2020).

Table 5.1 Summary of renewable energy support instruments and their assessed efficiency in a sample of EU member states

	FiT/FiP	*Efficient?*	*Green certificate*	*Efficient?*	*Auction/tender*	*Efficient?*	*CPPA*	*Efficient?*
Germany	Yes	Yes	Yes	Yes	Yes (for some technologies)	Yes	Yes	Yes
Spain	Yes	Yes, to an extent	Yes	Unassessed	Yes	Yes	Yes	Unknown
Denmark	Yes	Yes	Yes	Yes	Yes	Yes	No	-
Italy	Yes	No	Yes	Yes	Yes	No	Yes	No

Source: Author's elaboration.

It is pre-empting that Member States may not achieve sufficient progress towards their renewable energy targets for 2030, and allows the boosting of said progress through cooperative means. Effectively it links countries who voluntarily pay into the mechanism (called contributing countries) with those countries that agree to have new renewable energy project installations in their territory (called host countries). The participant countries do not need to negotiate between themselves to reach an agreement. Instead, the Commission facilitates the agreement setting the conditions and criteria that will determine if the projects will be supported or not (EC, n.d.). It is expected that the host countries will benefit from the mechanism through a number of advantages, such as local investment and job creation, reduction of greenhouse gas emissions and improved air quality, modernisation of their national energy systems and reduction of energy dependency, potentially free of costs (OJEU, 2020). The contributing countries will benefit from financing energy projects that are more cost-effective than producing renewable energy in their own territory, potentially gaining access to renewable energy production that would be otherwise absent (EC, n.d.). Effectively, this system follows the rationale used by the Kyoto Protocol for the implementation of Clean Development Mechanisms and Joint Implementation projects (UN, 1997), the so-called 'flexibility mechanisms', which allowed developed countries to invest in less developed or transition economies instead of their territories if it was cheaper to do so.

Importantly both host and contributing countries will benefit from the project implementation as the renewable energy sources financed through this mechanism will count towards the climate targets for renewable energy for both countries (EC, 2020), allocating the renewables statistics through a standard formula. The funding for this scheme may come not only from the payments made by the Member States but also from EU funding and private sector contributions (Maliszewska-Nienartowicz, 2024). In connection with the instruments described in previous sections, this mechanism is similar to some of them insofar it uses a competitive tendering process, in this case for the allocation of grants, by which the bids with the lowest price will be awarded first (EC, n.d.). The winning bid will determine the size of the grant, which can be used for the installation of a renewable production facility with a specified capacity (acting as investment support), or for the production of energy (in the form of operating support) (EC, n.d.).

It is still early to say if this new mechanism will be successful, but researchers have started analysing its potential. Some of them (Strunz et al., 2021) hint at the REFM as the direction of travel in terms of further increase of the EU institutionalisation of energy policy design, in detriment of Member States' prominent position in the regulatory framework. But the truth is that its reach is going to be limited, if the type of renewable energy projects to be financed is restricted to certain technologies. This is what can be observed at the moment, with the first decision on the type of projects that can be eligible for grants under this mechanism, approved in 2023 (EC, 2023), including only solar photovoltaic (PV) projects. In theory, however, projects could cover all eligible technologies under the Renewable Energy Directive of 2018 – RED II (Maliszewska-Nienartowicz, 2024). Only a couple of months before this decision was approved, the first step towards the implementation of the mechanism took place through a binding commitment between Finland and Luxemburg, which was followed by the first cross-border tender for renewables. In this first instance, the resulting grant will provide investment support for the installation of solar PV capacity in Finland with a minimum capacity of 5 MW and a maximum of 100 MW, to which Luxemburg contributes with €40 million (EC, n.d.).

The mechanism can be used to fill the gap that some Member States may suffer between their capacity to increase renewable energy production in their own territory and their individual renewable energy targets, as long as they have financial capability (Maliszewska-Nienartowicz, 2024). The question comes when the country may suffer from low renewable energy potential and low financial capability. In those cases, it is expected that these factors would have been taken into account to determine their targets and national contributions, but additional support measures may be necessary, or acceptance that energy dependence may continue in the longer term should be featured in further policy developments. A positive element of this mechanism is that it provides certainty in the funding available for the development of larger joint renewable energy projects, but its success is conditioned to the level of attractiveness of available projects for the investing (contributing) countries (Tedeschini et al., 2023).

It is hoped that this new mechanism will contribute to increasing the ambition of Member States to accelerate the transition of their energy systems. In conjunction with the rest of instruments covered by this chapter (and those to be analysed in the rest of the book), it would be reasonable to assume that there is a sufficient variety of instruments for countries to choose the ones that are better suited to their specific characteristics. Some authors argue that the lack of wider instrument harmonisation at EU level (Maliszewska-Nienartowicz, 2024) may reflect lower levels of ambition, as it happened when Member States opposed an EU-wide quota system (Strunz et al., 2021). But opting for instruments that may be perceived as less efficient is not necessarily resultant on less ambitious outcomes, as the case of Sweden demonstrates with its tradable green certificates (Maliszewska-Nienartowicz, 2024).

The new REFM also highlights the wider role that is expected from the private sector in the energy transition, since it can participate as both investor and project developer (EC, 2020). This is indicative of a wider trend in policy financing, at a time of limited budget availability by public institutions. It also provides a new development of inter-country cooperation (Tedeschini et al., 2023), strengthening the relationship between Member States and possibly opening a new avenue for further integration, at a time when Euroscepticism and national interests may have put into question the potential for such integration to happen.

All the measures discussed in this chapter have two elements in common: they use incentives to promote behavioural change in the market, whether affecting prices or quantities – in this case of energy; and they have the aim to increase the penetration of renewable energy in Member States' energy mix to reduce GHG emissions. This provides an indication of integration between the economic and environmental pillars of sustainability, unfortunately with very little attention to the social pillar.

Discussion questions

1. Do you think that feed-in-tariff support mechanisms should continue indefinitely or should progressively disappear?
2. Would you advocate for more command-and-control instruments or should market-based instruments be the only way forward?
3. To which extent the provision of incentives to act in a more sustainable manner is the responsibility of governments at the national and local levels as opposed to international or intergovernmental institutions?
4. Could the aims of the European Green Deal be achieved without economic incentives and financial support instruments?
5. Do you think it is possible to reach a balance between economic efficiency and social and environmental goals with single policy instruments or a combination of measures is unavoidable?

Further readings

Arent, D., Arndt, C., Miller, M., Tarp, F. and Zinaman, O. (eds) (2017) *The Political Economy of Clean Energy Transitions*. Oxford University Press: This book introduces the reader to a wide range of instruments used across the world to promote renewable energy penetration. It provides an interesting analysis of the instruments, institutions and actors at play, including perspectives from less developed countries, and presents an overview of the challenges ahead.

Fouquet, R. (ed) (2018) *The Economics of Renewable Energy,* The International Library of Critical Writings in Economics series, 347. Edward Elgar Publishing: This book is a nice collection of articles by international experts on energy economics, looking into the efficiency of different policy instruments, evidence cases around the world, and the direction of travel with regard to technological advances and the impact that the adoption of renewable energies has in different socio-economic contexts.

Zillman, D., Redgwell, C., Omorogbe, Y. and Barrera-Hernandez, L. K. (eds) (2008) *Beyond the Carbon Economy: Energy Law in Transition*. Oxford University Press: Though time has elapsed there are several chapters of this book that can be of interest for the reader insofar it provides overview of market-based instruments, in particular certificates, not so often covered by the literature. It also offers a different perspective, looking into the legal aspects of policy implementation.

References

Atanasoae, P. and Pentiuc, R. (2017) Considerations on the green certificate support system for electricity production from renewable energy sources, *Procedia Engineering*, 181 (2017): 796–803.

Beiser-McGrath, L. F., Bernauer, T. and Prakash, A. (2023) Command and control or market-based instruments? Public support for policies to address vehicular pollution in Beijing and New Delhi, *Environmental Politics*, 32 (4): 586–618.

Beiter, P., Kitzing, L., Spitsen, P., Noonan, M., Berkhout, V. and Kikuchi, Y. (2021) Toward global comparability in renewable energy procurement, *Joule*, 5 (2021): 1485–1500.

Bjørn, A., Lloyd, S. M., Brander, M. and Matthews, H. M. (2022) Renewable energy certificates threaten the integrity of corporate science-based targets, *Nature Climate Change*, 12 (2022): 539–546.

Böhringer, C., Cuntz, A., Harhoff, D. and Asane-Otoo, E. (2017) The impact of the German feed-in tariff scheme on innovation: Evidence based on patent filings in renewable energy technologies, *Energy Economics*, 67 (2017): 545–553.

Callan, S. J. and Thomas, J. M. (2013) *Environmental Economics & Management. Theory, Policy, and Applications* (6th edition). Mason: South-Western Cengage Learning.

Campoccia, A., Dusonchet, L., Telaretti, E. and Zizzo, G. (2014) An analysis of feed-in tariffs for solar PV in six representative countries of the European Union, *Solar Energy*, 107 (2014): 530–542.

Chrysikopoulos, S. K., Chountalas, P. T., Georgakellos, D. A. and Lagodimos, A. G. (2024) Green certificates research: Bibliometric assessment of current state and future directions, *Sustainability*, 16 (2024): 1129. https://doi.org/10.3390/su16031129

Clancy, D., Breen, J. P., Thorne, F. and Wallace, M. (2012) The influence of a renewable energy feed in tariff on the decision to produce biomass crops in Ireland, *Energy Policy*, 41 (2012): 412–421.

Doherty, R. and O'Malley, M. (2011) The efficiency of Ireland's renewable energy feed-in tariff (REFIT) for wind generation, *Energy Policy*, 39 (2011): 4911–4919.

European Commission (2013) Communication from the commission. Delivering the internal electricity market and making the most of public intervention. COM (2013) 7243 final. Brussels, 5.11.2013.

European Commission (2019) Communication from the commission to the European Parliament, the European council, the council, the European economic and social committee and the committee of the regions: the European Green Deal. COM (2019) 640 final. Brussels, 11.12.2019.

European Commission (2020) EU renewable energy financing mechanism, Fact Sheet. September 2020.

European Commission (2022a) Commission Recommendation of 18.5.2022 on speeding up permit-granting procedures for renewable energy projects and facilitating Power Purchase Agreements. C(2022) 3219 final. Brussels, 18.5.2022.

European Commission (2022b) *Study on the Performance of Support for Electricity from Renewable Sources Granted by Means of Tendering Procedures in the Union – 2022*, Directorate General for Energy, Brussels.

European Commission (2023) Commission decision of 14.4.2023 on the financing of the activities related to the Union renewable energy financing mechanism, and the adoption of the work programme for 2023. C(2023) 2437 final. Brussels, 14.4.2023.

European Commission (n.d.) EU renewable energy financing mechanism. Available from: https://energy.ec.europa.eu/topics/renewable-energy/financing/eu-renewable-energy-financing-mechanism_en

Fabra, N. (2023) Reforming European electricity markets: Lessons from the energy crisis, *Energy Economics*, 126 (2023): 106963. https://doi.org/10.1016/j.eneco.2023.106963

Fernandez, R. M. (2018) Conflicting energy policy priorities in EU energy governance. *Journal of Environmental Studies and Sciences*, 8(2018): 239–248. https://doi.org/10.1007/s13412-018-0499-0

Fernandez-Gonzalez, R., Arce, E. and Garza-Gil, D. (2021) How political decisions affect the economy of a sector: The example of photovoltaic energy in Spain, *Energy Reports*, 7 (2021): 2940–2949.

Gabrielli, P., Aboutalebi, R. and Sansavini, G. (2022) Mitigating financial risk of corporate power purchase agreements via portfolio optimization, *Energy Economics*, 109 (2022): 105980. https://doi.org/10.1016/j.eneco.2022.105980

Garcia-Alvarez, M. T. and Mariz-Perez, R. M. (2012) Analysis of the success of feed-in tariff for renewable energy promotion mechanism in the EU: Lessons from Germany and Spain, *Procedia - Social and Behavioral Sciences,* 65 (2012): 52–57.

Grafstrom, J. and Poudineh, R. (2023) No evidence of counteracting policy effects on European solar power invention and diffusion, *Energy Policy*, 172 (2023): 113319. https://doi.org/10.1016/j.enpol.2022.113319

Hanley, N., Shogren, J. and White, B. (2019) *Introduction to Environmental Economics* (3rd edition), Oxford, UK: Oxford University Press.

Held, A., Ragwitz, M., Huber, C., Resch, G., Faber, T. and Vertin, K. (2007) *Feed-In Systems in Germany, Spain and Slovenia – A Comparison,* Fraunhofer Institute, ARE and EEG. Karlsruhe, Germany, October 2007.

Held, A., Ragwitz, M., Gephart, M., Kleßmann, C. and de Visser, E. (2014) *D5.2: Best practice design features for RES-E support schemes and best practice methodologies to determine remuneration levels,* DIA-CORE Project, Work Package 5, Contract number: IEE/12/833/SI2.645735, Fraunhofer Institute, September 2014

Horton, M. and El-Hanainy, A. (2017) Fiscal policy: Taking and giving away. *Finance & Development, Back to Basics, Economic Concepts Explained,* International Monetary Fund. Available from: https://www.imf.org/external/pubs/ft/fandd/basics/pdf/horton_fiscal-policy.pdf

House of Commons (2016) *Energy: The Renewables Obligation*, Briefing Paper Number 05870, 22 July 2016, House of Commons Libray.

Hulshof, D., Jepma, C. and Mulder, M. (2019) Performance of markets for European renewable energy certificates, *Energy Policy,* 128 (2019): 697–710.

IRENA and CEM (2015) *Renewable Energy Auctions – A Guide to Design*. Abu Dhabi: IRENA and CEM.

Karakosta, O. and Petropoulou, D. (2022) The EU electricity market: Renewables targets, tradable green certificates and electricity trade, *Energy Economics*, 111 (2022): 106034. https://doi.org/10.1016/j.eneco.2022.106034

Kilinc-Ata, N. (2016) The evaluation of renewable energy policies across EU countries and US states: An econometric approach, *Energy for Sustainable Development*, 31 (2016): 83–90.

Klein, A., Pfluger, B., Held, A., Ragwitz, M., Resch, G. and Faber, T. (2008) *Evaluation of Different Feed-In Tariff Design Options – Best Practice Paper for the International Feed-In Cooperation* (2nd edition), EEG and Fraunhofer Institute. Available from: https://ledsgp.org/app/uploads/2015/07/best_practice_paper_feed-in-tariffs.pdf

Knodt, M., Ringel, M. and Müller, R. (2020) 'Harder' soft governance in the European Energy Union, *Journal of Environmental Policy and Planning*, 22 (6): 787–800.

Lamperti, F., Napoletano, M. and Roventini, A. (2016) *Preventing Environmental Disasters: Market-Based vs. Command-and-Control Policies,* ISI Growth, 24/2016 July.

Maliszewska-Nienartowicz, J. (2024) Renewable energy and its financing instruments in the European Union: New trends in development? *Journal of Contemporary European Studies,* 32 (1): 35–51.

Mazaheri, M., Bonnin Roca, J., Markus, A. and Walrave, B. (2022) Market-based instruments and sustainable innovation: A systematic literature review and critique, *Journal of Cleaner Production,* 373 (2022): 133947. https://doi.org/10.1016/j.jclepro.2022.133947

Menanteau, P., Finon, D. and Lamy, M.-L. (2003) Prices versus quantities: Choosing policies for promoting the development of renewable energy, *Energy Policy,* 31 (2003): 799–812.

Milanes-Montero, P., Arroyo-Farrona, A. and Perez-Calderon, E. (2018) Assessment of the influence of feed-in tariffs on the profitability of European photovoltaic companies, *Sustainability*, 10 (2018): 3427. https://dx.doi.org/10.3390/su10103427

Official Journal of the European Union (2009) Directive 2009/28/EC of the European parliament and of the council of 23 April 2009 on the promotion of the use of energy from renewable sources and amending and subsequently repealing Directives 2001/77/EC and 2003/30/EC. L140, 5.6.2009.

Official Journal of the European Union (2018a) Directive (EU) 2018/2001 of the European parliament and of the council of 11 December 2018 on the promotion of the use of energy from renewable sources (recast). L328, 21.12.2018.

Official Journal of the European Union (2018b) Regulation (EU) 2018/1999 of the European parliament and of the council of 11 December 2018 on the governance of the energy union and climate action, amending regulations (EC) No 663/2009 and (EC) No 715/2009 of the European Parliament and of the Council, Directives 94/22/EC, 98/70/EC, 2009/31/EC, 2009/73/EC, 2010/31/EU, 2012/27/EU and 2013/30/EU of the European Parliament and of the Council, Council Directives 2009/119/EC and (EU) 2015/652 and repealing Regulation (EU) No 525/2013 of the European Parliament and of the Council. L328, 21.12.2018.

Official Journal of the European Union (2019) Directive (EU) 2019/944 of the European parliament and of the council of 5 June 2019 on common rules for the internal market for electricity and amending Directive 2012/27/EU (recast). L158, 14.6.2019.

Official Journal of the European Union (2020) Commission implementing regulation (EU) 2020/1294 of 15 September 2020 on the Union renewable energy financing mechanism. L303, 17.9.2020.

Official Journal of the European Union (2023) Directive (EU) 2023/2413 of the European parliament and of the council of 18 October 2023 amending directive (EU) 2018/2001, Regulation (EU) 2018/1999 and Directive 98/70/EC as regards the promotion of energy from renewable sources, and repealing Council Directive (EU) 2015/652. L77, 31.10.2023.

Pablo-Romero, M. P., Sanchez-Braza, A., Salvador-Ponce, J. and Sanchez-Labrador, N. (2017) An overview of feed-in tariffs, premiums and tenders to promote electricity from biogas in the EU-28, *Renewable and Sustainable Energy Reviews*, 73 (2017): 1366–1379.

REN21 (2022) *Renewables 2022. Global Status Report,* Paris, France.

Ritzenhofen, I. and Spinler, S. (2016) Optimal design of feed-in-tariffs to stimulate renewable energy investments under regulatory uncertainty - A real options analysis, *Energy Economics,* 53 (2016): 76–89.

Ruderer, D. (2022) Infrastructure solutions: The power of purchase agreements, *European Investment Bank*, 12 July 2022, Part of the series 'Infrastructure Solutions'.

Ryan, L., Wheatley, J. and Saba, N. (2023) *A Review of Policies for the Rollout of Rooftop Solar PV in Ireland,* Climate Change Advisory Council, Working Paper no. 22.

Schallenberg-Rodriguez, J. and Haas, R. (2012) Fixed feed-in tariff versus premium: A review of the current Spanish system, *Renewable and Sustainable Energy Reviews*, 16 (2012): 293–305.

Sloman, J., Garratt, D. and Guest, J. (2022) *Economics* (11th edition). Harlow, UK: Pearson.

Srivastav, S. (2023) How are energy contracts affecting the transition to net zero? *Economics Observatory*, 16 February 2023. Available from: https://www.economicsobservatory.com/how-are-energy-contracts-affecting-the-transition-to-net-zero#:~:text=Around%20the%20world%2C%20a%20large,power%2C%20which%20is%20often%20cheaper.

Strunz, S., Lehmann, P. and Gawel, E. (2021) Analyzing the ambitions of renewable energy policy in the EU and its Member States, *Energy Policy*, 156 (2021): 112447. https://doi.org/10.1016/j.enpol.2021.112447

Tedeschini, F. R., Tuerk, A. and Frieden, D. (2023) Renewable cooperation mechanisms in the EU: Lessons learned and future perspectives, *Energies*, 16 (2023): 7410. https://doi.org/10.3390/en16217410

UN (1997) Kyoto protocol to the United Nations framework convention on climate change, 10 December 1997. FCCC/CP/1997/L.7/Add.1

Verbruggen, A. and Laes, E. (2021) Early European experience with tradable green certificates neglected by EU ETS architects, *Environmental Science and Policy,* 119 (2021): 66–71.

Wang, S., Huang, Y., Vorushylo, I. et al. (2020) Economic assessment of high renewable energy penetration scenario in 2030 on the interconnected Irish power system, *Energy Policy*, 145 (2020): 111774. https://doi.org/10.1016/j.enpol.2020.111774

Xydis, G. and Vlachakis, N. (2019) Feed-in-premium renewable energy support scheme: A scenario approach, *Resources*, 8 (2019): 106. https://dx.doi.org/10.3390/resources8020106

Yuliani, D. (2017) Is feed-in-tariff policy effective for increasing deployment of renewable energy in Indonesia? In Arent, D. and others (eds) *The Political Economy of Clean Energy Transitions*. Oxford: Oxford University Press: 144–162.

6 The European Emissions Trading System (ETS)

Introduction: emissions trading systems

Emission trading systems are part of *cap-and-trade systems*, by which companies are allocated a number of 'permits' that give them the right to pollute as a result of their daily operations, up to a level measured usually in tonnes of carbon dioxide equivalent (CO_2eq). The number of permits is determined by law, and so it is the provision of trading allowed between companies within specific economic sectors and within specific regions (Callan and Thomas, 2013). The key for the functioning of the system is the price of the permits: if the price of a permit is higher than the *marginal abatement cost* (cost of reducing one extra unit of pollution) for the company, this will incentivise said company to replace its production process by a less polluting one, with the potential to foster technological innovation. If on the contrary the price of the permit is lower than the marginal abatement cost, then the company will acquire permits in the market as it will be more cost-effective (Fernandez, 2023). There are also other elements very important in the design of the systems, including which greenhouse gases (GHG)s and which sectors they would regulate, the total allowances cap, how the system is going to be administered and monitored, particularly in terms of reporting and verification, and how are the permits going to be distributed – for example, for free or through an auction (Narassimhan et al., 2018).

As an economic instrument, emissions trading falls under the category of market-based instruments (MBIs) that were covered by Chapter 5, but it can be considered a hybrid between price-based and quantity-based instruments. The initial cap that determines the limit of how much it can be polluted is a quantity mechanism, but the trading of the permits, which is subject to demand and supply, is clearly a price-based mechanism.

Detractors of emissions trading tend to question if it is ethical to grant the right to pollute in exchange for a price, effectively buying the right to continue business as usual instead of making an effort to reduce pollution (Tietenberg and Lewis, 2009). But more widely there have been three categories of objections to emissions trading or carbon trading (since the unit of measurement is carbon dioxide): ethics, justice and effectiveness (Caney and Hepburn, 2011). This introduction and part of

DOI: 10.4324/9781003224785-8

the next section will look into the ethical and justice aspects, while the rest of the chapter will cover the effectiveness of the system.

Historically, the origins of emissions trading are set to emanate from the US Clean Air Act of the 1970s (Gorman and Solomon, 2002), while in practice it was the creation of a sulphur dioxide (SO_2) trading programme as a result of the 1990 Clean Air Act Amendments what pivoted the development of these schemes across the globe trying to replicate its success (Lane, 2012). On reflection, one of the questions that we should consider, given that this policy instrument and a number of policy instruments seen in the previous chapter have their origin in US policies, is to which extent it is appropriate to attempt their application (replication) elsewhere. We must bear in mind that the US economy is the clearest exponent of a market capitalist system which follows (for the most part) neoliberal approaches by which market efficiencies are predicated and government interventions reduced to the minimum expression (Weaver, 2021). There are clear differences between the US and particularly continental Europe, much more grounded on mixed economy approaches with government intervention in wide areas of economic activities and the establishment of different levels of social protection programmes (Molina and Rhodes, 2008). It would be no surprise then that the perceived success of MBIs at the other side of the Atlantic has not been achieved in the EU, for a number of reasons, including the complexity of reaching agreements and commitments among 27 very different sovereign countries.

One of the arguments against emissions trading from an ethical standpoint relates to the assumption that humans have property rights over the natural world (Caney and Hepburn, 2011), which would be gained if we 'pay a price' for certain elements of it. Turning pollution into a commodity may undermine the sense of shared responsibility over environmental goods (Sandel, 2005). Caney and Hepburn (2011) disregard this argument under the premise that the right to use a natural resource is not the same as a property right, and it is compatible with a stewardship function. I leave the readers to decide on what side of the debate they would position themselves. Another key argument against carbon trading relates to the problems it generates in terms of distributional justice (Farber, 2011): since emission allowances are allocated for free, at least in the initial stages of the scheme's implementation, this creates an overcompensation for companies, which would transfer the cost of the permits to consumers – who would pay higher prices – and would not really need to make an effort to comply. This could encourage older more polluting industries and production centres to continue operating, in detriment of the local communities where they are installed. In addition to this, regulation of emissions will always generate costs, and evidence is clear in indicating that these costs have a disproportionate negative impact over low-income consumers (Caney and Hepburn, 2011; Farber, 2011). Consciousness about these issues suggests that once more, in trying to strike a balance between environmental and economic pillars, the social pillar has been left behind. Notwithstanding this it will be interesting to explore how the EU ETS came to exist and how it has evolved overtime in an attempt to correct its shortcomings.

The origins of the EU ETS

The implementation of an emissions trading system in the EU is rooted in the approval of the Kyoto Protocol (UN, 1997), where said system was envisaged as part of the flexibility mechanisms included to help countries reach their emission reduction targets. Importantly, the flexibility mechanisms were introduced as suggested complementary actions to national reduction efforts, and the encouragement was given to those national or domestic interventions, which means that emissions trading has never been an obligation and once again, its inclusion took place on the insistence of the US (Skjærseth and Wettestad, 2009). Under the Protocol, which the EU and its 15 Member States at the time were signatories of, Annex B countries (industrialised economies) committed to reduce their GHGs by 5% with respect to 1990 as base year, during the first commitment period (2008–2012). Chapter 1 already explained how the Protocol listed six GHGs but actions have been focused on CO_2 as the one with the largest impact.

The Protocol didn't enter into force until 2005, as it was a condition that at least 55 countries (signatories of the United Nations Framework Convention on Climate Change) would sign, and that signatory parties would represent at least 55% of world emissions in industrialised countries (as of 1990) (UN, 1997). This condition was not fulfilled until Russia ratified the Protocol at the end of 2004 (Yagodin, 2021). The EU committed to reduce its emissions by 8% with respect to its 1990 levels, but as part of the flexibility to reach emissions reduction, the Protocol allowed that each Member State could reduce (or increase) emissions according to their circumstances (Eyckmans et al., 2002). A political agreement for the distribution of emissions reduction was reached in June 1998 (the Burden Sharing Agreement) and the percentages allocated to each Member State were published in a Commission Communication of 1999 (EC, 1999). Values for each Member State can be seen in Table 6.1.

As it can be observed, several Member States were allowed to increase their emissions levels, and these coincidentally were the four first countries who benefitted from the EU Cohesion Fund – -Spain, Portugal, Greece and Ireland (EC, 2023) – with a small increase allowed to Sweden too. One could argue that given the disadvantaged economic situation of these countries, there was an expectation that the market for emissions trading would be a success assuming that they would need to acquire permits (allowances) to undertake the economic activities that would facilitate their economic growth.

The EU took very seriously the opportunity to use emissions trading, and in its Green Paper (EC, 2000) it presented emissions trading as 'an integral and major part of the Community's implementation [of the Kyoto Protocol] strategy' (EC, 2000: 4). Interestingly, the Commission defined emissions trading as 'a new instrument for environmental protection' (EC, 2000: 4) but as if in need of further justification, it also presented an 'economic case' to defend the role of trading in the EU (EC, 2000: 11–12) estimating a potential cost saving of €1.7 billion a year (EC, 2000: 11–12), at the same time that it highlighted the need to protect the functioning of the internal market and avoid distortions in international trade.

Table 6.1 Distribution of emission reductions obligation under the initial 'Burden Sharing Agreement'

Member State	*Burden sharing (%)*
Austria	−13
Belgium	−7.5
Denmark	−21
Finland	0
France	0
Germany	−21
Greece	+25
Ireland	+13
Italy	−6.5
Luxembourg	−28
Netherlands	−6
Portugal	+27
Spain	+15
Sweden	+4
UK	−12.5%

Source: EC (1999).

Note: A plus (+) sign indicates that instead of reduction, the country is allowed to increase its emission levels.

The debates about burden sharing and emission trading had started early on, with a study in 1998 that proposed a bottom-up approach to allocate sectoral reduction targets which took into consideration national differences such as the composition of power production, the importance of energy intensive export industries and other domestic sectors (Eyckmans et al., 2002). This helped the publication of the Green Paper in 2000 showing a lot of thought on how emissions trading should begin. The initial ideas put forward for consultation (EC, 2000) envisaged that initially only carbon dioxide would be included in emissions trading, as it was estimated that at the time it represented 80% of EU total emissions (EC, 2000: 11). It also proposed a 'learning by doing' approach, justifying the beginning of trading before the initial Kyoto commitment period (EC, 2000: 10), and reflected over which sectors, emission-intensive ones, should participate in the scheme. The initial list (EC, 2000: 14) included electricity and heat production; iron and steel; refining; chemicals; glass, pottery and building materials – including cement; paper and printing – including paper pulping. Between these sectors it was estimated that 45.1% of the EU emissions would be covered by emissions trading (EC, 2000: 14). Finally, another important aspect considered by the Green Paper was the possible effects of a future EU enlargement (EC, 2000: 16), which materialised, as we know, more than once.

One of the most controversial and criticised aspects of emissions trading is the method of allocation of permits (called emissions allowances), since between the two main options – auction and grandfathering – the latter has been the preferred approach, at least in early stages (Caney and Hepburn, 2011), which translates on the allocation of allowances for free, in a number calculated based on historical levels of emissions (Wang et al., 2022). This usually leads to overallocation of allowances (Fernandez, 2023), and produces market inefficiencies, which have been all too present in the EU ETS case, as the next section will present.

Despite all the potential problems and criticisms outlined ex-ante, the emissions trading machine was working non-stop, and the initial regulatory framework saw the light in 2003 in the form of a Directive (2003/87/EC) on 'a scheme for greenhouse gas emission allowance trading *within* the Community' (italics by the author) (OJEU, 2003). Part of the reasons to pursue this policy instrument relate to the failed attempt to introduce an EU-wide eco-tax on CO_2 (Braun, 2009), but taxation will be the object of Chapter 7 of this book so the rationale of this aspect of the decision will not be discussed here.

Implementation phases of the EU ETS

Phases I and II

The EU ETS is recognised as the largest cap-and trade-scheme in the world in terms of traded value (Dechezleprêtre et al., 2023) but its beginnings were more modest. In addition to the potential issues as a methodology to reduce emissions, there were concerns about how this new scheme was going to affect the functioning of existing national trading systems – in France and the UK, which had wider scope and used relative instead of absolute targets (Boemare et al., 2003). Following the learning by doing principle, the EU decided to begin emissions trading in 2005 for three years (2005–2007) in what is considered a 'transition' period and now more widely known as Phase I (EC, n.d.). The 2003 Directive established the way in which trading was going to take place for the transition period and for Phase II, between 2008 and 2012 (OJEU, 2003), coinciding with the first commitment period of the Kyoto Protocol, but it also outlined the way forward beyond said period with some instructions or guidelines to be applied in subsequent five-year periods. From the beginning it was decided that the upcoming enlargement of the EU in 2004 to Eastern European countries would not modify the reduction commitments (Table 6.1) of existing Members, and these new Members ratified the Protocol and agreed on their own reduction targets of between 6% and 8% (EC, 2004).

The functioning of the system during these initial phases began with the establishment of a cap in the quantity of emissions allowed for the whole of the EU and then for each of the Member States, estimated through the grandfathering system previously described. Prior to the beginning of the trading period, each Member State had to submit National Allocation Plans (NAPs) on how they intended to distribute allowances among different industrial sectors to the approval of the Commission (Ghazani and Jafari, 2021), and if the Directive's criteria were not followed, the Plans had to go back to the Member State, which would be given three months to submit a revised version (OJEU, 2003). The need to resubmit NAPs was a reoccurring feature for several Member States (Skjærseth and Wettestad, 2009), and an example of the nuances of the procedure can be found in Box 6.1.

Box 6.1 Spain national allocation plan for EU ETS Phase II

Spain was allowed to increase its GHG emissions by 15% during the first commitment period of the Kyoto Protocol. As the chapter has already explained, this was a decision taken through the Burden Sharing Agreement, taking into consideration that at the time the country was still far from the EU GDP average. The expectation was that to achieve economic growth, immediate decoupling of emissions would not be possible, so there would be an increase, at least temporarily. As the graph indicates (Figure 6.1), Spain consistently went over the percentage allowed for its emissions increase through the whole period. In fact, emissions only started decreasing in 2008, as a result of the international economic crisis.

Time showed that Spain did not comply with its commitment with Kyoto, despite generous funding and special consideration from the EU, mostly due to the late action of its energy sector, with strong lobby power at the time (Solorio and Fernandez, 2017). It was concerning though, the way in which the government attempted to 'cheat' the National Allocation Plans procedure, in a way that more allowances could be allocated to different production sectors without the knowledge of the Commission (see Table 6.2).

Spain submitted its National Allocation Plan for the 2008–2012 period through the Royal Decree in the left column (BOE, 2006). This Plan was rejected by the Commission, so the country submitted the Plan in the middle column (BOE, 2007a), and this was approved. But the procedure had a loophole and there was an option to further modify the Plan without having to notify the Commission if the changes did not affect the total number of allowances assigned to the country. Spain made use of this option, approving

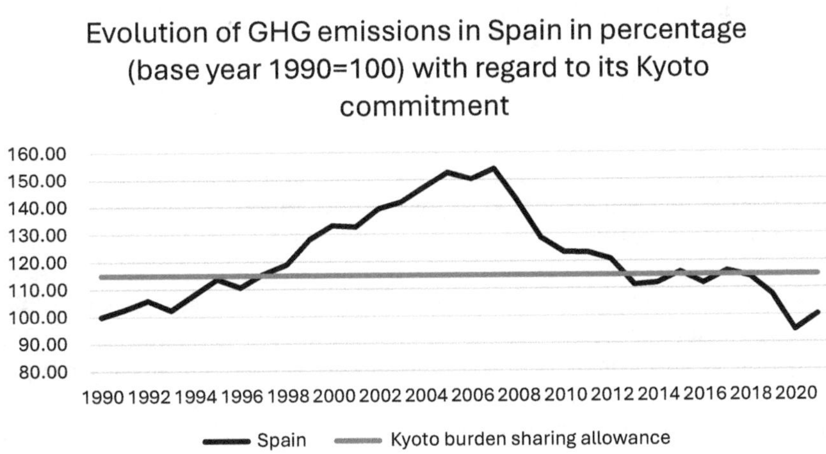

Figure 6.1 Evolution of Spain's greenhouse gas emissions (%)

Source: OECD.stats (extracted 29.04.2024 from https://stats.oecd.org/Index.aspx?DataSetCode =air_ghg).

Table 6.2 Spain's national allocation plan documentation 2008–2012

	RD 1370/2006	*RD 1030/2007*	*RD 1402/2007*
Total emissions/ allowances 2008–2012	144,848 $MtCO_2$/ year	144,425 $MtCO_2$/ year	145,973 $MtCO_2$/ year
Reserve for new entrants	5.40%	5.42% (7,825 $MtCO_2$/ year)	4.30% (6,277 $MtCO_2$/ year)
Sector level (electricity)	54.05 $MtCO_2$/year	53,630 $MtCO_2$/ year	54,420 $MtCO_2$/ year
Sector level (industrial sectors)	73.64 $MtCO_2$/year		73,885 $MtCO_2$/ year
Combustion installation	17.16 $MtCO_2$/year		17,668 $MtCO_2$/ year
Flexibility mechanisms (public service electricity production)	70%	42%	
Flexibility mechanisms (rest)	20%	7.9%	

Source: Boletin Oficial del Estado (2006, 2007a, 2007b).

a new Royal Decree (BOE, 2007b) that permitted the allocation of a number of emission allowances even higher than the ones initially rejected by the Commission. This was done to the detriment of the reserve for new entrants and the rest of flexibility mechanisms. In practice, it meant that the same type of industries had the opportunity to continue their business as usual.

The move in Phase III to a system without National Allocation Plans and more controlled centrally by EU institutions was a welcome change to prevent this type of occurrences.

Phase I was a tough learning experience, even if the Commission viewed it as a successful one (EC, n.d.). The Directive had confirmed some of the approaches outlined by the Green Paper, limiting the trade to one GHG (CO_2), and only the largest industrial emitters were obliged to participate in the scheme. Importantly, it was decided that allocation of allowances will be for free, at least 95% of them between 2005 and 2007, and 90% of them between 2008 and 2012 (OJEU, 2003: Art. 10). At the end of each period, allowances that had not been surrendered (used) would be cancelled, and this created one of the biggest problems for the efficiency of the system. When the first monitoring and verification exercises were conducted, it became apparent that an overestimation of emissions and hence over-allocation of allowances had taken place which, following basic laws of supply and demand, meant that with excess supply the price would go down, below what was considered necessary to incentivise active emissions reduction – around €30 per tonne of CO_2 (Adamolekun, 2024). The price of allowances during Phase I fluctuated between €0 and €30, with averages between €10 and €15 per tonne of CO_2 (Dechezleprêtre et al., 2023). It fell by 50% with the publication of the first emission verification figures (Narassimhan et al., 2018) and collapsed completely when at the end of the period the excess of allowances could not be transferred to the following one – a process called banking (Chevallier, 2010). Phase II attempted to correct this issue by reducing the cap and allowing banking, but it did not count on the economic crisis of 2007–2008 reducing economic activity and thus emissions to such a level that a new excess of allowances supply took place (Joltreau and Sommerfeld, 2019). Needless to say, even if the Directive had included penalties for non-compliance of €40 per tonne in 2005–2007 and €100 per tonne in 2008–2012 (OJEU, 2003), given the overflow of allowances in both periods, said penalties never came to effect.

In the spirit of commitment with the Kyoto Protocol, something that the EU wanted to see happening from the beginning was the possibility to open the emissions trading to third countries. This possibility was foreseen in the 2003 Directive, but a specific 'linking' Directive was approved in 2004 (OJEU, 2004). The idea was that Member States could benefit from credits from the joint implementation and clean development mechanism projects. However, since the Kyoto commitment period did not start until 2008, this option was not materialised in Phase I and was hardly used in Phase II (International Carbon Action Partnership [ICAP], 2022). What did happen in Phase II is that some Member States began using the auction system for the allocation of allowances and nitrous oxide emissions were also included as part of the GHG trading in some countries (EC, n.d.).

At the end of Phase II (January 2012) the aviation sector was included as part of the ETS (Scheelhaase et al., 2021), though the operational features needed separated arrangements and its own cap (ICAP, 2022). The system is supposed to cover flights within the European Economic Area (EEA) but lots of exceptions have been included to appease protests from both the sector and third countries (Euractiv, 2011). Modifications of these arrangements will be explored in the following paragraphs.

Phases III and IV

It could be argued that the beginnings of the EU ETS were tempestuous, full of good intentions but highly ineffective in their attempts to establish a market price for emissions allowances both stable and sufficiently high to incentivise producers' behavioural change. Necessarily changes were implemented, and a new Directive was introduced in 2009 (OJEU, 2009), which eliminated the NAPs and replaced them by a centralised cap for the period that would be progressively reduced year on year. Indeed, the five-year rule was abandoned, and Phase III covered the period 2013–2020 (Ghazani and Jafari, 2021). In addition to the lower cap and in an attempt to keep prices higher than in the previous period, auction of allowances was generalised, and mandated for the energy sector from 2013 (OJEU, 2009).

If allowances were to be allocated for free, they would follow a *benchmarking* system, by which an ex-ante amount of emissions per unit of productive output (Neelis et al., 2009) would be calculated Community (EU) wide, for specific sector or subsector, based on the average performance of the 10% most efficient installations in the years 2007–2008 (OJEU, 2009). Thought as an additional way of reducing the number of allowances to stabilise their market price, it is argued (Joltreau and Sommerfeld, 2019) that overallocation continued existing, since a lot of exceptions were applied for sectors susceptible of *carbon leakage*,[1] which represented between 85% and 95% of CO_2 emissions from manufacturing. Contrary to what happened in Phases I and II, where the price of allowances was close to zero, Phase III experienced a recovery and a bit of a boom in price levels. While at the beginning of this phase the allowances ranged between €5 and €7, the price increased above €20 from 2018, after a mechanism was introduced to prevent excessive banking (Dechezleprêtre et al., 2023). This was aided by the announcement that the EU would introduce a Market Stability Reserve (MSR) from 2019, which effectively meant to stop 900 million surplus allowances from getting into the market, 'backloading' them in case a hypothetical shortage was to happen (Narassimhan et al., 2018). The price of allowances reached €100/tonne in 2023, with average prices around €80/tonne (Florence School of Regulation [FSR], 2023).

While in Phase II the EU ETS expanded its application to Iceland, Liechtenstein and Norway, Phase III saw the official linking of the ETS to Switzerland. Some progress was made on the application of the ETS to the aviation sector, but still limited its functioning to flights within the EEA, adding also outgoing flights to Switzerland after the Linking Agreement (ICAP, 2022). Uncertainty over the EU ETS functioning for the aviation sector was introduced by the approval of a Carbon Offsetting and Reduction Scheme for International Aviation (CORSIA) by the International Civil Aviation Organization (ICAO) in 2016 (Efthymiou and Papatheodorou, 2019). As a concept, *offsetting* is the action of compensating for carbon emissions by financing a reduction of emissions elsewhere (IATA, 2022). This can be done by individuals or companies, on a voluntary basis, and commercial airlines have quickly embraced the system, with around 40 of them offering some type of offsetting programme (IATA, 2022). This adds another layer of complexity to what already presented a complicated picture: the international dimension of the EU ETS. On the one hand, integration with the Kyoto Protocol flexibility mechanisms allowed market participants to gain emission credits (equivalent to the emission allowances of the EU ETS) which contributed to more overflowing of the markets and lower prices. Hence the restrictions imposed in Phase II, with even tighter quantitative and qualitative measures for the use of international credits in Phase III, and their complete rule out for Phase IV (Verde and Borghesi, 2022). On the other hand, the Paris Agreement and the UN Sustainable Development Goals launched in 2015 provided grounds for further engagement in climate action beyond EU borders, thinking of alternative ways of encouraging policy change in third countries while protecting EU competitiveness.

In the last years of Phase III we have the approval of the European Green Deal (EC, 2019), with the Commission still committed to using the ETS as flagship initiative to tackle climate change, while proposing further reform in its functioning. The EGD hinted at the possibility to extend emissions trading to other sectors, and to set up reduction targets for emissions in sectors out of the ETS. It also proposed the implementation of a CBAM to address the risk of carbon leakage (EC, 2019: 5), for which compliance with World Trade Organization (WTO) rules would need to be guaranteed.

All these proposals take us to the current phase on the implementation of the EU ETS, Phase IV, which began in 2021 and will run until 2030 (ICAP, 2022). With more ambitious commitments for emissions reduction, energy efficiency and use of renewable energy for 2030 and 2050 (see Chapter 1 for details), the 'Fit for 55' package proposed in 2021 included the extension of the ETS to the maritime sector and the creation of a separate ETS for buildings and transport – this time with the complement of a Social Climate Fund to take care of negative social impacts (Oberthür and von Homeyer, 2023). Experts suggest (Pietzcker et al., 2021) that the tightening of the ETS will positively contribute to speed up the decarbonisation of the power sector (which as implied in Box 6.1 tends to lag behind in taking action). They anticipate a possible reduction in cumulative emissions of 54% and record increase in the price of carbon allowances to €129 per tonne of CO_2 by 2030 (Pietzcker et al., 2021).

The latest reform of the ETS has materialised in a new Directive approved in 2023 (OJEU, 2023), also amending the functioning of the MSR. It confirms the need for reform as part of the measures to comply with the 'Fit for 55' package, and reinforces the role of the ETS as 'cornerstone' of the EU climate policy and 'key' tool for cost-effective reduction of GHGs (OJEU, 2023). This reform is contextualised by the commitment to reach climate neutrality in the EU by 2050, but also justifies the need for change to address energy poverty issues linked to social impacts created by the Covid-19 pandemic so that society's resilience against external shocks can improve. In this regard, it can be argued that policy initiatives since the approval of the EGD are making an effort to include a social impact lens, in line with the UN SDGs moto of 'leaving no one behind', which is explicitly mentioned in the preamble paragraphs of the new Directive (OJEU, 2023).

What the summary presented in this section reflects is a dynamic of constant change and reform of an emissions trading system to make it more and more integrated with the rest of EU climate policy initiatives. The increase in the sectors covered by emissions trading, the tightening of conditions, the measures to prevent excessive supply of allowances, etc. are all testament of the recognition of a very imperfect initial design and the need for flexibility to adapt to changing circumstances. Instead, the way in which the functioning has been established relies on fixing targets and their specific modifications at predetermined timelines, not knowing if circumstances would have changed and the parameters are still appropriate to reach the initial goals. This risks the need for further modification along the way, and questions if the revisions and evaluation points are relevant or less stringency could be applied to make changes 'as needed'.

So far, within this Phase IV, there are several assessment points established (ICAP, 2022):

'By the end of July 2026, the European Commission will assess:

- *how negative emissions could be accounted for and covered under the EU ETS,*
- *the feasibility of lowering the 20 MW total rated thermal input thresholds for the activities under the EU ETS,*
- *effective accounting and avoidance of double counting of CCU products under the EU ETS,*
- *the feasibility of including municipal waste incineration under the EU ETS,*
- *the functioning of the EU ETS for aviation, including the functioning of CORSIA.*

By the end of December 2027, the Commission will assess the possibility of the scope of the EU ETS to include non-CO_2 aviation emissions'.

It is worth checking then if with so many changes, the ETS is fit for purpose or other policy instruments should be considered, in light of the progress (or lack thereof) in the implementation of the Paris Agreement, but also of the proliferation of carbon markets in other economies.

Is the EU ETS fit for purpose?

The EU ETS is repeatedly considered as the largest carbon market in the world (Jan Venmans, 2016; Aus dem Moore et al., 2019). It applies to over 17,000 installations (EC, 2021) belonging to heavily-polluting sectors, mostly energy intensive industries and electricity generation companies, covering around 40% of the EU GHG emissions (Verde and Borghesi, 2022). Assessing its effectiveness or fitness for purpose is not an easy task. Based on the information provided in the previous sections, it cannot be said that the purpose of creating a price for carbon emissions sufficiently high and stable enough to incentivise active emissions reduction (through innovation and modification of production processes) has been achieved, particularly if one looks at price levels for Phases I, II and most of Phase III. Hence, as a MBI, it still has room for improvement, even if the latest reforms aim to correct most of the shortcomings of the initial designs.

If one looks at the EU ETS as part of its climate governance framework, the increase in stringency conditions to access emissions allowances, through progressive reductions in the cap levels, the introduction of auctioning and benchmarking and the elimination of the option to use international carbon credits, speak positively of the level of ambition of the scheme, covering two of the most common criteria (ambition and stringency) used to assess the adequacy of EU climate governance instruments (Oberthür and von Homeyer, 2023). However, it also speaks of increasing levels of supranational regulation and monitoring, which is not welcomed by everyone. When analysing the possible negative effects of the ETS over Member States, carbon leakage comes to the forefront of potential impacts – which the EU has tried to limit. Here Poland stands out as the country who has spoken more loudly against the ETS, to the point of asking for its suspension in 2021 (Kosc, 2021). But looking at the evidence, the complaints do not seem to be justified: the economic performance of the country has improved, and research (Dechezleprêtre et al., 2023) confirms positive and statistically significant impacts of the EU ETS on Poland's revenue and fixed assets, at the same time that it has decreased the likelihood of firms' closure in the country. It is true that in a country whose energy sector still depends heavily on coal, the financial situation of some coal-powered stations is set to worsen, particularly if the price of emissions allowances keeps going up as expected, but gas-fuelled combined heat and power plants are less vulnerable to the ETS associated costs (Skoczkowski et al., 2018). If the country aims to comply with its international obligations it will have to change its approach to energy, and the ETS is trying to push in that direction.

Still subject to debate is the contribution of the ETS to GHG emissions reduction, which is supposed to be its main purpose. It is uncontroversial that emissions in the EU have decreased considerably since 2005, the beginning of the ETS. Up to 2020, there has been a 21% reduction of 'regulated' emissions, but the aim is to force a 62% reduction by 2030 (FSR, 2023). On one side of the debate we find those who claim that a large proportion of the emissions reduction achieved in the period, particularly in Phases I and II, was more related to the international economic crisis of 2007–2008 than to the correct functioning of the ETS (Bel and Joseph, 2015). In general, it can be found that while at the beginning of the ETS the terminology used for the evaluation of carbon trading talked about 'carbon markets', this changed relatively quickly to 'carbon pricing' (see for instance the reports on 'State and Trends of…' by the World Bank). This is because many countries started introducing carbon taxes as a complement or replacement of carbon trading. Studies suggest (Green, 2021) that carbon taxes tend to perform better than carbon trading for emissions reduction, even if the reductions achieved tend to be modest in both cases. On the other side of the debate, there are researchers (Bayer and Aklin, 2020) who defend the role of the EU ETS in reducing emissions despite the low prices that allowances reached for most of the period considered. According to their analysis, even accounting for the effects of the economic crisis, the increase in the stringency of the ETS is what caused larger emissions reduction than what we would have had without the ETS in place, particularly from 2008 onwards. Since there is heterogeneity in the methods used to reach these seemingly contradicting conclusions, it is helpful to look at other variables beyond emissions reduction to get a better understanding of the efficiency of the ETS.

One such variable is the effect of the ETS on innovation and technological change, usually measured (not without limitations) in terms of the number of patents in the industries regulated by the emissions trading. Evidence (Teixido et al., 2019) seems to indicate that the ETS has had a positive effect, but only from Phase III onwards, which concurs with the analysis of other variables insofar the effectiveness or efficiency is linked to more stringent conditions for the functioning of the market, or in other words, for the system to work, allocation of allowances should not take place for free. Given that the risk of carbon leakage, with its potential negative effect on employment in specific industries and regions, has been one of the justifications for exceptions and differentiated treatment of sectors and countries within the ETS, it would be relevant to assess the possible impacts of the ETS on industry competitiveness and employment across the EU in general. As already pointed out, the EU ETS has increased innovation activity in low-carbon technologies within the regulated sectors by around 30%, but innovation does not guarantee that the competitiveness of innovative industries will improve (Dechezleprêtre et al., 2023). On the other hand, the same study concludes that the ETS led to an increase in revenue and fixed assets of the regulated firms which is statistically significant, while there is also a positive effect on employment, but this time not statistically significant (Dechezleprêtre et al., 2023). Effects on employment are also linked to the perceived increase in costs for the regulated sectors, which may decide in turn to decrease production and make staff redundant. But evidence suggests (Aus dem Moore et al., 2019) that this has a less than 10% occurrence, and it is not observed in countries like Germany. With the expansion of the ETS to more sectors such as the aviation and maritime sector (the latter an addition in Phase IV), it is reassuring that current estimations indicate low levels of employment loss (European Parliament, 2021). Instead, what is expected is more a shift of employment between companies and sectors, which is common and already anticipated as part of a sustainable transition.

All in all it could be argued that the EU ETS has experienced a learning curve that has improved its performance overtime, and its current operating framework is probably better positioned now than it has ever been to make a significant contribution to a sustainable transition in Europe (and beyond, since it is being used as example by other countries). Emissions reduction has taken place and allowance prices have begun to take off. But this could also be related to the increase in energy prices caused by the conflict in Ukraine. Whatever the reason, the higher the price of allowances the greater the incentive to take measures. The issue is that the moment additional costs appear there are calls to shelve the plans for the expansion of the scheme to prevent extra burdens. There are some (see Poland in Kosc, 2021) who consider the ETS a de facto tax, and it is well known that politically speaking taxes are a non-desirable measure. Others (Cornago, 2022), however, argue that high energy prices provide additional incentives to act, innovate, and move towards more sustainable behaviour, including the reduction in energy consumption. The negative impact over vulnerable groups will need to be cushioned through complementary policy measures. This is something that is still under development with the ETS. With all the new Climate Action packages being approved, together with the special budgetary provisions to help with the recovery from the Covid-19 pandemic, it once more becomes apparent that the ETS as policy instrument cannot be considered in isolation. The provisions for the allocation of (a percentage of) the revenues coming from the auctioning of emission allowances to address climate challenges are a step in the right direction, but more could be done to address current social inequalities.

For a policy instrument considered a cornerstone, a flagship initiative, the centre of policy efforts, etc., it cannot be said that its performance is outstanding, and previous paragraphs lead to the conclusion that at best the EU ETS is an 'adequate' average tool, but more was expected. It should not be considered enough that its negative impacts are limited, if the positive effects are limited too. We will have to wait and see how the changes to be implemented between now and 2030 will play out, but the current geopolitical instability created by several armed conflicts (and threats of more to come) around the world may once more affect the initial planning and the need for readjustment of both measures and targets. It is good in that sense that the EU is taking steps to act more decisively in the area of taxation, as the next chapter will discuss, as given the multifaceted challenges that we face, it would be naïve to think that one specific instrument can be the key towards better outcomes. Perhaps the term 'cornerstone' should not be the one to use for the ETS in the coming future. This is all without entering into the debate about the ethical issues presented by emissions trading and effectively buying the right to continue polluting. In a way, this would go hand in hand with the 'polluter pays principle' if effectively firms had been paying for the emissions allowances, but this is still not the case with a large percentage of allowances being allocated for free, even if this proportion is set to be reduced. While this does not change and all allowances are paid for, the balance between economic, environmental and social aspects of sustainability will not be reached, and the economic pillar will continue to take precedence over any other.

Discussion questions

1 Is the introduction of the Carbon Border Adjustment Mechanism enough to prevent the potential carbon leakages caused by the ETS?
2 Have the reforms of the ETS gone far enough to ensure an adequate allocation of emission allowances?
3 Should the ethical considerations around the right to pollute take a more prominent role in the debates about the future of the ETS?
4 Should we accept that now that the ETS has been created it should continue existing instead of exploring what would happen if emissions trading was no longer an option?
5 Should emissions trading replace national emission reduction efforts on the groups of 'cost' efficiency or other social and environmental aspects should be considered?

Note

1 Carbon leakage occurs when production shifts from a carbon-constrained region (through regulation, such as the EU ETS) to those regions that do not have constraints, so outputs formerly produced domestically are replaced by relatively cheaper imported products. This definition by Juergens et al. (2013) includes a nice explanation with economics terminology with regard to the types of 'substitution effect'.

Further readings

Gronwald, M. and Hinterman, B. (eds) (2015) *Emissions Trading as a Policy Instrument: Evaluation and Prospects.* MIT Press: This book provides an insightful review of the functioning of the EU ETS during its first two phases. It uses economic terminology and arguments to analyse the differences between the two periods and the interaction between the ETS and other policy instruments existing at national level.

Unger, C. (2021) *Linking the European Union Emissions Trading System. Political Drivers and Barriers.* Routledge: Interesting assessment of how the European ETS has been linked with other regional ETS, analysing the reasons for successful linking (such as in the case of Switzerland) or failing attempts (such as the Californian case). It helps reflecting over the possibility for the integration of carbon markets around the world.

Verbruggen, A (2021) *Pricing Carbon Emissions. Economic Reality and Utopia.* Routledge: This book introduces the reader to a comprehensive analysis of the ETS under the premise that its role is more to keep the business as usual activities of industrial sectors in the EU instead of fostering innovation for the decarbonisation of production technologies.

References

Adamolekun, G. (2024) Carbon price and firm greenhouse gas emissions, *Journal of Environmental Management,* 349 (2024): 119496. https://doi.org/10.1016/j.jenvman.2023.119496

Aus dem Moore, N., Großkurth, P. and Themann, M. (2019) Multinational corporations and the EU emissions trading system: The specter or asset erosion and creeping deindustrialization, *Journal of Environmental Economics and Management*, 94 (2019): 1–26.

Bayer, P. and Aklin, M. (2020) The European emissions trading system reduced CO2 emissions despite low prices, *PNAS*, 117 (16): 8804–8812.

Bel, G. and Joseph, S. (2015) Emission abatement: Untangling the impacts of the EU ETS and the economic crisis, *Energy Economics*, 49 (2015): 531–539.

BOE (2007a) Real Decreto 1030/2007, de 20 de julio, por el que se modifica el Real Decreto 1370/2006, de 24 de noviembre, por el que se aprueba el Plan Nacional de Asignación de derechos de emisión de gases de efecto invernadero, 2008–2012. 21.07.2007.

BOE (2007b) Real Decreto 1402/2007, de 29 de octubre, por el que se modifica el Real Decreto 1370/2006, de 24 de noviembre, por el que se aprueba el Plan Nacional de Asignación de derechos de emisión de gases de efecto invernadero, 2008–2012. 30.10.2007.

Boemare, C., Quirion, P. and Sorrell, S. (2003) The evolution of emissions trading in the EU: Tensions between national trading schemes and the proposed EU directive, *Climate Policy*, 3S2 (2003): S105–S124.

Boletin Oficial del Estado [BOE] (2006) Real Decreto 1370/2006, de 24 de noviembre, por el que se aprueba el Plan Nacional de asignación de derechos de emisión 2008–2012. 25.11.2006.

Braun, M. (2009) The evolution of emissions trading in the European Union – The role of policy networks, knowledge and policy entrepreneurs, *Accounting, Organizations and Society*, 34 (2009): 469–487.

Callan, S. J. and Thomas, J. M. (2013) *Environmental Economics & Management. Theory, Policy, and Applications* (6th edition). Mason, OH: South-Western Cengage Learning.

Caney, S. and Hepburn, C. (2011) Carbon trading: Unethical, unjust and ineffective? *Centre for Climate Change Economics and Policy Working Paper* No. 59, *Grantham Research Institute on Climate Change and the Environment Working Paper* No. 49, June 2011.

Chevallier, J. (2010) The European carbon market (2005–2007): Banking, pricing and risk-hedging strategies. *HAL Open Science,* halshs-00458787. Available from: https://shs.hal.science/halshs-00458787/document

Cornago, E. (2022) High energy prices threaten the EU emissions trading system. *Centre for European Reform, CER Insight,* Open Society European Policy Institute. 23 March 2022.

Dechezleprêtre, A., Natchtigall, D. and Venmans, F. (2023) The joint impact of the European Union emissions trading system on carbon emissions and economic performance,

Journal of Environmental Economics and Management, 118 (2023): 102758. https://doi.org/10.1016/j.jeem.2022.102758

Efthymiou, M. and Papatheodorou, A. (2019) EU emissions trading scheme in aviation: Policy analysis and suggestions, *Journal of Cleaner Production*, 237 (2019): 117734. https://doi.org/10.1016/j.jclepro.2019.117734

Euractiv (2011) China opposes including its airlines in EU's ETS, 11 May *Euractiv.* Available from: https://www.euractiv.com/section/transport/news/china-opposes-including-its-airlines-in-eu-s-ets/

European Commission (1999) Communication from the commission to the council and the European parliament "Preparing for Implementation of the Kyoto Protocol". COM(1999) 230 final. Brussels, 19.05.1999.

European Commission (2000) *Green Paper on Greenhouse Gas Emissions Trading Withing the European Union*, COM (2000) 87 final. Brussels, 8.3.2000.

European Commision (2004) Kyoto protocol, MEMO/04/03. Brussels, 4.3.2004.

European Commission (2019) Communication from the commission to the European parliament, the European council, the council, the European economic and social committee and the committee of the regions: The European Green Deal. COM (2019) 640 final. Brussels, 11.12.2019.

European Commission (2021) European Emissions Trading System (ETS) – Calculations on the regional employment impact of ETS installations. *Analytical and methodological report. Directorate-General for Regional and Urban Policy.* https://doi.org/10.2776/792141

European Commission (2023) 30th anniversary of the Cohesion Fund: €179 billion for convergence and sustainable development. Newsroom, 03 April 2023. Available from: https://ec.europa.eu/regional_policy/whats-new/newsroom/04-03-2023-30th-anniversary-of-the-cohesion-fund-eur179-billion-for-convergence-and-sustainable-development_en

European Commission (n.d.) Development of the EU ETS (2005–2020). Available from: https://climate.ec.europa.eu/eu-action/eu-emissions-trading-system-eu-ets/development-eu-ets-2005-2020_en

European Parliament (2021) The aviation and maritime sectors and the EU ETS: Challenges and impacts. Final study. Research for Tran Committee. *Policy Department for Structural and Cohesion Policies, Directorate-General for Internal Policies.* PE 690.897 – October 2021.

Eyckmans, J., Cornillie, J. and Van Regemorter, D. (2002) Efficiency and equity in the EU burden sharing agreement, Katholieke Universiteit Leuven Center for Economic Studies, *Energy Transport & Environment Working Paper Series* No. 2000-02.

Farber, D. A. (2011) Emissions trading and social justice, *Berkeley Program in Law and Economics, Working Paper Series,* 20.09.2011.

Fernandez, R. M. (2023) Economics for a low-carbon future. In Moltan-Hill, P. (ed) *Sustainable Management. A Complete Guide for Faculty and Students* (Third edition). The Principles for Responsible Management Education Series, Abingdon: Routledge: 237–265.

Florence School of Regulation (2023) EU Emission Trading System (EU ETS), Cover the Basics Type. Available from: https://fsr.eui.eu/eu-emission-trading-system-eu-ets/

Ghazani, M. M. and Jafari, M. A. (2021) The efficiency of CO2 market in the phase III EU ETS: Analyzing in the context of a dynamic approach, *Environmental Science and Pollution Research*, 28 (2021): 61080–61095.

Gorman, H. S. and Solomon, B. D. (2002) The origins and practice of emissions trading, *The Journal of Policy History*, 14 (3): 293–320.

Green, J. F. (2021) Does carbon pricing reduce emissions? A review of ex-post analysis, *Environmental Research Letters*, 16 (4): 043004. https://doi.org/10.1088/1748-9326/abdae9

IATA (2022) *Aviation Carbon Offsetting. Guidelines for Voluntary Programs,* Version III-April 2022.

International Carbon Action Partnership (2022) EU Emissions Trading System (EU ETS). Available from: https://icapcarbonaction.com/en/ets/eu-emissions-trading-system-eu-ets

Joltreau, E. and Sommerfeld (2019) Why does emissions trading under the EU emissions trading system (ETS) not affect firms' competitiveness? Empirical findings from the literature, *Climate Policy*, 19 (4): 453–471.

Jan Venmans, F. M. (2016) The effect of allocation above emissions and price uncertainty on abatement investments under the EU ETS, *Journal of Cleaner Production,* 126 (2016): 595–606.

Juergens, I., Barreiro-Hurle, J. and Vasa, A. (2013) Identifying carbon leakage sectors in the EU ETS and implications of results, *Climate Policy,* 13 (1): 89–109.

Kosc, W. (2021) Poland rakes in the carbon cash it pretends to hate, 20 December, *Politico.* Available from: https://www.politico.eu/article/poland-emission-trading-eu/

Lane, R. (2012) The promiscuous history of market efficiency: The development of early emissions trading systems, *Environmental Politics,* 21 (4): 583–603.

Molina, O. and Rhodes, M. (2008) The reform of social protection systems in mixed market economies, *Pôle Sud,* 28 (1): 9–33.

Narassimhan, E., Gallagher, K. S., Koester, S. and Rivera Alejo, J. (2018) Carbon pricing in practice: A review of existing emissions trading systems, *Climate Policy,* 18 (8): 967–991.

Neelis, M., Worrell, E., Mueller, N. and Angelini, T. (2009) Developing benchmarking criteria for CO2 emissions, *Ecofys Netherlands and Fraunhofer Institute for Systems and Innovation Research*, February 2009.

Oberthür, S. and von Homeyer, I. (2023) From emissions trading to the European Green Deal: The evolution of the climate policy mix and climate policy integration in the EU, *Journal of European Public Policy,* 30 (3): 445–468.

Official Journal of the European Union (2003) Directive 2003/87/EC of the European parliament and of the council of 13 October 2003 establishing a scheme for greenhouse gas emission allowance trading within the community and amending council directive 96/61/EC. L275, 25.10.2003.

Official Journal of the European Union (2004) Directive 2004/101/EC of the European parliament and of the council of 27 October 2004 amending directive 2003/87/EC establishing a scheme for greenhouse gas emission allowance trading within the community, In respect of the Kyoto Protocol's project mechanisms. L338, 13.11.2004.

Official Journal of the European Union (2009) Directive 2009/29/EC of the European parliament and of the council of 23 April 2009 amending directive 2003/87/EC so as to improve and extend the greenhouse gas emission allowance trading scheme of the community. L140, 5.6.2009.

Official Journal of the European Union (2023) Directive (EU) 2023/959 of the European parliament and of the council of 10 May 2023 amending directive 2003/87/EC establishing a system for greenhouse gas emission allowance trading within the union and decision (EU) 2015/1814 concerning the establishment and operation of a market stability reserve for the Union greenhouse gas emission trading system. L130, 16.5.2023.

Pietzcker, R. C., Osorio, S. and Rodrigues, R. (2021) Tightening EU ETS targets in line with the European green deal: Impacts on the decarbonization of the EU power sector, *Applied Energy*, 293 (2021): 116914. https://doi.org/10.1016/j.apenergy.2021.116914.

Sandel, M. J. (2005) Should we buy the right to pollute? In *Public Philosophy: Essays on Morality in Politics.* Cambridge, MA: Harvard University Press: 93–96.

Scheelhaase, J., Maertens, S. and Grimme, W. (2021) Options for improving the EU emissions trading scheme (EU ETS) for aviation, *Transportation Research Procedia,* 59 (2012): 193–202.

Skjærseth, J. B. and Wettestad, J. (2009) The origin, evolution and consequences of the EU emissions trading system, *Global Environmental Politics,* 9 (2): 101–122.

Skoczkowski, T., Bielecki, S., Weglarz, A., Wlodarczak, M. and Gutowski, P. (2018) Impact assessment of climate policy on Poland's power sector, *Mitigation and Adaptation Strategies for Global Change,* 23 (2018): 1303–1349.

Solorio, I. and Fernandez, R. (2017) Spain and renewable energy promotion: Euopeanization upside down. In Solorio, I and Jorgens, H. (eds) *A Guide to EU Renewable Energy Policy. Comparing Europeanization and Domestic Policy Change in EU Member States.* Chelteenham: Edward Elgar: 141–161.

Teixido, J., Verde, S. F. and Nicoli, F. (2019) The impact of the EU emissions trading system on low-carbon technological change: The empirical evidence, *Ecological Economics*, 164 (2019): 106347. https://doi.org/10.1016/j.ecolecon.2019.06.002.

Tietenberg, T. and Lewis, L. (2009) *Environmental and Natural Resource Economics* (8th edition). Boston, MA: Addison-Wesley.

UN (1997) Kyoto Protocol to the United Nations Framework Convention on Climate Change, 10 December 1997. FCCC/CP/1997/L.7/Add.1.

Verde, S. F. and Borghesi, S. (2022) The international dimension of the EU emissions trading system: Bringing the pieces together, *Environmental and Resource Economics*, 83 (2022): 23–46.

Wang, Z., Wang, F. and Wang, Y. (2022) Grandfathering or benchmarking: Which is more viable for the manufacturer's low-carbon activities? *Frontiers in Environmental Science,* 10 (2022): 991827. https://doi.org/10.3389/fenvs.2022.991827.

Weaver, T. P. R. (2021) Market privilege: The place of neoliberalism in American political development, *Studies in American Political Development*, 35 (2021): 104–126.

Yagodin, D. (2021) Policy implications of climate change denial: Content analysis of Russian national and regional news media, *International Political Science Review,* 42 (1): 64–77.

7 The elephant in the room: Taxation to promote sustainable behaviour

Introduction: taxation as part of wider fiscal systems

Taxes are integral parts of the functioning of nation states. They are vital for the financing of essential public services and provide the opportunity to fund social programmes, also playing a redistribution of income role to reduce inequalities (Winer and Hettich, 2004). This does not prevent people from perceiving taxes as a financial burden or punishment instead of a service – or the means to a service (Mohammed and Tangl, 2024). The design of the tax becomes an essential element to ensure not only that the necessary resources are collected but that any potential negative consequence associated with the tax is minimised (Fernandez, 2023a). This is why tax acceptance is maximised when the tax is perceived to be simple, fair, and people can see the benefits of their tax contributions (Mohammed and Tangl, 2024).

As part of a policy mix, Chapters 5 and 6 already classified taxes among the market-based instruments (MBIs) that governments can use, for the purpose of this book, with the specific aim to incentivise change that supports a sustainability transition. But there are many types of taxes, so within this chapter we will focus on those more commonly associated with sustainability transitions, widely known as *environmental or green taxes*, as part of 'green fiscal systems' and 'environmental tax (or fiscal) reforms'. In terms of efficiency as policy instrument, it was already established in Chapter 6 that for the purposes of greenhouse gas emissions reduction MBIs are more efficient than command-and-control measures (see also Fernandez, 2023b), and within MBIs carbon taxes are more efficient than carbon trading. Knowing this, one could question why is taxation not used more often to reach certain policy targets? And the answer is that when it comes to taxation rules coming from a supranational entity such as the EU, things are not that simple, as the next lines will show.

Taxation debates in the EU

If one searches for taxation information in EU websites the first thing one can read is that the EU does not collect or set taxes directly and taxation is a responsibility and competence of the governments of Member States (see for instance Angerer, 2024 or EC, n.d.a). This is why the EU has focused on harmonisation.

DOI: 10.4324/9781003224785-9

What is more, if any decision on taxation is to be made at EU level, it requires to be approved by unanimity of the Council (EC, n.d.b), which is more difficult to reach each day given the increase in the number of Member States over time. The unanimity rule, while seen as a guarantee of democratic sovereignty, it is also seen as a hindrance to make progress when adaptations are necessary to include new requirements or flexibility to accommodate citizens' requests, which may happen at the national level (Jaakkola, 2019).

Debates about the move from unanimity to qualified majority voting on taxation matters in the EU have existed for many years. The first voices were raised by the Commission following the Intergovernmental Conference on the Future of Europe that discussed the failed Constitution document. It issued an opinion communication (EC, 2003) listing areas where unanimity should not be needed, which were mostly related to the operation of the internal market, but importantly for the topic of this book 'taxation in respect of the environment' (EC, 2003: 7). Member States have disagreed with proposals presented so far, particularly those countries where tax rates are comparatively low (Wasserfallen, 2014). The Commission considered that insufficient progress towards the elimination of the unanimity rule had taken place so it submitted a new proposal in 2019 with a roadmap for the progressive move to qualified majority voting (EC, 2019a). It argued once more that the rule is a barrier for the completion of the Single Market, which touches on the economic rationale for decision-making (and the economic pillar of sustainability). It provided examples of taxation initiatives incomplete due to the lack of agreement by unanimity, including the costs of inaction in those areas (EC, 2019a: 4): the Value Added Tax (VAT) Definitive Regime, the Common Consolidated Corporate Tax Base; the Financial Transactions Tax (proposed in 2011) and the Digital Services Tax (proposed in 2018). Interestingly, while the 2003 Communication focused mostly on economic and financial aspects, in 2019 the justification for the move away from unanimity includes wider perspectives. Here the Commission argues in favour of a fairer tax system that qualified majority decision-making would facilitate, while taxation is described as central 'in a fair and inclusive society' (EC, 2019a: 1). The need for change on environmental grounds is also addressed, while the initial proposal to reform the Energy Tax Directive failure is provided as yet another example of lack of progress due to the unanimity rule (EC, 2019a: 5).

If this was not considered sufficient incentive for change, another clear endorsement came with the approval of the EGD (EC, 2019b), in which taxation is listed as one of the policy areas where a rethink is required to deliver it. The second objective of the EGD (Greening national budgets and sending the right price signals) includes the explicit mention of 'well-designed tax reforms' as those that 'can boost economic growth and resilience to climate shocks and help contribute to a fairer society and to a just transition' (EC, 2019b: 17). We have here a perfect example in which the three pillars of sustainability are put together in a complementary balanced way.

From the economic point of view, taxation is part of the wider narrative that was introduced in Chapter 2 about the limitations in the resources that the EU budget could obtain to finance the sustainability transition, which directly connects with one of the questions this book aims to address: how are all the sustainability transformations going to be paid for? In that regard, there are arguments in favour of increasing the fiscal capacity of the EU (i.e. grant 'federal' fiscal powers to the EU institutions) so that sufficient resources can be collected and distributed for green transition projects (Georgiou, 2023). The EGD starts paving the way in that direction with the proposal for new taxes, such as the already in force plastic tax and the consideration of taxes for different modes of transport (EC, 2019b: 10–16). These are examples of environmental/green taxes, so it would be fair to say that if plans come true, we will see a wider variety of this type of taxes in the near future. Another element in the wider narrative positions the modification of the fiscal systems and frameworks as enablers of a green economy (Pekanov and Schratzenstaller, 2020), which will be addressed in Chapter 8.

Fiscal reforms for the sustainability transition

Basic concepts

A simple definition of environmental tax reform is 'the restructuring of the tax system to more effectively promote environmental objectives' (Heine et al., 2012). But taxes are only one element of the fiscal system, so full fiscal system reforms include actions such as the elimination of harmful subsidies like those received by the fossil fuel industry, and despite numerous international commitments and pledges – including by the EU, this is something far from being achieved (Heyl et al., 2022). To complicate matters further, there are multiple definitions of what an environmental tax is. In fact, sometimes a definition is not used, and what we find is an enumeration of taxes that are going to be classified or treated as such. The EU defines environmental tax as 'A tax whose tax base is a physical unit (or proxy of a physical unit) of something that has a proven specific negative impact on the environment' (OJEU, 2011), to which Eurostat adds 'and which is identified in ESA [European System of Accounts] as a tax' – bracket by the author (Eurostat, 2013). This definition follows the '*polluter pays principle*' first outlined by the OECD in the 1960s (Vicha, 2011). However, in the development of tax systems there is another principle commonly used, the '*beneficiary pays principle*', according to which, in the area of climate change policy 'states benefiting most from activities that cause climate change should bear the greatest burden in terms of the costs of preventing dangerous climate change' (Page, 2012). In this case the payers would be states instead of private actors. But some (Abeysuriya et al., 2008) defend the '*user pays principle*' as a special case of the beneficiary pays principle, arguing that those who benefit for a service should pay for it. In this case the payer is a private actor on the grounds that most of the benefits of the service go to private users. The same principle would not be applicable for something like sanitation, since the benefits of it are for the general population more than for private individuals (Abeysuriya et al., 2008). The beneficiary pays principle emerged with the climate justice literature, when some started opposing to the use of the polluter pays principle. The basis was that the beneficiaries principle could account better for historical causes of pollution or climate change damages in the sense that it would not matter if those who caused the damage were conscious or ignorant of the consequences of their actions. But some argue that similar objections to those associated with the polluter pays principle can also apply to the beneficiary pays principle (Garcia-Portela, 2023). In economic terms, one way or another the negative externalities created by day-to-day activities (both in production and consumption) need to be internalised. The problem for the regulator is how to find the right level for the taxes (or any other instrument), since in general there is information asymmetry and a reluctance on the side of the polluter to reveal their marginal abatement costs. It is not the purpose of this chapter to elaborate on the economic theory in this area, but helpful explanations including graphical representations can be found in Fernandez (2023b). In terms of who is paying for the tax, to some extent again economic theory helps explain that it does not matter who is the tax imposed on because both producers and consumers will share its burden in different proportions, depending on the elasticity of supply and demand, what is called the 'tax incidence' (Sloman et al., 2022).

Given the difficulties associated to the calculation of the right levels of taxation, both researchers (for instance: Elshamy and Sayed Ahmed, 2017; Schlegelmilch and Joas, 2015) and officials (for instance: Heine et al., 2012; OECD, 2020) insist on the need for 'well-designed' tax policies, and green fiscal reforms in general. This is because environmental taxes are usually accused of being regressive (i.e., affect more negatively to disadvantaged or low-income groups), but again this is very much connected with the design of the tax and how it fits within the wider fiscal and governance structures (Domguia, 2023). On the other side of the debate are those who defend the potential of environmental taxes to create a 'double dividend', which means that they can create both an environmental benefit (incentivising behavioural change towards a less polluting or more environmental-friendly one) and an economic benefit – since they can be used to reduce other taxes and the revenue collected can be recycled for sustainability-related projects (Wesseh Jr and Lin, 2019). But since the literature seems to find evidence in favour and against both characteristics (regressivity and double dividend), insofar they are both context and design dependent, one could wonder why there seems to be a preference for this policy instrument emerging in recent years. For this researcher the answer is clear: since environmental degradation across the world has worsened and evidence of human responsibility for climate change becomes more undisputable each day, softer mechanisms for action – including those that create markets for pollution (like the ETS) have proved insufficient, and regulators aim to provide stronger signals of the need for change with an instrument whose mere mention provokes strong reactions. If those reactions go in the necessary direction is something only observable in the longer term.

Environmental fiscal reforms in the EU

All the previous paragraphs refer to environmental taxes in relation to their function over the effects that certain activities have on the environment. But in addition to what is already a high level of complexity, environmental taxes can be classified according to the purpose stated by the regulator, the name given to the tax, or the earmarking of the revenue collected for environmental purposes (Eurostat,

2013). One could argue, however, that some regulators may approve a so-called environmental tax aiming for public acceptance of what could be a pure revenue collection exercise – as observed with the increase experienced in Greece after the economic crisis of 2007–2008 on their environmental tax revenue as a percentage of total tax revenue (Fernandez, 2023a) or it could be the case that the tax is created with several purposes in mind. Classifications according to those variables are more difficult and do not allow for international comparisons, hence the generalised use of the effects of the tax on the costs of the activities and prices of products with a negative effect on the environment. This involves the establishment of tax bases – usually linked to national accounts, and all taxes levied on those specific tax bases will be considered environmental taxes (Eurostat, 2013).

Green fiscal reforms do not necessarily involve the creation of new taxes (though this often happens), but the restructuring of the existing fiscal systems. This means that there are possibilities for action in four areas (Schratzenstaller, 2023): revenue (covered by this book in Chapters 5–7), expenditure (mainly Chapters 2 and 3 but also Chapter 4), governance (seen throughout but further developed in Chapter 8: Green economy) and debt (Chapter 9: Green finance). In the revenue side is where we find taxes, with four main types of environmental taxes: energy taxes (including fuel for transport), transport taxes (excluding fuel for transport), pollution taxes, and resource taxes (Eurostat, 2013; Schlegelmilch and Joas, 2015). This chapter focuses on the revenue aspects of fiscal reforms, particularly in the area of environmental taxation – but it will combine information of the actions at Member State level, since as it has been established, taxation is a national competence, with the so far limited but significant actions at EU level, as outlined in Figure 7.1.

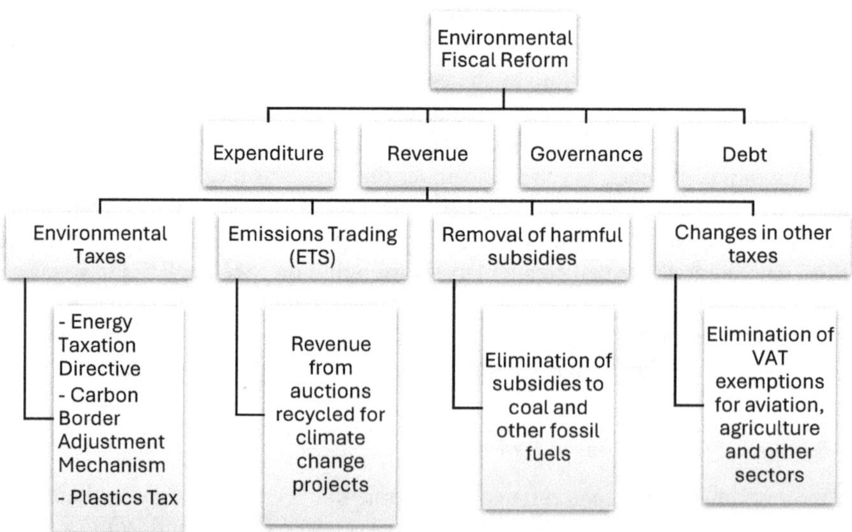

Figure 7.1 Components of environmental tax reform at EU level

Source: Author's elaboration.

The support packages approved at EU level to assist in the recovery from the Covid-19 pandemic played with the expenditure side of fiscal reforms, outlining where and how different funding was going to be spent, but also recognising that new resources were necessary to pay for the extraordinary funding required. It is in this context that apart from existing own resources such as the customs duties, Member States contributions to VAT and Contributions based on gross national income (GNI) a new own resource is introduced (EC, n.d. c): the new Directive on Single-Use Plastics (as it was covered in Chapter 2). But it is also in this context that reforms of existing taxes are discussed – such as the reform of the Energy Taxation Directive, and debates about how much taxes some private corporations pay and where, become more prevalent. Additionally, the EU had no other option but to borrow money in open markets (EC, n.d. c) which means more careful consideration of the use of financial resources in the future to be able to pay that debt back (Details of this will be covered in Chapter 9). While not part of a green fiscal reform per se, and definitely not part of environmental taxes, it is worth mentioning the Commission Communication on 'Business Taxation for the 21st Century' (EC, 2021a), since it is part of a circular economy approach (Comelli, 2022), and calls for a reform of the international corporate taxation framework to create both 'fair and sustainable' growth and business environments (EC, 2021a: 2–3). A more straightforward link can be found in the proposals to modify the current VAT system, which is based on the sales price of a product or service, to one that assigns VAT rates according to the environmental impact of the products through their life-cycle (Timmermans and Achten, 2018). Other suggestions for green tax reforms consider that reduced VAT rates and VAT exemptions in certain products or sectors act effectively as harmful subsidies, so they could be eliminated (Schlegelmilch and Joas, 2015). Examples include reduced VAT rates for the meat and dairy industry and VAT exemption for international aviation in Germany, or reduced VAT rate for fuel and power in the UK, within Europe. Changes introduced in Phase IV of the ETS try to counteract some of these harmful subsidies by including sectors like the maritime industry as part of the system and accelerating the full incorporation of the aviation industry.

More relevant as part of a green fiscal reform is the revision of the Energy Taxation Directive (in place since 2003), which is blocked by the need to achieve unanimity, as it has been previously mentioned. The Commission submitted a new proposal in the context of the implementation of the EGD, as part of the 'Fit for 55' package (EC, 2021b). The proposed recast (EC, 2021c) is part of the efforts to reach the goals of the European Climate Law to make the EU climate neutral by 2050. The evaluation of the current Directive, included to provide contextualisation to the new proposal, concluded that it did not align with climate and energy objectives and did not promote GHG emissions reduction, among other reasons because it taxes new less carbon-intensive fuels as their fossil equivalent, 'de facto' favouring fossil fuels use (EC, 2021c: 2). Bearing in mind that this recast was proposed in 2021 and at the time of writing (2024) it is still embroiled in negotiations, it is debatable that it would achieve its goals, particularly those aiming to contribute to the 40% GHG emissions reduction for 2030. If and when the new Directive gets approved, it would mean that fuels will start being taxed according to their energy content and environmental performance instead of their volume, exemptions for home heating will be phased out, and fossil fuels used for intra-EU air transport, maritime transport and fishing will no longer be 'fully' exempt from energy taxation (EC, 2021c). This should contribute to help businesses and consumers to make cleaner, more climate-friendly choices (European Parliament, 2024). In 2022, during the Czech Presidency of the Council, negotiations concluded with several points still needing work to reach a compromise (European Parliament, 2024):

- Pace of implementation.
- Abolition of some exemptions for aviation and maritime sectors.
- Minimum levels of taxation (which were also part of the Discussions at the end of 2023 during the Spanish Presidency).
- Interaction of the Energy Taxation Directive with other initiatives of the Fit for 55 package.

By the end of 2023 it was concluded that positions among Member States were 'still divergent on several crucial issues' (European Parliament, 2024). This delay has not prevented researchers from trying to assess the consequences of the implementation of the proposed changes. For instance, with regard to effects over the fishing fleets – which will be affected by the elimination of exemptions for the maritime sector, it is concluded (Carvalho and Guillen, 2021) that since the Directive would only be applied to EU territorial waters, the largest effects would be for those small-scale fleets that deploy their fishing activities closer to the coast. However, the largest proportion of fuel consumed corresponds to large-scale and distant-water vessels, with small-scale vessels representing only 7% of the fuel consumed by the fishing fleets in the EU (Carvalho and Guillen, 2021). This would mean a limited effect of this directive on the reduction of GHG emissions and on the collection of tax revenue. In any case, since the fishing fleet cannot get adapted to less pollutant fuels immediately, it is recommended (Carvalho and Guillen, 2021) a progressive implementation of the Directive in this area.

The Commission itself (EC, 2021c) recognises that the Directive can have regressive effects, that is, have more negative impact over lower-income groups. Interestingly, it proposes revenue recycling in the form of lump-sum transfers, which their analysis suggests would turn the changes caused by the Directive progressive (EC, 2021c: 11). This would need careful consideration insofar previous research (Chiroleu-Assouline and Fodha, 2014) has suggested that lump-sum transfers are less effective than other options to achieve progressivity.

The impacts of environmental tax reforms had already been analysed by the European Environment Agency (EEA, 2011), in particular the distributional impacts for different income groups. Though effects vary considerably between countries, taxes and income groups, there are certain aspects that are generally shared: energy taxes are the ones that tend to be more regressive, with motor fuel taxes affecting more middle-income groups and disproportionately rural communities. When the proposals for the modification of the EU ETS aim to create a separate

ETS for buildings and road transport, whose role is considered by Scenario 3 of the Energy Directive recast (EC, 2021c), the social consequences for disadvantaged groups of this type of taxation need to be carefully calibrated. The proposal also takes account of the changes that are taking place across Europe as the energy system evolves away from fossil fuels, which would make the revenue collected by Member States decrease by almost 32% (EC, 2021c: 11). The proposed change to tax energy content and energy performance instead of volume aims to mitigate this potential loss of revenue. However, the EEA (2022) warns about the fact that the decarbonisation of the European economies will erode the current tax base, since what is being taxed now are fuel fossils and carbon generating energies and activities, something already observable in Sweden. It suggests that to future proof the tax system there needs to be a balance between achieving the goals of the sustainability transition and maintaining revenue stability, and for this it suggests finding new revenue sources. In the bigger picture, the revenues coming from the VAT own resource and the new plastics packaging waste contribution are very modest, so current analyses (Schratzenstaller, 2023) situate both the new ETS and the Carbon Border Adjustment Mechanism (CBAM) – to be covered in the last section of this chapter, as the best opportunities for the EU to keep a stable revenue stream in the future. This is because there is a need for coordinated implementation of other new green levies in the Member States and given the delay in the adoption of the reviewed Energy Taxation Directive it will take some time for proposals in this area to find their way into the EU agenda. Since differences among Member States are conditioning progress in overall green fiscal reforms at EU level, it is worth looking at what the Member States have been doing in their own territories to move forward in their fiscal systems.

The use of environmental taxes across the EU

The key recommendations for a green or environmental fiscal reform include the transfer of the tax burden from labour to environment, which reinforces the possibility of creating a double dividend (Markandya et al., 2013). But how those transfers happen will depend on the specific structure of the country in question, and there are plenty of differences, including among EU Member States. Another recommendation is the recycling of the tax revenue collected through environmental taxes to modify the progressivity of other tax rates and the general tax system, since that would conduct to Pareto-improving situations (Chiroleu-Assouline and Fodha, 2014). This translates on an environmental tax reform that takes care of the three pillars of sustainability by improving economic, environmental and social outcomes.

It is traditionally recognised that the first environmental fiscal reforms (EFRs) in Europe took place in the Nordic countries (Gazzani, 2021; Heine et al., 2012), even if in Germany they had been conceptualised in 1983. Implementation there was delayed until the late 1990s due to the reunification process (OECD, 2005). The most common indicator of the implementation of said fiscal reforms is the percentage share of environmental tax revenue with respect to total tax revenue collected in a country, including social contributions. The problem that we can observe is that in most EU Member States that percentage has been decreasing over time instead of increasing, something more notable in countries considered as frontrunners on environmental taxation such as Sweden and Denmark (EEA, 2022). This has to do, among other things, with the different design and implementation of the EFRs in each country.

Early pioneers such as the Nordic countries, Germany, France or Italy began their reforms by launching new environmental taxes, mostly over energy consumption and CO_2 emissions, at the same time that they reduced income taxes and other labour costs. But in addition to those steps, Denmark and the Netherlands also increased their already existing taxes on waste disposal (Gazzani, 2021). In terms of revenue collected (and recycled), the uses also differ from country to country. In Germany they were used to lower pension payments, which were increasing labour cost and causing unemployment (Schlegelmilch and Joas, 2015). In Latvia, for instance, the revenue collected from electricity taxes was used for a new Electricity Customer Support Fund to offset the increase in electricity costs associated with the wider use of renewable energy (Streimikiene et al., 2018). Another feature of environmental tax reforms is that of specific 'tax incentives' (as opposed to creating new taxes) for the promotion of renewable energy. The increase in the proportion of renewables in countries energy mixes has been mostly attributed to other MBIs such as the FiT or green certification systems that were covered in Chapter 5, but most Member States created additional incentives in the form of tax exemptions. These include (Cansino et al., 2010): exemptions on the payments of excise duties in electricity if it is generated from renewable sources in Denmark, Germany, Poland, Romania, Slovakia and Sweden; personal income tax incentives have been available in Belgium, Czechia, France and Luxembourg; deductions in corporate profit taxes are less common but were implemented in Belgium, Czechia, Greece and Spain; lower VAT rates were used in France, Italy and Portugal and finally Spain was the only Member State to implement tax incentives in property taxation (Cansino et al., 2010). Box 7.1 provides a review of environmental tax reforms in Croatia, the latest country to become an EU Member State in 2013, as it tends not to be featured in early analyses.

Box 7.1 Environmental fiscal reforms in Croatia

While in most EU Member States environmental tax revenues come mainly from energy taxation, they made only between 50% and 55% in Croatia in 2012 (together with Malta, Ireland and the Netherlands). Conversely, while pollution and resource taxes tend to play a minor role (4% on average), in Croatia their importance has been traditionally higher, amounting to 20% of environmental tax revenues in 2012 (Schlegelmilch and Joas, 2015). This has progressively changed and now energy taxes account for 80% of the environmental tax revenue in the country (International Monetary Fund [IMF],

2023). It is one of the Member States where a shift from labour taxation to environmental taxation is observable through an increase in environmental tax revenue higher than the increase in labour tax revenue (EEA, 2022). This shift is not consistently kept over time and between 2010 and 2011 the movement was in favour of labour taxes (Dyduch and Stabryla-Chuczio, 2019). But even if there has been a small move towards the decrease of environmental tax revenue as a proportion of total tax revenues, as observed in many EU Member States, Croatia presents the smallest of these trends (EEA, 2022) and still averages much higher levels than most of the EU, with 9.15% as opposed to 5.76% EU average in 2019 (EC, 2021d). As already pointed out, there is not much academic research covering the progress of the country in its sustainability transition. In studies that compare 'old' and 'new' Member States (Sikic and Hodzic, 2023) results applicable to Croatia indicate that environmental taxes have a negative impact on final energy consumption, which is desirable for the reduction of GHG emissions, but this impact is smaller than in old Member States, and more stringent regulations and institutional and regulatory reforms are recommended. One of the main issues is that Croatia is still heavily dependent on fossil fuels and fuel imports, even renewable energy, and as a country it requires high level of infrastructure investment to facilitate the penetration of renewables (IMF, 2023). While it is praised by its early adoption of plastic packaging taxation and waste management system, which includes a deposit-refund scheme for bottles, together with a Forest Public Benefit Function Fee in place since 1983 (EC, 2021d), latest analyses conclude that the country's environmental tax policy is not aligned with EU climate targets and goals and is in need of wider reforms. This is necessary if Croatia wants to benefit from the Recovery and Resilience Facility funds that the EU has put in place after the Covid-19 pandemic (IMF, 2023).

The worrying trend that is being observed in recent years is that while labour tax revenue collection has increased overtime in all EU Member States, to see a green fiscal reform or environmental tax reform, there should have been a shift from labour taxes to environmental taxes indicated by an increase in environmental tax revenues that is higher than the increase in labour tax revenues. Instead, in a considerable proportion of Member States (Slovakia, Malta, Cyprus, Ireland, Lithuania, Czechia, Luxembourg, Spain, Hungary, Sweden and Austria) the opposite has happened, and even worse, in Germany, Denmark and Portugal there has been an increase in labour tax revenue at the same time that there has been a decrease in environmental tax revenue (EEA, 2022). As previously stated, given that behavioural changes towards consumption of greener products, including greener fuels, have started eroding the tax base at the root of most of the existing environmental tax reforms, this decrease on environmental tax revenues should not come as a surprise or be taken as a negative without further consideration and specific country by country analysis. The uptake of electric vehicles that is being promoted through new regulations on the ban of petrol and diesel cars for 2035 (Frost, 2023) can only further the erosion of the current tax base. As usual, any negative effect would be felt differently in each EU Member State, and recent studies suggest that Slovenia, for instance, is particularly exposed to the consequences of the decarbonisation of the transport sector (OECD, 2019). This is related to the high proportion of the total tax revenue that road transport taxes represent in the country (14.6% in 2016). A suggestion to counteract the estimated decrease in tax revenue is the gradual phase-in of 'distance charges', which will tax road transport from another perspective and would create a tax base resilient to electrification of transport (OECD, 2019). The creation of a second ETS for buildings and transport that is currently under development goes in the same direction. But once again, careful account of potential regressive effects of these proposed new instruments would be necessary.

To some extent, it could be argued that the options to increase environmental taxation are running short, at least from the point of view of environmental justification. If the priority is given to the revenue collection function, the implementation of new taxes or the application of taxes to new tax bases could be justified, but then their classification as environmental could and should be challenged, particularly if the revenue collected is not recycled for environmental, climate or biodiversity purposes.

New environmental fiscal instruments: the Carbon Border Adjustment Mechanism

These limitations over additional possibilities of taxation within EU borders to EU citizens and companies oblige regulators to be innovative. It could be argued that the creation of a CBAM falls under this innovative category. It has already been mentioned that the CBAM was conceived to try and limit the risk of carbon leakage that the EU ETS could create, to protect the Member States from potential competitiveness disadvantages if other parts of the world did not share similar levels of climate ambitions to those of the EU. This is the narrative used by the Commission in the EGD (EC, 2019b). Unsurprisingly, the mere proposal spiked rejection from the EU's main commercial competitors, including China (Xu and Stanway, 2021), and even if there have been modifications to the initial proposal, international criticisms persist. As a tax, the CBAM could be described as a mix between an environmental tax and a trade (import) tax. While environmental taxes are relatively well received, import taxes are not allowed under the World Trade Organization (WTO) rules, hence the insistence of the EU that its CBAM is designed to comply with WTO rules (EC, 2019b) while China has attempted to gather support to push back against it within WTO discussions (Yin, 2023) claiming that the opposite is true. The WTO Deputy Director-General (WTO, 2021) did not seem to share the concerns but advocated for an international agreement on carbon pricing.

Detractors of the CBAM argue, among other things, that it would affect more negatively developing countries whose economies are more carbon intensive (Yin, 2023). Some studies seem to confirm those fears simulating different implementation approaches of the mechanism, concluding (Beaufils et al., 2023) that middle- and low-income countries for which the EU is a considerable export market would be the most affected. BRIC countries (Brazil, Russia, India, China) consider the CBAM discriminatory, unilateral, and also in violation of WTO rules (Majkut, 2023) since it would clearly make them less competitive against the EU. For the US the situation is a bit different. Not only its economy is already more competitive and less carbon intensive than that of the aforementioned countries, it is also planning to have its own CBAM (Reinsch and Duncan, 2022), which could facilitate that both EU and US cooperate to reach higher climate ambitions and lead the way for the rest of the world (Majkut, 2023). However and despite several proposals put forward to the legislators in the US, none of them have been approved yet (Gangotra et al., 2023), which gives the upper hand to the EU, at least temporarily.

After several revisions, the EU CBAM Regulation was approved in 2023 (OJEU, 2023) and has already entered into force but in a transitional mode. This transition period will run until 31 December 2025, and between January 2026 and 2034 there will be a full phase-in of the CBAM coinciding with the phase-out of free allocation of allowances in the EU ETS (Beharab, 2023). The GHGs covered by the EU CBAM will be the same covered by the EU ETS Directive (OJEU, 2023) so it is clear that both instruments are expected to complement each other. Importantly, for the good functioning of both instruments it is necessary that the price of carbon remains high because it will be the determinant of the CBAM certificates that importing countries will need to obtain. That carbon price will be determined by the price of allowances in the EU ETS, which is a difference, for instance, with the CBAM proposed in the US (Reinsch and Duncan, 2022). Initially the EU CBAM will apply to imports of goods whose production is carbon intensive, which have previously been identified as at risk of carbon leakage: cement, iron and steel, aluminium, fertilisers, electricity and hydrogen (EC, 2024). The Regulation gives room for the list of products included to be modified if necessary.

This is because as it happened with the EU ETS the transition period will become a learning process which will require a proper assessment to evaluate the need for adjustments. Regular reports will need to be produced, among other reasons, to assess the possible impact into developing countries (particularly least developed countries) whose trade with the EU is dominated by the goods or products affected by the CBAM. In theory, the EU is expecting that the CBAM will contribute to reduction in emissions in third countries, encouraging them to adopt greener technologies (OJEU, 2023). The transition period will also help determine which countries are more likely to engage with or support CBAM, which is something necessary to ensure its success in the longer term. Preliminary studies (Sabyrbekov and Overland, 2024) indicate lists of countries most likely to become supporters of the EU CBAM with different motivations:

- Among the largest world economies, potential allies include: Japan, South Korea, Singapore, Canada, Colombia, Mexico, Vietnam, South Africa, Kazakhstan and Ukraine.

- Among the main EU aid recipients, the most likely potential allies would be: Cote d'Ivoire, Colombia, South Africa, Serbia, Ukraine, Turkey, Cameroon, Madagascar, Ecuador and Senegal.
- Among countries particularly concerned by climate change effects, there would also be potential allies such as: Japan, Korea, Singapore, Israel, Cote d'Ivoire, Canada, Colombia and Mexico (Sabyrbekov and Overland, 2024).

The CBAM Regulation also foresees what to do if attempts to circumnavigate the mechanism are detected (OJEU, 2023), but already there are countries exempted from its application, notably Switzerland (OJEU, 2023) since it has linked its ETS with the EU one. Since the system is now in its infancy, we will have to wait at least until the end of the transition period to make proper assessments of its functioning and potential, but thinking of its role among the MBIs and the whole fiscal system in the EU, one could already extract some preliminary thoughts: we are again in front of a new policy instrument that is based on prices (and quantities through its direct link to the ETS), which is trying to correct issues caused (or potentially caused) by another instrument. The three chapters in this section have shown that the design of MBIs has not managed to reach expectations despite decades of experience, since there are always pitfalls and negativities that require a complementary instrument to correct said negative effects. Those negative impacts tend to concentrate on low-income groups, whether regionally or internationally, depending on which instrument we are referring to, which puts into question to which extent the wish to pursue an integration of environmental and economic aspects keeps leaving the social pillar of sustainability behind. On paper, the pillar is not totally forgotten, if we account for the creation of the Just Transition Mechanism and its related Just Transition Fund, also introduced in 2021 as part of the implementation of the EGD (EC, 2019b). But social inequalities need to be addressed in wider debates about the consequences of the sustainable transition, and this means going beyond the consideration of aspects such as employment. Other indicators need to emerge to reflect the proper balance (or lack thereof) between the three pillars of sustainability in the planning and implementation of new policy instruments.

A concern from the analysis of materials in this chapter is that the shift of EFRs to prioritise environmental outcomes seems to be reversing somehow, and worries about less revenue collection as the green transition progresses seem to overshadow the achievements so far. One cannot but wonder if it could be worth considering that if the transition is successful, GHG emissions get reduced, the penetration of renewable energies is maximised and the goal of becoming a carbon neutral economy is fulfilled we may not be needing that much tax revenue being collected as we could achieve the desired level of internalisation of externalities. If environmental tax revenues begin being used to cover purposes other than environmental and climate ones, first the taxes should stop being called environmental, and second there would be an indication that the fiscal system is (still) not properly designed.

Discussion questions

1 Can a tax still be called 'environmental' if its purpose is purely revenue collection?
2 Which approaches could be helpful to move forward in the elimination of the unanimity rule for taxation decisions in the EU? Will it ever happen?
3 Are EU Member States ready to decrease income taxation in favour of environmental taxes?
4 Which steps could be given to counteract the negative perception of taxes? Is it something that could be done at the supranational level?
5 Among the different proposals for new taxes and reform of existing taxes, which ones do you think will have the largest impacts (assuming they get implemented)? Will those impacts be mainly environmental or economic and social too?

Further readings

Milne, J. E. and Andersen, M. S. (eds) (2014) *Handbook of Research on Environmental Taxation.* Edward Elgar: This is a helpful introduction to environmental taxation concepts and processes, organised by themes that help the reader follow the logic of the regulator: Concept – Design-Acceptance-Implementation-Impact. Case studies contribute to visualising the bigger picture and the appreciation of different contexts.

Panayi, C. H. J. I., Haslehner, W. and Traversa, E. (eds) (2020) *Research Handbook on European Taxation Law.* Edward Elgar: Presented as following an interdisciplinary approach, this book provides insights into a wide range of taxation issues in a number of areas, including businesses and personal income. It complements the content of this chapter since environmental taxation is not covered.

Pistone, P. and Villar Ezcurra, M. (eds) (2021) *Energy Taxation, Environmental Protection and State Aids.* IBDF: This book provides nice case studies from around the world looking into the different approaches to energy and environmental taxation. It even considers the transnational effects of taxation by introducing the topic of the border adjustment mechanisms.

References

Abeysuriya, K., Mitchell, C. and Willetts, J. (2008) Expanding economic perspectives for sustainability in urban water and sanitation, *Development*, 51 (2008): 23–29.

Angerer, J. (2024) General tax policy. Fact sheets on the European Union – 2024, *European Parliament*, 10/2023.

Beaufils, T., Ward, H., Jakob, M. and Wenz, L. (2023) Assessing different European carbon border adjustment mechanism implementations and their impact on trade partners, *Communications Earth & Environment*, 4 (2023): 131. https://doi.org/10.1038/s43247-023-00788-4

Beharab, R. (2023) Navigating the CBAM transitional period: Understanding the latest developments, and enhancing preparedness, *Policy Center for the New South,* Policy Brief PB-29/23, July 2023.

Cansino, J. M., Pablo-Romero, M. P., Roman, R. and Yñiguez, R. (2010) Tax incentives to promote green electricity: An overview of EU-27 countries, *Energy Policy,* 38 (2010): 6000–6008.

Carvalho, N. and Guillen, J. (2021) Economic impact of eliminating the fuel tax exemption in the EU fishing fleet, *Sustainability,* 13 (2021): 2179. https://doi.org/10.3390/su13052719

Chiroleu-Assouline, M. and Fodha, M. (2014) From regressive pollution taxes to progressive environmental tax reforms, *European Economic Review*, 69 (2014): 126–142.

Comelli, A. (2022) Environmental taxation from a European Union perspective, after the Covid-19 crisis. In Weishaar, S., Milne, J., Andersen, M. and Ashiabor, H. (eds) *Green Deals in the Making. Perspective from Across the Globe.* Critical Issues in Environmental Taxation series. Cheltenham: Edward Elgar: 2–13.

Domguia, E. N. (2023) Taxing for a better life? The impact of environmental taxes on income distribution and inclusive education, *Heliyon,* 9 (2023): e21443. https://doi.org/10.1016/j.heliyon.2023.e21443

Dyduch, J. and Stabryla-Chuczio, K. (2019) Fiscal impacts of environmental tax reform in selected EU member states, *EKONOMIA I ŚRODOWISKO,* 1 (68): 114–126.

Elshamy, H. M. and Sayed Ahmed, K. I. (2017) Green Fiscal reforms, environment and sustainable development, *International Journal of Applied Economics, Finance and Accounting,* 1 (1): 48–52.

European Commission (2003) Communication form the commission: A constitution for the union – Opinion of the commission, pursuant to Article 48 of the Treaty on European Union, on the Conference of representatives of the Member States' governments convened to revise the Treaties. COM (2003) 548 final. Brussels, 17.9.2003.

European Commission (2019a) Communication form the commission to the European parliament, the European council and the council, *Towards a More Efficient and Democratic Decision Making in EU Tax Policy.* COM (2019) 8 final. Strasbourg, 15.1.2019.

European Commission (2019b) Communication from the commission to the European parliament, the European council, the council, the European economic and social committee and the committee of the regions: The European Green Deal. COM (2019) 640 final. Brussels, 11.12.2019.

European Commission (2021a) Communication on business taxation for the 21st century: Key messages and next steps. Platform for tax good governance. DOC: Platform/43/2021/EN. Directorate-General Taxation and Customs Union.

European Commission (2021b) Communication from the commission to the European parliament, the council, the European economic and social committee and the committee of the regions. 'Fit for 55': delivering the EU's 2030 Climate Target on the way to climate neutrality. COM (2021) 550 final. Brussels, 14.7.2021.

European Commission (2021c) Proposal for a council directive restructuring the Union framework for the taxation of energy products and electricity (recast). COM (2021) 563 final. Brussels, 14.7.2021.

European Commission (2021d) *Ensuring That Polluters Pay – Croatia.* Luxembourg: Publications Office of the European Union.

European Commission (2024) Carbon border adjustment mechanism. Available from: https://taxation-customs.ec.europa.eu/carbon-border-adjustment-mechanism_en

European Commission (n.d.a) Taxation. Towards fair, efficient and growth-friendly taxes. Available from: https://european-union.europa.eu/priorities-and-actions/actions-topic/taxation_en#:~:text=The%20EU%20does%20not%20have,the%20collected%20taxes%20are%20spent.

European Commission (n.d.b) Taxation and qualified majority voting. The Intergovernmental Conference of 2003–2004. Available from: https://taxation-customs.ec.europa.

eu/taxation-and-qualified-majority-voting_en#:~:text=Unanimity%20v.&text=That%20is%2C%20all%20Member%20States,Council%20of%20Ministers%20is%20reached.
European Commission (n.d.c) Recovery plan for Europe. Available from: https://commission.europa.eu/strategy-and-policy/recovery-plan-europe_en
European Environment Agency (2011) *Environmental Tax Reform in Europe: Implications for Income Distribution*, EEA Technical report No. 16/2011.
European Environment Agency (2022) *The Role of (Environmental) Taxation in Supporting Sustainability Transitions*, Briefing no. 22/2021. Published 07 February 2022.
European Parliament (2024) Revision of the Energy Taxation Directive (ETD)-Q2 2021 [Blocked]. Legislative Train 04.2024.
Eurostat (2013) *Environmental Taxes. A Statistical Guide* (2013 edition). Eurostat Manuals and Guidelines. Luxembourg: Publications Office of the European Union.
Fernandez, R. M. (2023a) Green fiscal systems – Their role in the European green deal. In Dyrhauge, H. and Kurze, K. (eds) *Making the European Green Deal Work. EU Sustainability Policies at Home and Abroad*. Abingdon: Routledge: 29–44.
Fernandez, R. M. (2023b) Economics for a low-carbon future. In Moltan-Hill, P. (ed) *Sustainable Management. A Complete Guide for Faculty and Students* (third edition). The Principles for Responsible Management Education Series, Abingdon: Routledge: 237–265.
Frost, R. (2023) EU 2035 petrol and diesel car ban: Germany reaches deal on synthetic fuels. *Euronews,* March 22. Available from: https://www.euronews.com/green/2023/03/22/eu-to-ban-petrol-and-diesel-cars-by-2035-heres-why-some-countries-are-pushing-back
Gangotra, A., Carlsen, W. and Kennedy, K. (2023) 4 US congress bills related to carbon border adjustments in 2023, *World Resources Institute,* 13 December. Available from: https://www.wri.org/update/4-us-congress-bills-related-carbon-border-adjustments-2023
Garcia-Portela, L. (2023) Backward-looking principles of climate justice: The unjustified move from the polluter pays principle to the beneficiary pays principle, *Res Publica,* 29 (2023): 367–384.
Gazzani, F. (2021) Transition to social-ecological sustainability using the environmental fiscal reform, *International Journal of Social Economics,* 48 (5): 675–692.
Georgiou, C. (2023) Federal fiscal capacity and the challenge of the green transition in the EU, *Journal of European Integration,* 45 (6): 871–887.
Heine, D., Norregaard, J. and Parry, I. W. H. (2012) Environmental tax reform: Principles from theory and practice to date, *IMF Working Paper,* WP/12/180. International Monetary Fund. July 2012.
Heyl, K., Ekardt, F., Sund, L. and Roos, P. (2022) Potentials and limitations of subsidies in sustainability governance: The example of agriculture, *Sustainability,* 14 (2022): 15859. https://doi.org/10.3390/su142315859
International Monetary Fund (2023) Energy security and climate change: Challenges and opportunities for Croatia. In *Republic of Croatia: Selected Issues*, Country Report 2023/234. https://doi.org/10.5089/9798400246937.002
Jaakkola, J. (2019) A democratic dilemma of European power to tax: Reconstructing the symbiosis between taxation and democracy beyond the state? *German Law Journal,* 20 (2019): 660–678.
Majkut, J. (2023) The United States should learn to live with EU CBAM, *Center for Strategic and International Studies,* Comentary, 17 January. Available from: https://www.csis.org/analysis/united-states-should-learn-live-eu-cbam

Markandya, A., Gonzalez-Eguino, M. and Escapa, M. (2013) From shadow to green: Linking environmental fiscal reforms and the informal economy, *Energy Economics,* 40 (2013): S108–S118.

Mohammed, H. and Tangl, A. (2024) Taxation perspectives: Analyzing the factors behind viewing taxes as punishment – A comprehensive study of taxes as service or strain, *Journal of Risk and Financial Management,* 17 (5). https://doi.org/10.3390/jrfm17010005

OECD (2005) *Environmental Fiscal Reform for Poverty Reduction, A DAC Reference Document. DAC Guidelines and Reference Series.* Paris: OECD Publishing.

OECD (2019) The fiscal implications of the low-carbon transition. *2019 Green Growth and Sustainable Development Forum.* Greening heavy and extractive industries Issue Paper, 26 & 27 November, Paris: OCDE.

OECD (2020) Green budgeting and tax policy tools to support a green recovery. *Tackling coronavirus (COVID-19): Contributing to a global effort.* 9 October 2020.

Official Journal of the European Union (2011) Regulation (EU) N. 691/2011 of the European parliament and of the council of 6 July 2011 on European environmental economic accounts. L192, 22.7.2011.

Official Journal of the European Union (2023) Regulation (EU) 2023/956 of the European parliament and of the council of 10 May 2023 establishing a carbon border adjustment mechanism. L130, 16.5.2023.

Page, E. A. (2012) Give it up for climate change: A defence of the beneficiary pays principle, *International Theory,* 4 (2): 300–330.

Pekanov, A. and Schratzenstaller, M. (2020) *The Role of Fiscal Rules in Relation with the Green Economy.* European Parliament, Study Requested by the ECON committee. Economic Governance Support Unit and Policy Department A. PE 614.524 – September 2020.

Reinsch, W. A. and Duncan, E. (2022) Trade tools for climate: Transatlantic carbon border adjustments, *Center for Strategic and International Studies,* Critical Questions, 20 July. Available from: https://www.csis.org/analysis/trade-tools-climate-transatlantic-carbon-border-adjustments

Sabyrbekov, R. and Overland, I. (2024) Small and large friends of the EU's carbon border adjustment mechanism: Which non-EU countries are likely to support it? *Energy Strategy Reviews*, 51 (2024): 101303. https://doi.org/10.1016/j.esr.2024.101303

Schlegelmilch, K. and Joas, A. (2015) Fiscal considerations in the design of green tax reforms, *Green Growth Knowledge Platform, Third Annual Conference, Fiscal Policies and the Green Economy Transition: Generating Knowledge – Creating Impact*, Venice-Italy, 29030 January 2015.

Schratzenstaller, M. (2023) Elements of a European green fiscal policy, *Intereconomics,* 58 (6): 300–304.

Sikic, T. J. and Hodzic, S. (2023) Can environmental taxes decrease final energy consumption in the old and new EU countries? *ECONOMIC RESEARCH-EKONOMSKA ISTRAŽIVANJA,* 36(3): 2271968. https://doi.org/10.1080/1331677X.2023.2271968

Sloman, J., Garratt, D. and Guest, J. (2022) *Economics* (11th edition). Harlow: Pearson.

Streimikiene, D., Siksnelyte, I., Zavadskas, E. K. and Cavallaro, F. (2018) The impact of greening tax systems on sustainable energy development in the baltic states, *Energies*, 11 (2018): 1193. https://doi.org/10.3390/en11051193

Timmermans, B. and Achten, W. M. J. (2018) From value-added tax to a damage and value-added tax partially based on life cycle assessment: principles and feasibility, *International Journal of Life Cycle Assessment,* 23 (2018): 2217–2247.

Vicha, O. (2011) The polluter-pays principle in OECD recommendations and its application in international and EC/EU law, *CYIL*, 2 (2011): 57–67.

Wasserfallen, F. (2014) Political and economic integration in the EU: The case of failed tax harmonization, *Journal of Common Market Studies*, 52 (2): 420–435.

Wesseh Jr, P. K. and Lin, B. (2019) Environmental policy and 'double dividend' in a transitional economy, *Energy Policy*, 134 (2019): 110947. https://doi.org/10.1016/j.enpol.2019.110947

Winer, S. L. and Hettich, W. (2004) The political economy of taxation: Positive and normative analysis when collective choice matters. In Rowley, C. K. and Schneider, F. (eds) *The Encyclopedia of Public Choice*. Boston, MA: Springer, https://doi.org/10.1007/978-0-306-47828-4_15

World Trade Organisation (2021) DDG Paugam: WTO rules no barrier to ambitious environmental policies. *News*, 16 September. Available from: https://www.wto.org/english/news_e/news21_e/ddgjp_16sep21_e.htm

Xu, M. and Stanway, D. (2021) China says EU's planned carbon border tax violates trade principles. *Reuters*, 26 July. Available from: https://www.reuters.com/business/sustainable-business/china-says-ecs-carbon-border-tax-is-expanding-climate-issues-trade-2021-07-26/

Yin, I. (2023) China lays groundwork for pushback against EU's cross border carbon tax, *S&P Global*, 19 July. Available from: https://www.spglobal.com/commodityinsights/en/market-insights/latest-news/energy-transition/071923-china-lays-groundwork-for-pushback-against-eus-cross-border-carbon-tax

Part III

Latest developments

Green economy, green finance and the challenges ahead

8 Circular and green economy

Introduction

The economy: circular and green

In Chapter 1 we made reference to and defined a 'low-carbon economy'. Another common notation found in many EU documents is that of 'green economy', with 'green' being used as a synonym of sustainable. The United Nations Environment Programme (UNEP) links all these notations by defining green economy as 'low carbon, resource efficient and socially inclusive' (UNEP, 2011), which also blends the three pillars of sustainability. For the purpose of this chapter it is also helpful to look at the characteristics of said green economy, where

> growth in employment and income are driven by public and private investment into such economic activities, infrastructure and assets that allow reduced carbon emissions and pollution, enhanced energy and resource efficiency, and prevention of the loss of biodiversity and ecosystems services.
>
> (UNEP, 2011)

It is commonplace to find expressions referring to 'greening' economic activities and after all, the document this book uses as a framework includes the word in its title: European 'Green' Deal. Despite multiple informal definitions of the term, the one that has been more widely and formally used is also provided by UNEP (2011) understanding green economy as 'the one that results in improved human well-being and social equity, while significantly reducing environmental risks and ecological scarcities'. So even if there are EU Member States considered pioneers on green economy initiatives, its operational framework is more global and in that sense it is practical to approach the analysis of green economy in the EU in terms of its embeddedness of the UN approaches. To begin with, the title of European Green Deal (EGD) is mirroring the one coined by the UN as a result of the international economic crisis of 2007–2008, with a Green Economy Initiative launched in 2008, and a 'Global Green New Deal' launched in 2009 (UNEP, 2009). In that sense, the ideas of the EGD are not new, since the proposal of initiatives that advocate the consideration of environmental aspects to get out of crises has been previously

DOI: 10.4324/9781003224785-11

used, including green fiscal reforms – the object of Chapter 7, and the inclusion of environmental factors in macroeconomic policy decision-making in general. The EU is adamant that the EGD is key for the recovery from the crisis created by the Covid-19 pandemic (European Committee of the Regions, 2021), hence there are parallelisms between the two 'deals' as crises solving instruments.

Achieving a green, low carbon economy is not possible if the same things keep being done, nor if they are done in the same way that it is now known to damage the planet. Hence the calls for a circular economy, term used to make reference mainly to a whole systems approach to production and consumption. Again, this is not a new concept, and was introduced in the 1990s (Heshmati, 2015), as an attempt to formulate the connections between the environment and economic activities. The European Environment Agency [EEA] (2016) started systematising the knowledge base about the circular economy and has been trying to measure the progress towards its main aim of 'living well but within the limits of the planet'. A circular economy approach calls for respect of the planetary boundaries by 'increasing the share of renewable or recyclable resources while reducing the consumption of raw materials and energy and at the same time cutting emissions and material losses' (EEA, 2016: 6). The term is used in numerous occasions in the EGD (EC, 2019), as it commits to the creation of a Circular Economy Action Plan, which saw the light in 2020 (EC, 2020a), and even if it has been said that for the sustainability transition the participation of all stakeholders is necessary, the circular economy messages are mainly directed towards the industrial sectors of the EU, so that any industrial strategy is based on its principles. This makes sense insofar it is production processes within global value chains the ones using resources (raw materials and land, human resources and capital) in a way that is damaging and depleting, compromising the possibility of reaching sustainable development. Since it is recognised that it takes 25 years to 'transform an industrial sector and all the value chains' (EC, 2019: 7) it makes sense to take action as soon as possible to reach the EU goal of climate neutrality in 2050.

Links to other concepts and approaches

In this context, it becomes easy to connect both green economy and circular economy with the UN SDGs and particularly with SDG12 'Responsible consumption and production' (UN, 2015). It is not the purpose of this chapter or book to delve into the management side of businesses and production processes, but there is an extensive branch of literature that covers the role of businesses in sustainable development (including sustainable value chains), rooted in the concept of 'corporate social responsibility' (Carroll, 2016) and business ethics (for instance Crane and Matten, 2010). The latest developments in this area lean towards environment, social and governance (ESG). These are areas or topics that companies need to report on (see for instance Janicka and Sajnog, 2022) so that their stakeholders, particularly potential investors, can make decisions based on companies' impacts, in what is now called Socially Responsible Investment (SRI), which in turn will condition their access to financial resources (for an overview of the European framework on SRI, see Martini, 2021). The EU has enacted regulations in this area too (Corporate Sustainability Reporting Directive and others) but our concern in this chapter is more linked to how EU institutions facilitate investments in the sectors and activities required to make economies green and circular.

Perhaps a better link with the concept of circularity can be found in what has become a widespread phenomenon in Economics – the 'economics of the doughnut' (the one with a whole in the middle) or 'Doughnut Economics' (Raworth, 2022). It breaks with the traditional paradigm that focus on the maximisation of economic growth and Gross Domestic Product (GDP). Instead, it presents the economy as a safe space for humanity's development (as opposed to growth), with a social foundation and an ecological ceiling. In that regard it conciliates the three pillars of sustainability (economic, social, environmental – also called ecological). Interestingly it characterises the economy as both 'regenerative' and 'distributive' (Raworth, 2022). A regenerative economy aims at leaving things better than they were before, respecting living systems (Morseletto, 2020). Incidentally, a circular economy is defined as one that is regenerative by design (Ellen MacArthur Foundation, 2013), and is also associated with the term 'restorative'. The distributive element is the one that connects the doughnut with the social pillar of sustainability, insofar it describes an economy 'that shares value and opportunity more equitably with all who co-create it' (Sahan et al., 2022). It could be argued that all the concepts are interrelated (see Figure 8.1) or that they simply represent the same ideas from different perspectives.

Hand in hand with the debates about what type of growth economies should have to become sustainable (green growth and green economy) we find those who defend 'degrowth' as the only option to save the planet, considering sustainability incompatible with economic growth (Schneider et al., 2010). Since the EU is using the terms green and circular economy, it is safe to say that its belief is more aligned

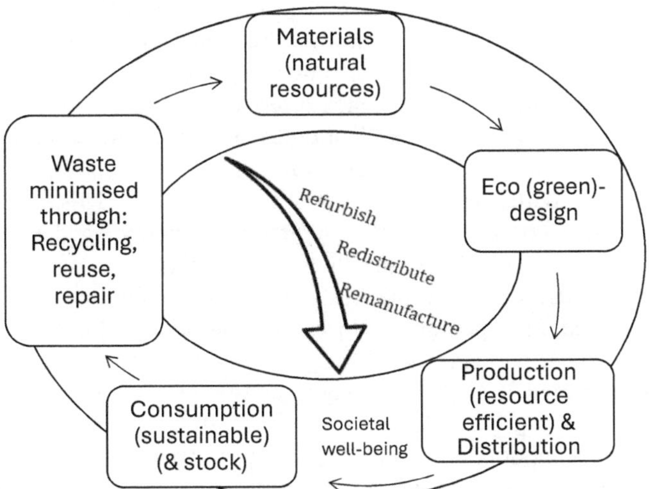

Figure 8.1 Green-circular-doughnut framework

Source: Author's elaboration.

with the idea that growth is compatible with sustainable development, as long as we respect the limits of our planet. Without entering into the debate between green growth or degrowth, this chapter lets the reader decide if the postulates of green and circular economy are situated within the strong or weak sustainability frameworks.

In this chapter we will analyse what steps have been taken by the EU to transform economies into green and circular, and we will pay attention to the EU institutions who play a prominent role in this transformation.

Green and circular economy in the EU

The role of the European Environment Agency

When the EEA started developing the knowledge base on circular economy (EEA, 2016), it was contextualised as part of the policy mix constituting the 7th Environment Action Programme (see Chapter 3) with one of its objectives being to 'turn the EU into a resource-efficient, green and competitive low-carbon economy'. The objectives are said to reflect a 'green economy policy concept' (EEA, 2016: 31), by which there should be a decoupling between economic growth and environmental pressures. But from what we have already seen in previous chapters, the decoupling between economic growth and greenhouse gas emissions has not been achieved. It is at that point (2016) that there is a recognition of the need to widen the focus of action beyond the so-called 'core' circular aspects, that is, waste management, waste prevention and resource efficiency, to achieve full ecosystem resilience and human well-being (EEA, 2016). The Commission developed a Circular Economy Package in 2018 (European Parliament, 2018), with several legislative proposals related to raw materials, plastics and monitoring framework, but with the emphasis put on waste. As part of its mission, the EEA started looking at wider global drivers for change that could influence the EU's plans to achieve sustainable development. The warnings were made public right after the launch of the EGD (EEA, 2020) which in theory should have served at informing the policy initiatives that have been launched thereafter. Said warnings referred to the fact that in a globalised world and with the EU being dependent on the import of raw materials, with the expansion of economic systems everywhere it may not be possible to keep the goal of reducing environmental pressures (EEA, 2020: 52). This, in other words, means that the focus on waste of the first circular economy legislative package is not going to be enough to address the challenges we face.

As part of its research work, the EEA continues looking into the latest developments, evidence and approaches, to expand the knowledge base on sustainability issues, and it publishes its findings in regular reports. One of the latest (EEA, 2021 – updated 2023) conveys some striking messages: one of them is that 100% circularity is not possible, as we cannot fully decouple economic growth and resource consumption. But another interesting remark is that 'doughnut economics, post-growth and degrowth are alternatives to mainstream conceptions of economic growth that offer valuable insights' (EEA, 2021). Could this be an indication that some of the less generally accepted economic approaches may become mainstream in the near future? Time will tell. The role of the Agency in this case is to provide visibility to debates and topics related to sustainability that are usually complex and affected by uncertainty (Kovacic and Benini, 2022).

The progress towards circular economy needs to be measured and monitored. To that end, Eurostat and the European Commission have developed a monitoring framework which includes five thematic areas (Eurostat, 2024):

- Production and consumption
- Waste management
- Secondary raw materials
- Competitiveness and innovation
- Global sustainability and resilience

For each thematic area a series of indicators have been developed (for instance, resource productivity, food waste and generation of plastic packaging waste per capita).

The EEA has developed its own Circularity Metrics Lab (CML) which provides data on additional indicators following the Bellagio Declaration on Circular Economy Monitoring Principles (EEA et al., 2020). These indicators are:

- Material footprints in Europe
- Consumption footprints
- Circular material use rate
- Waste generation and decoupling in Europe
- Diversion of waste from landfill in Europe
- Waste recycling in Europe

It is worth noting that at the time of writing not all the indicators are fully functioning. It can be observed that Eurostat indicators cover production more comprehensively and the CML seems to be more focused on consumption/consumption-related behaviour. Some data on the progress that Member States are making in this area according to these indicators will be provided in the following paragraphs.

While the EEA produced all these reports, the Commission continued with the development of the regulatory framework for a circular economy, following the guidelines established by the EGD (EC, 2019). Importantly, the objective set up by the EDG relates to 'Mobilising industry for a clean and circular economy' (EC, 2019: 7) which reinforces the narrative of measures being directed towards the private productive sectors. The Action Plan approved in 2020 (EC, 2020a) situates circularity as a prerequisite to achieving climate neutrality. But if as the EEA (2021) states total circularity is not possible, the wider areas for action defined for a green economy will require tighter focus. There are several relevant points to be extracted from the Action Plan (EC, 2020a):

1 As its subtitle indicates, aims to make Europe 'more competitive', which highlights the economic component of the initiative;

2 It recognises that efforts are needed at the local and international level (besides EU, national and regional): at local level it considers the need to reduce dependence from third country suppliers in light of recent disruptions in global value chains – while at the international level it recognises that for most of the goals and targets international cooperation and agreements will be necessary;
3 It presents a list of key sectors where urgent action is needed: electronics and ICT; batteries and vehicles; packaging; plastics; textiles; construction and buildings; food, water and nutrients.

The implementation of the Action Plan has resulted in a myriad of legislative initiatives, including updates on proposals for waste management regulation, and very recently (EC, 2023) a Regulation on Critical Raw Materials. The choice of instrument in the form of Regulation instead of Directive, which requires adaptation to national regulatory frameworks, gives an idea of the urgency detected to take action in this area. This is contextualised in the speech of Ursula von der Leyen on the State of the Union in 2022 (EC, 2022), where the challenges created by the conflict in Ukraine and the disruption of global supply chains due to the pandemic and other crises are pointed out as threats for the EU competitiveness. It is worth noting that the Council has just given the green light (April 2024) so we will soon have this Regulation added to the list of implementation instruments of the EGD.

In the meantime, it is worth reflecting on the role of the EEA in the transition to a green and circular economy. As an agency it provides information without creating policy, but it can also issue recommendations that EU institutions may choose to follow or ignore. Bearing in mind that it is supposed to create a knowledge base and monitor progress against established indicators, it is significant that its reports do not usually generate the policy outputs one would expect based on evidence but also on innovative suggestions, sometimes disruptive. Instead, policy recommendations become nuanced since they need to strike a balance between what may be opposing institutional needs (Kovacic and Benini, 2022). As incidental evidence of its limited influence, in the EGD text references from the EEA are only mentioned twice (EC, 2019), while only one reference is used in the Circular Economy Action Plan (EC, 2020a) and there is no mention in the recent critical raw materials regulation proposal (EC, 2023). Another question for reflection (in addition to the ones the reader can find at the end of each chapter) is if there is scope for the EEA to have a more authoritative role within the governance framework of the sustainability transition in Europe, or if there is always going to be a mismatch between science and politics/policy (similarly to what we find in the measures taken internationally to tackle climate change).

EU Member States' transition to circular and green economies

In Chapter 7, we explored the progress that Member States and the EU as a whole have made in the reform of their fiscal systems so that they could contribute to the achievement of greener economies. The main indicator analysed was environmental tax revenues, for which it became apparent that both increase and decrease of its value could indicate a positive change. If we think of the indicators mentioned in

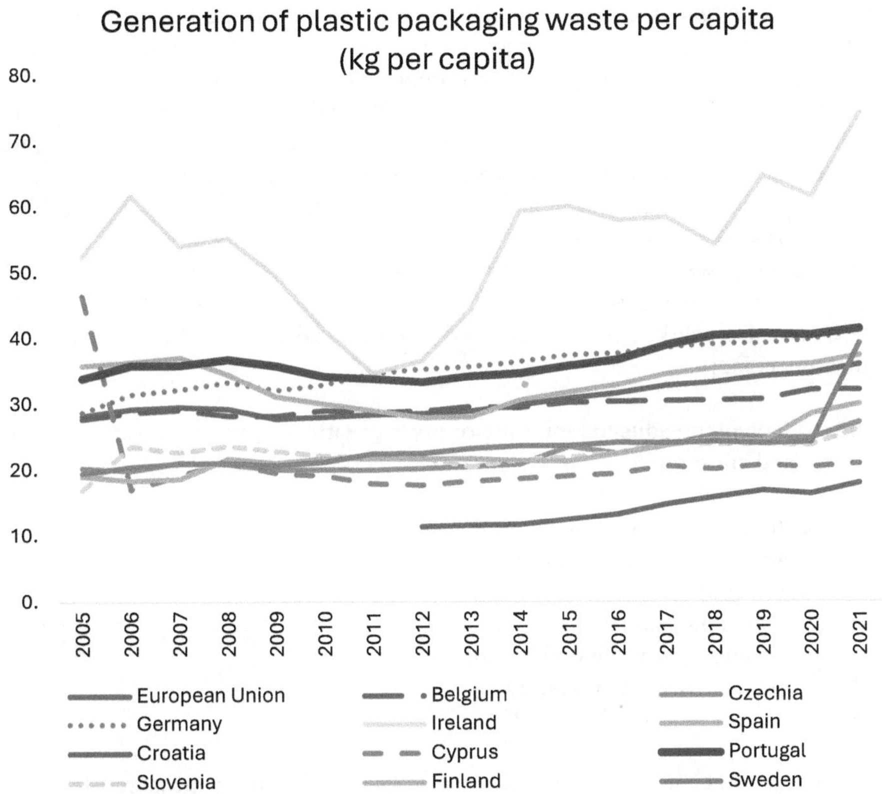

Figure 8.2 Generation of plastic packaging waste per capita (2005–2021)

Source: Eurostat.

Note: Croatia since 2012.

the previous section, the most obvious to look at are ones related to the generation of waste. See Figure 8.2 for the evolution of plastic packaging waste.

Though the progression is quite uneven among Member States, with Ireland by far the worst performer, it is apparent that the trend shown so far is increasing, while if a green and circular economy approach had been taken, or had been effective, we would be observing a decreasing trend (or at least a flat rate per year). However, these are not the type of data that most governments are concerned about, and priority tends to be given to indicators related to green 'growth'. The current EU monitoring framework, first launched in 2018 and updated in 2023, is very limited in terms of assessing circularity (Pacurariu et al., 2021), not just because of the indicators' practical applicability, but because they seem to be constrained to waste generation and recycling processes, leaving out of scope important indicators with regard to prolonging or extending the life cycle of products and materials.

For the evaluation of policies related to green growth and green economy, said policies need to be conducive to investment and innovation, at the same time that productivity, employment, greenhouse gas emissions and pollution in general, improve. In the end, a circular economy model and the progress of Member States in its implementation is going to be determined by variables that are very different from country to country. These variables include (Busu, 2019): resource productivity, labour employed in environmental protection-related activities, recycling rate of municipal waste, and renewable energy use. The OECD has developed a series of green growth indicators which can complement the ones Eurostat and the EEA have been working on. According to its set of indicators, before the EGD was launched, there were four EU Member States (plus the UK, Member at the time) leading the improvements towards green growth in comparison to the year 2000. These were Denmark, Estonia, Italy and Slovakia (OECD, 2017), with the main indicators being:

- Environmentally adjusted multifactor productivity
- Low land consumption
- Low air pollution exposure
- Environmentally related innovation
- Environmentally related taxation
- GDP per capita
- Low-income inequality
- CO_2 productivity (production based)
- CO_2 productivity (demand based)
- Material productivity (OECD, 2017)

Not all these indicators are new (income inequality has been measured for decades), and the appropriateness of some of them has been put into question (for instance, GDP keeps being used, when it is simply a measure of production and not of well-being; and as already mentioned, the direction of environmental taxation values is not the best indication of their performance). But it is interesting to see the behaviour with regard to CO_2 in production and consumption, since the production side has been the focus of most policies in the past. It can be noted though that both institutional and academic indicators share main common elements (productivity, employment, waste, renewable energy).

In using the EU own indicators, early analysis (Mazur-Wierzbicka, 2021) suggests the emergence of a two-speed Europe in the transition towards green and circular economy. On one side, we find the old Member States (the analysis includes the UK), in particular Germany, Belgium, Spain, France, Italy and the Netherlands, leading the way in their operation according to circular economy principles. On the opposite side, we have Cyprus, Czechia, Malta, Lithuania, Latvia, Hungary, Ireland, Slovakia, Romania, Estonia, Croatia and Bulgaria, showing the slowest pace of circular economy transformation. As it can be observed, with the exception of Ireland, these 'laggards' are mostly Eastern European countries gaining accession after the year 2000. The economies of both groups of countries are significantly different, with high levels of industrialisation and movement towards a service economy in the first group. This is also the reason why these old Member

States perform worse with regard to the excessive generation of waste, exhaustive use of resources, increasing consumerism attitudes and unbalanced consumption (Mazur-Wierzbicka, 2021) though unfortunately the group of new Member States may be only experiencing a delay in the increase in value of these indicators, which would not be a good sign. It is worth noting that two of the indicators used in this analysis are 'Private investments, jobs and gross value added related to circular economy sectors' and 'Patents related to recycling and secondary raw materials' (Mazur-Wierzbicka, 2021). The former is associated with economic growth and employment and the latter is a common variable used as a proxy to measure innovation. Both variables are also indicators of green growth as measured by the OECD (2017). Interestingly, some studies (Aldieri and Vinci, 2018) point to a negative effect of innovation related to the green economy over employment through what is called knowledge spillovers, mostly linked to the displacement of workers (due to the displacement of old products no longer demanded). They recommend stronger actions to boost employment creation relative to environmental activities, in addition to economic incentives to allow a transition to cleaner technologies.

The scarce academic literature combined with official statistics and reports present an interesting picture in relation to green and circular economy in Europe. On one side it could be argued that despite many years trying to avoid a two-speed Europe, in the sustainability transition this is still the case. Only one country appears as leading performer in this area both in academic literature and institutional reports, Italy, which grants further research as it has been traditionally considered a laggard with regard to environmental policy integration. Importantly, the literature seems to agree with the assessment of the inaccuracy of the indicators used to measure progress towards circular and green economy, which in itself could also be the confirmation of a trend that has been observed in other policy areas: holistic (Friant et al., 2021) and ambitious policy discourses are not followed by the same type of actions, limiting the solutions proposed to 'end of pipe' ones that do not address the deeper socio-ecological implications and impacts of the transition.

Investments for a green economy transition: the role of the European Investment Bank

At the core of this book has always been the understanding that the sustainability transition requires financial resources, in addition to those already dedicated to any other policy or action. The question posed in that regard is where is the funding going to come from. The EU and its EGD are not alien to this fact and had conservatively estimated that reaching the climate and energy targets for 2030 would necessitate €260 billion of additional annual investment (EC, 2019). More recent estimates increase that figure to €520 billion per year until 2030 (EEA, 2023). It is patently obvious that public resources will not be enough to reach that large amount, hence the intention of EU institutions to create the right environment to foster private investment too (EC, 2019). The EGD already envisioned the creation of a 'Sustainable Europe Investment Plan', which saw the light early in 2020 (EC,

2020b). Its main target is to mobilise €1 trillion over a decade, not only in the energy and climate areas, but also on key sectors such as agriculture and digitalisation, the latter as 'enabler' of the EGD (EC, 2020b: 3–4). Importantly, the Commission sees the Just Transition Mechanism, which has been mentioned in previous chapters, as part of the investment plan, with the purpose of helping those regions negatively affected by the transition (EC, 2020b). In that regard, at least in paper, the Plan aims to be consistent with and help achieving the UN SDGs core goal of leaving no one behind, addressing the social pillar of sustainability.

To mobilise private funding the EGD foresees the creation of the InvestEU Programme, which would use the EU's budget guarantee mechanism to be used as leverage for the crowding in of private investment resources. Further details about its functions are provided in the Sustainable Europe Investment Plan (EC, 2020b), but its regulation was not approved until 2021 (OJEU, 2021). Even if its creation was part of the EGD, its functioning has been very much conditioned by the Covid-19 pandemic, as part of the NextGenerationEU and the multiannual financial framework (which we discussed in Chapter 2). InvestEU has three main components (OJEU, 2021): the InvestEU Fund, InvestEU Advisory Hub and InvestEU Portal. The InvestEU Fund, arguably the most important component funding wise, works through financial partners (i.e. it is not all left to EU institutions). Those partners will invest in projects (i.e. will provide financial instruments – loans and others, which will be covered in Chapter 9) and will get the protection of the funding they provide through the EU budget guarantee. In that regard, €26.2 billion of said guarantee acts as backup for the investment of the financial partners, called 'implementing partners', in a way that increase their risk-bearing capacity. The aim is to mobilise around €372 billion in additional investment (EC, n.d.).

The type of projects that can be financed for the green transition through InvestEU need to be consistent with the EU Taxonomy (EC, 2020b), which as we know has brought controversy after including as 'sustainable' certain fossil fuel investments, and in fact has been taken to the European Court of Justice by environmentalist groups because of that (McNally, 2023). In addition, but also in relation to this controversy, investors find the Taxonomy confusing for certain sectors and activities (Lucarelli et al., 2023) and it is this uncertainty about eligibility criteria what can hinder the achievement of its main purpose, the increase of corporate investment in sustainability projects. One study (Papari et al., 2024) looking at how the EU Taxonomy could help increase the finance for urban nature-based solutions concludes that it is necessary for the eligibility criteria to be very explicit and clear in the Taxonomy, as otherwise there would be doubts if the projects do not completely fit with existing investment classes. In general, the main conclusion is that communication about which projects are eligible needs to improve (Lucarelli et al., 2023; Papari et al., 2024), opening the door to facilitate not only private investment projects but public-private cooperation (Papari et al., 2024), something that the Investment Plan already mentioned as worthy of consideration (EC, 2020b). But if the goal of the initiative is to bring in more private investment, the call for public or institutional investors may defeat the purpose. Importantly, the distribution of investment between public and private investors is expected to vary between

Member States, ranging in proportions of 1 in 5 (1:5) to 1 in 2 (1:2) (EEA, 2023). Estimations by the European Investment Bank (EIB) project that in Central and Eastern Europe around 60% of the additional investment needed for the green transition will come from public sources, while this percentage will decrease up to 37% in Western and Northern EU Member States (EIB, 2021a). An example of how Member States are approaching circular and green economy transition, together with the funding received for it according to EGD-related programmes can be seen in Box 8.1.

Box 8.1 Green and circular economy in Poland

Poland belongs to the group of EU Member States that according to several studies seen in the chapter are lagging behind in the efforts to transition into a green and circular economy. However, the country has received support from the EIB since 1990, both in finance and expertise, totalling €93.71 billion in 606 projects (EIB, 2024d) mostly linked to transport but also related to the opening of credit lines services and the energy sector. Just in 2023 Poland received €5.1 billion from the EIB group, including €632 million from the European Investment Fund (EIF). The projects financed targeted regional development, clean energy and business growth (EIB, 2024e), with particular emphasis in the energy transition projects under the REPowerEU and InvestEU initiatives.

While Poland has begun its efforts late, and mostly linked to its accession to the EU (Iskandarova et al., 2021), in the last years it has accelerated its green economy actions, particularly in the energy sector. Subject to the EU ETS regime, companies started realising that in case of inaction they could end bankrupt (Koehne, 2024) so they recognise the need to invest in renewable energies, and experts consider that the country has potential for a competitive development in this area, which will allow its decarbonisation and the breaking of its dependence from coal (Koehne, 2024). This was not helped by the approval of the 'Anti-Wind Turbine Act' in 2016, after a few years of consistent development (Iskandarova et al., 2021). Public opinion about the effects of climate change in health have also forced a change in the investment environment for sustainable projects. Studies (Petelczyc, 2022) show that there is interest and potential for green investment from private retail investors, though the wish for financial profit is still dominant. It is for this reason that the development of green investments is heavily dependent on subsidies (Iskandarova et al., 2021) and public funds from the EU or domestic institutions.

The controversy around the Taxonomy and what is classified as a sustainable activity is not new. There have been multiple attempts at defining what is understood as 'green' and what is understood as 'investment', so it could be argued that it may have different meanings in different contexts. Taking the elements used by the OECD in its own attempt at definition (Inderst et al., 2012) it can be said that a green investment is the commitment of money or capital to an endeavour (business, project, asset) with the expectation of obtaining an additional income or profit. Importantly, the endeavour needs to be linked to climate change mitigation or adaptation, or more generally to enable sustainable development [the addition of sustainable development by the author]. The understanding of the term gets more complicated when distinctions are made between investors being institutional or public investors and private investors. As already stated, Invest EU and the EGD Investment Plan address their communications and tools to the private sector, but it is equally important to think that governments also act as investors, making use of their annual budgets to decide, for instance, which infrastructure projects they can finance. This side of institutional investment is linked to the concept of green budgeting, defined in Chapter 2, but with more academic approaches, such as 'the integration of environmental concerns into government fiscal cycles' (Wilkinson et al., 2008). In this sense we can link green investment with the environmental fiscal reforms covered in Chapter 7, referring to what type of projects is the environmental tax revenue collected going to finance – which should be a green project (green investment) so that the double dividend can be achieved through the revenue recycling.

The European Investment Bank

Institutionally, both the EGD (EC, 2019) and the Investment Plan (EC, 2020b) consider that the EIB is set to become Europe's 'climate bank', even if collaboration with other financial institutions is deemed also necessary. In fact, in the creation of the InvestEU Programme, the EIB is included as the main partner of the InvestEU Advisory Hub (OJEU, 2021). It launched in 2019 a new climate strategy and Energy Lending Policy (EIB, 2019) by which it committed to ending the financing of fossil fuel energy projects, including gas, from the end of 2021, which adds controversy to the decision of the EU Taxonomy to include gas as sustainable activity under certain circumstances. The EIB also committed to gradually increasing the percentage of its financing dedicated to climate action and environmental sustainability to reach 50% of its operations in 2025 (EIB, 2019), from around 30% in 2019 (EC, 2020b). In addition to those goals, the Bank committed to align its financing activities with the principles and goals of the Paris Agreement, and to doing so by the end of 2020, all of it as part of its 'Climate Bank Roadmap'. In 2023, the Bank financed a total of €44.3 billion worth of projects related to climate action (€22.6 bn), environmental sustainability (€2.5 bn) or a combination of both (€19.2 bn) (EIB, 2024a), even if its assessment of the situation facing the private sector in Europe is not the most optimistic (EIB, 2024b). These are remarkable amounts for an entity that was not born with sustainability in mind, and it may well mean that it has already reached its 50%

target, though several years of observation will be required to determine if there is consistency in the figures.

The EIB is one of the longest serving EU institutions. Its origins are linked to the creation of the common market in the 1950s for what it became the European Economic Community (EEC) through the Treaty of Rome, but the initial negotiations aimed to create a 'European Investment Fund', not a bank (EIB, 2008). Its initial years were dedicated to the finance of infrastructure projects, particularly road connectivity, with 60% of its lending to the then six Members going to Italy in the 1960s (EIB, 2018). But facilitating innovation has been at the heart of its activities, with participation in the Airbus consortium for the development of a technologically new aircraft (the A300) in the 1970s, or the CERN and the Large Hadron Collider in the early 2000s (EIB, 2018). With regard to sustainability and climate change is in the last 20 years when the EIB has stepped up its actions, financing SMEs projects, photovoltaic and wind energy projects and others, even when due to the international economic crisis (2007–2008) investing in new projects could be considered too risky for commercial financial institutions.

Importantly, the EIB does not limit its activity to the EU territory, and has participated in projects in over 160 countries, where it offers not only finance, but also advisory support and awareness-raising, especially with regard to the circular economy (EIB, 2024c) concluding nevertheless that the progress of the EU is very slow in this area. Despite what is presented as an impressive record, the bank has been criticised for the way it approached the Covid-19 pandemic (Howarth and Kavvadia, 2024), since it continued applying the same set paths for lending usually towards low-risk lending activities. In that regard, it failed to increase lending to the public health sector. Others argue (Liebe and Howarth, 2020) that it has acted as a policy entrepreneur in the promotion of public-private partnership (PPP) investments, through the engagement of British 'norm entrepreneurs' within the Bank. This would not be a surprise given the proliferation in the use of this instrument since the privatisation of public services in the UK in the 1980s (Phang, 2013). The EIB should be careful on this approach though, since the collapse of Carillion in 2018 (Neate and Davies, 2020) speaks volumes about the need for proper governance processes in the use of PPPs.

An example of the involvement of the EIB beyond European territory is its collaboration with other international financial institutions. These include, among others, the World Bank and the European Bank for Reconstruction and Development (EBRD) (EIB et al., 2022). The advice provided also serves at assessing the situation of other parts of the world with regard to the progress they make towards greening their economies. The MENA (Middle East and North Africa) region provides evidence of the challenges these economies face, being highly dependent on fossil fuels for their economic growth, and with poor levels of ESG standards and practices (EIB et al., 2022). This does not prevent international financial institutions from getting engaged with these countries as they detect potential for collaboration in an area of geopolitical importance. But it could be argued that the approach from the EIB to these engagements may be different to that of the EBRD, which was created later with an environmental mandate embedded as part of its priorities for action (Weber, 1994). This mandate has been maintained over the years despite several updates on its founding documents, and it is also publicised through its social media presence (Ambrosio et al., 2022). The EBRD began operations in 1991, being owned by the EU and the EIB, as well as 69 countries. It provides support for entrepreneurial activities, facilitating investments in the regions where it operates to improve the governance of their economies, making them greener, resilient and integrated (EIB, 2021b). Despite the European origin and mandate of both EIB and EBRD, their activities beyond the EU are substantial and are set to continue (EIB, 2021b), which provides an international dimension to this side of the fiscal governance structure in the EU.

This is not the only element of complexity with regard to the EIB functioning. Similarly to the World Bank, it is not just one institution but a 'group'. The readers may have spotted the mention of the EIF in Box 8.1. Well, this is another institution part of the EIB Group (EIF, 2024), specialised in providing 'risk finance' particularly to SMEs across Europe. It has some similarities with the EBRD insofar its shareholders are also the EIB and the EU (represented by the Commission), together with public and private banks and financial institutions (EIF, 2024) – in the case of the EBRD these were 'countries', implying public shareholders.

Concluding remarks

The previous paragraphs have provided only an overview of the complexity involved in trying to take European countries into the path of greener and circular economies. The financial resources required to reach the level of investment that the green transition demands highlight the need to mobilise funds beyond what any local, national and even supranational institution could achieve. A green and circular economy aims also to be 'local' to reduce the demand on natural resources and materials, which seems to be at odds with the movement towards supranational cooperation, coordination and integration, but it is necessary to ensure that no one is left behind. The proliferation of regulatory initiatives coming from the EU and the design of supporting mechanisms, involving a growing number of institutions and stakeholders, may well create in itself barriers in particular for smaller enterprises, who will find the navigation through processes and regulations confusing. And this is without going into the detail of specific financial instruments (loans, bonds, guarantees …) at the disposal of private companies (sometimes public institutions too), which will be the focus of Chapter 9. But without having gone too deep into the analysis it becomes apparent that the divide between more and less industrialised economies within the EU is not being solved, and one wonders if it would be worth simplifying 'de facto' some of the structures and mechanisms used. In paper, through the approval of legislative acts, the EU gives the impression that it does not stop and it accelerates its commitment to the sustainable transition. In practice, all indicators suggest that progress is not being made, or not by everyone, or not enough. The EEA warns (EEA, 2023) that the international geopolitical environment is becoming more complex and there is a risk of slower pace in the sustainability transition, which is highly undesirable. Regardless of the contextual environment the climate emergency is not going to disappear so long-term commitments and immediate actions should be the order of the day.

Researchers have already identified a clear dichotomy between the EU discourses and actions, whose ambition tends to get diluted in the name of political compromise. The EU institutions reviewed here represent another layer of complexity in purpose, with the EIB focused on financial aspects and the EEA prioritising environmental concerns. This is understandable to an extent, but there could be more and better use of the resources of the EEA to inform policy and economic decision-making. In any case these two institutions would cover the economic and environmental pillars of sustainability, while the Just Transition Mechanism (without institutional range) is in between to address social issues. There does not seem to be a balance between the three pillars, and the fact that the latest reports (EIB, 2024b) emphasise the push for competitiveness suggest that the economic pillar may be at the top of the agenda once more.

Discussion questions

1 Will the ideas behind 'Doughnut Economics' take centre stage in mainstream Economics or will they be left aside for non-economist audiences?
2 Is there scope for more EU institutions to intervene in facilitating green investments or should they be handled at national and regional levels?
3 Do you think there is confusion among policymakers between the concepts of green and circular economy?
4 Do the rules about sustainable or SRI need a supranational governance framework?
5 Does the green economy approach cover sufficiently social perspectives and impacts?

Further readings

Fairbrass, J. and Vasilakos, N. (eds) (2021) *Emerging Governance of a Green Economy. Cases of European Implementation.* Cambridge University Press: This book introduces an interdisciplinary approach to the conceptualisation of governance for a green economy, exemplified through a number of case studies. Interestingly the cases cover national, sub-national and regional tiers of governance, which allows the reader to observe the role of multiple stakeholders.

Fung, H.-G., Law, S. A. and You, J. (eds) (2010) *Socially Responsible Investment in a Global Environment.* Edward Elgar: Though anything related to socially responsible investment (SRI) has evolved very quickly in the last decade, this book provides a very nice introduction to some of the issues 'green' investment still suffers. It explores the perspectives of institutional as well as private investors and covers the complexity of governance of SRI in a context where the movement of funds is international.

Lehman, H., Hinske, C., de Margerie, V. and Nikolova, A. S. (eds) (2023) *The Impossibilities of the Circular Economy. Separating aspirations from Reality.* Routledge: This very recent volume provides a myriad of case studies offering a critical lens to the analysis of the implementation of circular economy policies and projects. Reality in this context serves at identifying the limitations we face when trying to apply principles to practice.

References

Aldieri, L. and Vinci, C. P. (2018) Green economy and sustainable development: The economic impact of innovation on employment, *Sustainability,* 10 (2018): 3541. https://doi.org/10.3390/su10103541

Ambrosio, T., Hall, S. G. F. and Obydenkova, A. (2022) Sustainable development agendas of regional international organizations: The European bank of reconstruction and development and the Eurasian development bank, *Problems of Post-Communism,* 69 (4–5): 304–316.

Busu, M. (2019) Adopting circular economy at the European Union level and its impact on economic growth, *Social Sciences*, 8 (2019): 159. https://doi.org/10.3390/socsci8050159

Carroll, A. B. (2016) Carroll's pyramid on CSR: Taking another look, *International Journal of Corporate Social Responsibility*, 1 (2016): 3. https://doi.org/10.1186/s40991-016-0004-6

Crane, A. and Matten, D. (2010) *Business Ethics* (third edition). Oxford University Press.

Ellen MacArthur Foundation (2013) *Towards the Circular Economy. Opportunities for the Consumer Goods Sector*. Report 2/2013.

European Commission (2019) Communication from the commission to the European Parliament, the European council, the council, the European economic and social committee and the committee of the regions: The European Green Deal. COM (2019) 640 final. Brussels, 11.12.2019.

European Commission (2020a) Communication from the commission to the European parliament, the European council, the council, the European economic and social committee and the committee of the regions: A new circular economy action plan. For a cleaner and more competitive Europe. COM (2020) 98 final. Brussels, 11.3.2020.

European Commission (2020b) Communication from the commission to the European parliament, the European council, the council, the European economic and social committee and the committee of the regions: Sustainable Europe Investment Plan – European Green Deal Investment Plan. COM (2020) 21 final. Brussels, 14.1.2020.

European Commission (2022) 2022 State of the Union Address by President von der Leyen. Strasbourg, 14 September 2022. Available from: https://ec.europa.eu/commission/presscorner/detail/en/speech_22_5493

European Commission (2023) Proposal for a regulation of the European parliament and of the Council establishing a framework for ensuring a secure and sustainable supply of critical raw materials and amending Regulations (EU) 168/2013, (EU) 2018/858, 2018/1724 and (EU) 2019/1020. COM (2023) 160 final. 2023/0079 (COD). Brussels, 16.3.2023.

European Commission (n.d.) InvestEU. Available from: https://investeu.europa.eu/investeu-programme_en

European Committee of the Regions (2021) The European Green Deal remains the compass of the EU's COVID-19 recovery plan. Press Release 01/02/2021. Available from: https://cor.europa.eu/en/news/Pages/European-Green-Deal-compass-EU-COVID-19-recovery-plan.aspx

European Environment Agency (2016) *Circular Economy in Europe. Developing the Knowledge Base.* EEA Report No. 2/2016. Copenhagen.

European Environment Agency (2020) *Drivers of Change of Relevance for Europe's Environment and Sustainability*. EEA Report No 25/2019.

European Environment Agency (2021) Growth without economic growth. Part of the series 'Narratives for Change'.

European Environment Agency (2023) *Investments in the Sustainability Transition: Leveraging Green Industrial Policy Against Emerging Constraints.* Briefing no. 20/2023, 7 November 2023.

European Environment Agency, EPA Network, ISPRA and Sistema Nazionale per la Protezione dell'Ambiente (2020) Bellagio Declaration. Circular Economy Monitoring Principles.

European Investment Bank (2008) *The Creation of the European Investment Bank.* EIB GraphicWorkshop -03/2008 – EN.

European Investment Bank (2018) *A History of Europe in 6 Projects.* European Investment Bank.

European Investment Bank (2019) EU Bank launches ambitious new climate strategy end energy lending policy, Press Release 2019-313-EN, 14 November 2019.

European Investment Bank (2021a) Building a smart and green Europe in the COVID-10 era. Investment Report 2020/2021.

European Investment Bank (2021b) EIB and EBRD to deepen cooperation outside EU: Presidents Hoyer and Renaud-Basso sign framework agreement. Press Release, 11 October 2021. Available from: https://www.eib.org/en/press/all/2021-335-eib-and-ebrd-to-deepen-cooperation-outside-eu-presidents-hoyer-and-renaud-basso-sign-framework-agreement

European Investment Bank (2024a) EIB climate action explained. Available from: https://www.eib.org/en/projects/topics/climate-action/explained

European Investment Bank (2024b) Transforming for competitiveness. Investment Report 2023/2024.

European Investment Bank (2024c) Circular economy overview 2024. Available from: https://www.eib.org/attachments/lucalli/20240104_circular_economy_overview_2024_en.pdf

European Investment Bank (2024d) Poland and the EIB. Available from: https://www.eib.org/en/projects/country/poland

European Investment Bank (2024e) Poland received €5.1 billion from EIB Group in 2023 to bolster economy. Available from: https://www.eib.org/en/press/all/2024-128-poland-received-eur5-1-billion-from-eib-group-in-2023-to-bolster-economy#:~:text=Polish%20regions%20and%20cities%20have,amounted%20to%20%E2%82%AC2.33%20billion.

European Investment Bank, European Bank for Reconstruction and Development and World Bank (2022) Unlocking sustainable private sector growth in the Middle East and North Africa. Evidence from the Enterprise Survey. https://doi.org/10.2867/4598

European Investment Fund (2024) Financing start-ups and scale-ups in Europe. Available from: https://www.eif.org/who_we_are/index.htm

European Parliament (2018) Circular economy package. Four legislative proposals on waste. Briefing. EU Legislation in Progress, March 2018. PE 614.766.

Eurostat (2024) Circular economy monitoring framework. Available from: https://ec.europa.eu/eurostat/web/circular-economy/monitoring-framework

Friant, M. C., Vermeulen, W. J. V. and Salomone, R. (2021) Analysing European Union circular economy policies: Words versus actions, *Sustainable Production and Consumption*, 27 (2021): 337–353.

Heshmati, A. (2015) A review of the circular economy and its implementation. IZA Discussion Paper No. 9611, December 2015.

Howarth, D. and Kavvadia, H. (2024) The European investment bank to the rescue? COVID-related lending as incremental change, *Journal of Economic Policy Reform,* 27 (1): 25–44.

Inderst, G., Kaminker, C. and Stewart, F. (2012) Defining and measuring green investments: Implications for institutional investors' asset allocations. *OECD Working Papers on Finance, Insurance and Private Pensions*, No.24, OECD Publishing.

Iskandarova, M., Dembek, A., Fraaije, M. et al. (2021) Who finances renewable energy in Europe? Examining temporality, authority and contestation in solar and wind subsidies in Poland, the Netherlands and the United Kingdom, *Energy Strategy Reviews*, 38 (2021): 100730. https://doi.org/10.1016/j.esr.2021.100730

Janicka, M. and Sajnog, A. (2022) The ESG reporting of EU public companies – Does the company's capitalisation matter? *Sustainability*, 14 (2022): 4279. https://doi.org/10.3390/su14074279

Koehne, D. (2024) Poland's long journey towards a green transition. *Legal500.* Available from: https://www.legal500.com/global_green_guide/polands-long-journey-towards-a-green-transition/#:~:text=The%20Polish%20government%20has%20shown,phased%20out%20completely%20by%202049.

Kovacic, Z. and Benini, L. (2022) Striking the balance: Sustainability and institutional transitions in the European environment agency, *Futures*, 141 (2022): 102984. https://doi.org/10.1016/j.futures.2022.102984

Liebe, M. and Howarth, D. (2020) The European investment bank as policy entrepreneour and the promotion of public-private partnerships, *New Political Economy*, 25 (2): 195–212.

Lucarelli, C., Mazzoli, C., Rancan, M. and Severini, S. (2023) The impact of EU taxonomy on corporate investments, *Journal of Financial Management, Markets and Institutions*, 11 (1): 2350004. https://doi.org/10.1142/S2282717X23500044

Martini, A. (2021) Socially responsible investing: From the ethical origins to the sustainable development framework of the European Union, *Environment, Development and Sustainability,* 23 (2021): 16874–16890.

Mazur-Wierzbicka, E. (2021) Circular economy: Advancement of European Union countries, *Environmental Sciences Europe*, 33 (2021): 111. https://doi.org/10.1186/s12302-021-00549-0

McNally, F. (2023) EU hit with legal action over 'green' label for gas in taxonomy. *Responsible Investor,* 19 April. Available from: https://www.responsible-investor.com/eu-hit-with-legal-action-over-green-label-for-gas-in-taxonomy/#:~:text=The%20NGOs%20have%20filed%20a,the%20taxonomy's%20inclusion%20of%20gas.&text=Four%20environmental%20groups%20have%20taken,green%E2%80%9D%20in%20the%20EU%20taxonomy.

Morseletto, P. (2020) Restorative and regenerative. Exploring the concepts in the circular economy, *Journal of Industrial Ecology,* 24 (2020): 763–776.

Neate, R. and Davies, R. (2020) Carillion collapse: Two years on, 'government has learned nothing'. *The Guardian,* 15 January. Available from: https://www.theguardian.com/business/2020/jan/15/carillion-collapse-two-years-on-government-has-learned-nothing

OECD (2017) *Green Growth Indicators 2017. Highlights*. June 2017.

Official Journal of the European Union (2021) Regulation (EU) 2021/523 of the European parliament and of the council of 24 March 2021 establishing the InvestEU programme and amending regulation (EU) 2015/1017.

Pacurariu, R. L., Vatca, S. D., Lakatos, E. S., Bacali, L. and Vlad, M. (2021) A critical review of EU key indicators for the transition to the circular economy, *Environmental Research and Public Health*, 18 (2021): 8840. https://doi.org/10.3390/ijerph18168840

Papari, C-A., Toxopeus, H., Polzin, F., Bulkeley, H. and Menguzzo, E. V. Can the EU taxonomy for sustainable activities help upscale investments into urban nature-based solutions?

Environmental Science and Policy, 151 (2024): 103598. https://doi.org/10.1016/j.envsci.2023.103598

Petelczyc, J. (2022) The readiness for ESG among retail investors in central and eastern Europe. The example of Poland, *Global Business Review*, 23 (6): 1299–1315.

Phang, S.-Y. (2013) Public-private partnerships. In *Housing Finance Systems.* London, UK: Palgrave Macmillan. Macmillan Publishing: 97–108.

Raworth, K. (2022) *Doughnut Economics. Seven Ways to Think Like a 21st-Century Economist* (2nd edition). London: Random House Business.

Sahan, E., Sanz Ruiz, C. Raworth, K., van Winden, W. and van den Buuse, D. (2022) *What Doughnut Economics Means for Business: Creating Enterprises That Are Regenerative and Distributive by Design.* Oxford and Amsterdam: Doughnut Economics Action Lab and Centre for Economic Transformation.

Schneider, F., Kallis, G. and Martinez-Alier, J. (2010) Crisis or opportunity? Economic degrowth for social equity and ecological sustainability. Introduction to this special issue. *Journal of Cleaner Production,* 18 (2010): 511–518.

UN (2015) Resolution adopted by the general assembly on 25 September 2015. Transforming our world: the 2030 agenda for sustainable development. A/RES/70/1.

UNEP (2009) *Global Green New Deal. Policy Brief.* March 2009.

UNEP (2011) *Towards a Green Economy: Pathways to Sustainable Development and Poverty Eradication.* Nairobi: UNEP.

Weber, S. (1994) Origins of the European bank for reconstruction and development, *International Organization*, 48 (1): 1–38.

Wilkinson, D., Benson, D. and Jordan, A. (2008) Green budgeting. In Jordan, A. and Lenschow, A. (eds) *Innovation in Environmental Policy? Integrating the Environment for Sustainability.* Cheltenham: Edward Elgar: 70–93.

9 Green and sustainable finance

Introduction: the concept and context of green finance

While the concept of sustainable development has been among us for a considerable time, green finance is a much more recent concept, to the extent that there is no agreed definition, and we are at a point in which proposals are presented for said definition (Lindenberg, 2014), and debates are open about the feasibility of a universal definition, the development of a specific one for a country or group of countries, or the endorsement of an existing one (EC, 2017). It is no surprise that in this context, academic empirical research on green finance is only starting to emerge. What is more, there is confusion in the approach to green finance conceptualisation, as some experts have been focused on the instruments and tools for green finance (green finance 'products'), namely debt and equity in different forms (Global Environment Facility [GEF], 2017); while others put the emphasis on the aims of said instruments, renaming the concept as 'climate finance' (Cui and Huang, 2018; UNEP, 2014). In the EU, another notation can also be found through the concept of 'sustainable finance', which again is defined in terms of what it includes (EIB, 2023): 'Sustainable finance is about including environmental, social and governance considerations in investment decisions'. Surprisingly enough, the 'economic' component of development has been omitted, and the focus has been given to awareness and transparency (similarly to the accountability factor remarked by the UN), as well as to the role of financial and corporate actors to reduce the risks for the sustainability of the financial system through appropriate governance. This requirement is undoubtedly linked to the consequences of the economic crisis of 2008, where the bail out of financial institutions across the EU put in risk the European integration project (Hall, 2016). We will look into this conceptualisation puzzle throughout the chapter, but since the aims of the instruments have been discussed elsewhere in this book, namely the support of the sustainability transition, we will focus here on the instruments themselves.

Through the exploration of the use of green finance, an additional argument will be presented, which is that the aims and purposes of green finance at international level have changed overtime, from the purely 'growth' argument to leave the 2008 economic crisis behind, mostly thought for the Western developed countries, to the global aims of the Sustainable Development Goals (SDGs) approved in 2015

DOI: 10.4324/9781003224785-12

(UN, 2015a) and the international agreement signed in Paris the same year to fight against climate change (UN, 2015b). In that regard it could be said that we are currently in a transition period for green finance and its full potential to contribute to the achievement of the SDGs cannot be reached until said transition is completed. This view at the global level can be translated to the European context as a before and after the EGD (EC, 2019a), given its explicit commitment to both the SDGs and the Paris Agreement. Even if the EGD only mentions 'green finance' once, it repeats the term 'sustainable finance' several times in ways that have sparked action: on the one hand, the EGD entrusts the Commission to present a 'renewed sustainable finance strategy' (EC, 2019a: 17), something that happened in 2021 (EC, 2021). On the other hand, and with the purpose of mobilising (attracting) international investors, it aims to use the International Platform on Sustainable Finance to coordinate efforts related to 'environmentally' sustainable finance initiatives, but also stating that it will contribute to set up a financial system that supports 'global sustainable growth'. This has implications for the way in which both the EU and its Member States approach financial decisions: are they going to aim for their own domestic sustainable growth (first?) or will they use these financial instruments in support of other countries?

Important at this point is to decide if 'green' and 'sustainable' are synonyms here. And while many may use both terms interchangeably (see definitions in Chapter 1), it becomes apparent that the Commission is not doing so, with the EGD mentioning, as already remarked, green and sustainable finance, but also green and sustainable investments:

> The Commission will present a Sustainable Europe Investment Plan to help meet the additional funding needs. It will combine dedicated financing to support sustainable investments, and proposals for an improved enabling framework that is conducive to green investment.
>
> (EC, 2019a: 15)

The international level of governance provides help in clarifying terms. UNEP began an 'Inquiry into the design of a Sustainable Financial System' in 2014, which brought forward a roadmap in 2017 (UNEP and World Bank, 2017), and a conceptual document in 2016 (UNEP, 2016). In a summarised way, sustainable finance includes environmental, social, governance and economic aspects, while green finance excludes social and economic aspects (focusing on the environmental) and includes climate finance (as a subset of environmental/green finance) (UNEP 2016 as summarised by International Organisation for Standardization [ISO], 2022). Simple as it seems, it is not clear that the terms are being used with those meanings, given the inclusion of social considerations when speaking about green investment projects (see Chapter 8).

It is important to note that terms such as green economy, green growth and even green finance only started taking centre stage in the public debate during the last couple of decades. As it has been explained in previous chapters, some developed countries had been implementing green fiscal reforms in the 1990s, such as in the case of Sweden (Shmelev and Speck, 2018), but the appeal to generalise this approach to macroeconomic issues came from the Global Green New Deal in 2009 (UNEP, 2009a). This was a plan directed to the implementation of domestic policies and specific fiscal stimulus during 2009 and 2010 in an attempt to bring economic growth back after the deep international economic crisis of 2008, this time in a sustainable way. There are several conclusions that can be extracted from what happened at the time: first of all the Global Green New Deal was aimed mainly to governments, for them to take action in the domestic arena and to some extent in the international sphere too, through coordination activities. This means that the main actors in the governance system were public actors and institutions. A second conclusion that can be inferred is that since it was Western developed nations the ones most badly affected by the economic crisis, the policy proposals were also mostly aimed at developed countries. The fact that a specific update was created for the G20 summit (UNEP, 2009b) supports this view. How to finance all the required expenditure at the domestic/national level was, however, very loosely mentioned, other than through the need to remove perverse subsidies and create tax incentives (UNEP, 2009a). Financing was mostly left for the international context, where developing countries are mentioned, as a responsibility for developed countries to help them progress towards more sustainable ways of economic development (UNEP, 2009a). The use of global carbon markets (such as the EU ETS) and the creation of global markets for ecosystem services (not within the scope of this book) were part of this international framework, as it was the encouragement for governments and 'international financial institutions' to create financing mechanisms in support of 'developing countries and countries with economies in transition' (UNEP, 2009a). This wording seems to indicate that there was an assumption that developed countries did not need to modify their financial sectors in order to reach the green growth path. Ironic if we bear in mind the changes in the regulation of the financial sector that came about precisely because of how the international economic crisis originated (in the financial sector).

We know that the availability of financial resources by governments is limited, and it soon became apparent that the participation of private actors in this sustainability effort was required. But for this private involvement to happen, it was necessary to adapt the discourse to make the green economic sectors attractive to them. This is when the language begins to shift, to promote renewable energy, energy efficiency, recycling and others, as 'investment' opportunities (Doval and Negulescu, 2014; Voica et al., 2015). How to obtain funding to participate in these new investment opportunities is what originated a demand for new financial products that took into consideration not only the economic returns but the social and environmental effects of those projects. This paved the way for closer links between 'sustainable development' and the financial sector, and indeed for a greater involvement of the private sector in the green economy.

With the approval of the SDGs and the Paris Agreement part of the focus has shifted from developed to less developed/developing countries and economies in transition. So we are in a situation, particularly after the Covid-19 pandemic and the cost of living crisis, where there are two parallel international (and EU) discourses:

finance is needed to make (developed – should be all) economies resilient to crises, competitive and green, and to transition to climate neutrality (by 2050 in the case of the EU) AND Finance is needed to help developing countries dealing with the effects of climate change, improve their living standards and economic growth in a sustainable way. This means that green and sustainable finance products can be issued and acquired to fund projects internationally (in and out of the EU), depending on the type of instrument and the issuer, but also that these financial products can be issued by institutional investors (such as the EIB or national governments) or by private companies to finance their own sustainability transformation. While there will be mention of both sets of instruments, the focus of this chapter will be institutional green/sustainable finance. In doing so it will be observed that most instruments are classified as 'green' more than sustainable, which should take the reader to reflect on the narrow approach that financing the sustainability transition has followed to date.

The regulatory framework of green and sustainable finance in the EU

The new EU Sustainable Finance Strategy (EC, 2021) emphasised the need for what is called a 'Sustainable Finance Framework', whose components will be (are) the EU Taxonomy (OJEU, 2020); a disclosure regime which includes Disclosure Regulation (already in place since 2021) and a Corporate Sustainability Reporting Directive [CSRD] (in force since 2023); a system of tools to help and guide companies, market participants and financial intermediaries to develop sustainable investment solutions, at the same time that greenwashing is prevented. The main purpose of the Strategy is to help attract funding from private actors, private investors, to support the sustainability transition. This requires first a definition of what is considered a sustainable activity, which the EU Taxonomy aims to provide, but already in the Strategy the lines start blurring, since it is proposed that more activities are added to the list if they contribute to give steps into the transition (EC, 2021). In reality, this constitutes a lifeline for companies whose activities would not be initially considered as sustainable ones, and the Strategy mentions gas specifically (EC, 2021: 5–6), which as you may remember from Chapter 8 is widely contested. Most of the instruments and frameworks allow for the participation of large companies in the transition (whether to act as investors or to receive the resources from the investors for their own projects), so it is refreshing to see that the Strategy begins a reflection on how to include citizens and small companies in sustainable finance, though it could also be argued that this could just be another way of increasing the financialisation of everyday life (Storm, 2018), a controversial debate out of the scope of this book but worth considering.

The EU Taxonomy (OJEU, 2020) makes reference to Sustainable Finance Disclosure Regulation (OJEU, 2019), which is aimed at the financial sector directly. Taken together with the CSRD, what we have is a set of rules that tells us what is considered sustainable so that if financial resources are required to achieve it the financial sector can classify those resources as such (sustainable/green), and a set of rules to let companies know how to report their sustainability impacts, risks and activities so that there is transparency and accountability, but also so that potential investors get the right information to be able to make investment decisions. On the positive side, the obligation to disclose information will force companies to analyse what impact climate risks can have on their performance (financial and otherwise), so in theory the need to comply will make them prepare and act on said impacts and risks. Once again, however, there is a mixed message insofar what seems to be happening is a transference or duplication of rules that have been guiding public institutions (governments) into the private sector, so for the lay person it may be difficult to distinguish what the announcements about these changes mean or who they apply to.

For clarification purposes, the classification of what constitutes sustainable activities according to the EU Taxonomy is listed here (OJEU, 2020: Art. 3 and Art. 9 mainly). An economic activity will be qualified as environmentally sustainable where said activity:

- Contributes substantially to one or more of the environmental objectives set out in Art. 9 [namely: climate change mitigation; climate change adaptation; the sustainable use and protection of water and marine resources; the transition to a circular economy; pollution prevention and control; and the protection and restoration of biodiversity and ecosystems].
- Does not significantly harm any of the environmental objectives mentioned above.
- Is carried out in compliance with the minimum safeguards laid down in Art. 18.
- Complies with technical screening criteria that have been established by the Commission.

Interestingly in the context of difficulties to define what circular economy is (as seen in Chapter 8), the Taxonomy Regulation includes its own definition (OJEU, 2020: Art. 2 (9)): *'circular economy' means an economic system whereby the value of products, materials and other resources in the economy is maintained for as long as possible, enhancing their efficient use in production and consumption, thereby reducing the environmental impact of their use, minimising waste and the release of hazardous substances at all stages of their life cycle, including through the application of the waste hierarchy*. It can be observed that waste is only mentioned in the final part of said definition, which puts into question why so much emphasis has been placed on this aspect when enacting regulations and proposing new initiatives.

In 2023 the Commission updated the 'Sustainable Finance Framework' (EC, 2023) precisely to confirm the need to keep altering the Taxonomy to facilitate inclusion of transition activities. Unsurprisingly, it also highlighted the need to simplify access to sustainable finance and the related processes for SMEs and to keep working with international financial institutions and other international partners, in line with the commitment of leaving no one behind. Its assessment of the existing framework is that it works, but it could be argued that if it needs continuous adjustments and additions it really needs further simplification. Given how recent all these regulations and modifications are, there is little academic research that assess their performance. Early studies (Schütze and Stede, 2024) point out that when looking at the screening criteria that the Taxonomy uses, thresholds for 'transition activities' are not on track to be able to say that they are supporting a transition towards climate neutrality. In fact, their recommendations suggest that for new investments in said transition activities the criteria could be stricter than for current activities.

Nevertheless, and in addition to the financial support that the EU provides to less developed countries through different mechanisms, its initiative for sustainable finance focuses on the provision of funding for EU countries and regions, with the initial purpose to mobilise through the EIB €500 billion by 2020 (EIB, 2017), actioned through the European Fund for Strategic Investments (EFSI), whose lifespan ended in 2020. Its sustainable development approach at the time was reinforced by the requirement to include a climate action component, with projects being eligible in areas such as energy and resource efficiency or the environment, among others (EIB, 2017). The EU was also making progress in line with its international commitments, with an agreement reached (EC, 2019b) to create two new low-carbon benchmarks in order to bring investment portfolios in line with the goal of the Paris Agreement to limit global temperature increase to 1.5° above pre-industrial levels. These benchmarks support the goals of the EU 'Capital Markets Union', with the aim to become a leader in the 'shift and scale up of private investment towards the objectives of the Paris Agreement' (EC, 2019b). Indeed, the benchmarks are part of the set of tools designed to form the sustainable finance framework outlined in the previous paragraphs.

Meanwhile internationally, the World Bank, through the International Finance Corporation (IFC) identified the need to scale up investments that provide environmental benefits, which is the definition they give to green finance (IFC, 2017). In their view to transition into a sustainable global economy, the financial sector needs to undergo changes. The lack of a consistent definition of green finance, as identified at the beginning of this chapter, becomes a difficulty to track the existing funding gap. It also became apparent in their assessment that though there are numerous so-called green finance initiatives, many of them fail to be implemented, and the reasons behind this failure need to be analysed at the micro level (IFC, 2017).

This interconnection between the European and the international levels of governance may complicate compliance for firms, particularly multinationals. Further complexity is added when standards are not fully compatible, and at the moment we have several initiatives being used around the world. In line with the CSRD the EU approved its own sustainability reporting standards in 2023, with reporting requirements for different sectors and companies being currently developed. Internationally we have the International Sustainability Standards Board and the Global Reporting Initiative, among others. The EU aims to reach interoperability with their standards too, but going into the detail of how that may work is in itself another book. The key point is that the compliance with reporting obligations will allow companies to show which efforts they are making to align with the goals of the EGD, and accordingly have access to sustainable financial resources. The form of those resources is what the following section will cover.

Green and sustainable financial products: definitions and use in Europe

The EU Sustainable Finance Disclosure Regulation (OJEU, 2019) provides a list of the 'investment' products it covers, with short descriptions to try and prevent confusion, but as the reader will observe, this is not an easy task. On one side, we have the type of investment from the point of view of the investors or potential investors: investment funds, alternative funds, insurance-based investment products, pension funds and pan-European personal pension funds. The classification of these investments as sustainable financial products or not is going to depend on their purpose. Here the regulation distinguishes two main types (OJEU, 2019: Art. 2(17)): investments in an economic activity that contributes to an environmental objective; or investments in an economic activity that contributes to a social objective (such as tackling inequality, or investments in human capital or economically or socially disadvantaged communities). The Regulation then separates investment products between those in said activities with environmental or social objectives per se (Art. 9), and those that simply 'promote' environmental or social characteristics (Art. 8), which some (Brühl, 2022) call 'dark green' and 'light green' investments.

On the other hand, we have the classification of sustainable or green financial products from the point of view of those who issue the product, the ones who need the financial resources. As such we could have equity-type products, which would make the investor partial owner or co-owner of the company, in a similar way to that of shareholders in any corporation. Green equity products are however very new, and aim to facilitate funds from those investors guided by a green agenda (Grönroos, 2023) to those companies that have sustainable business models. The main characteristic for a product to receive the 'green equity' classification is that the issuers (the company) need to generate more than 50% of their annual revenue from activities that contribute to the green economy (World Federation of Exchanges [WFE], 2023). As already stated, green equity products are only nascent, so most of the sustainable or green financial products fall under the category of debt-based. Among those, the most widely known products would be green loans and green bonds, though other products exist.

Green loans (Gilchrist et al., 2021) are lending products (or investments for those who get them as part of their savings portfolio) designed to support the transition to net-zero carbon economy by funding environmentally responsible projects or climate change mitigation. Again, their development is limited, particularly in comparison to green bonds, so we are going to provide more attention to them, also given the role of the EU in their implementation across the world. It is possible however to find some examples of green loans provided by the EIB that may give the reader some idea of how this particular instrument works: one such example is the agreement reached by Iberdrola and the EIB for a €700 million green loan with the purpose of expanding the company's electricity distribution grid in Spain (EIB, 2024a). In this case the loan is part of the support of the EIB to the REPowerEU initiative (EIB, 2024a). It is debatable if the loan should be classified as green or sustainable (not really used in the literature for loans), because in addition to the purpose of improving energy efficiency and energy security, the project is expected to contribute to the maintenance of 10,000 jobs per year in 12 Spanish autonomous regions during the implementation period. This is consistent with the commitments of the EIB to support economic, social and territorial cohesion (i.e. not environmental purposes), confirming that more than 65% of the investment is arriving to Spanish regions where the per capita income is below the EU average (EIB, 2024a). Another example is a green loan to the company Ørsted in the Netherlands, of €500 million, to support its increased capex programme on renewable energy projects (Kamau, 2021). A feature of these examples is that the companies receiving the loans are big corporations. Digging for news trying to establish a trend on who are the recipients of these green loans, a common occurrence is for big financial institutions (ING [ESG, 2023], ABN Amro [ABN Amro, 2024]) to receive the funding from the EIB so that these financial institutions can dedicate those resources to help SMEs in their sustainability journey. This is an indication that the green loan market is not totally accessible to small businesses, which is something that the latest sustainable finance framework (EC, 2023) points out as a pending issue.

Green bonds are defined (Flammer, 2020) as debt instruments 'whose proceeds are committed to the financing of low-carbon, climate-friendly projects'. Something we haven't touched on yet is the fact that they can be issued not only by corporations but also by municipalities, government entities or supranational institutions (Flammer, 2020). Here is where the EU becomes a key actor, through the EIB. The world's first green bond was issued by the EIB in 2007, with the denomination of 'Climate Awareness Bond' (CAB), beginning the process of looking at the classification of financial products according to 'the use of proceeds' (EIB, 2021). That first green bond had a value of €600 million, and set the stepping stone for the creation of what is now a fully functioning Green Bond Market (Halder, 2023) and the development of a complementary financial product in the form of 'Sustainability Awareness Bond' (SAB). The main difference between the CAB and SAB is that the former covers environmental projects while the latter expands its reach to environmental and social projects (EIB, 2022).

With such a quick market development, it is not surprising that calls for regulation and standardisation began. So at EU level we now have the 'European Green Bond Standard', through another regulation approved at the end of 2023 (OJEU, 2023). According to this new regulation there will be a supervisory framework for external reviewers of European green bonds, and a registration system is established. Additionally, provisions for voluntary disclosure requirements are established to prevent greenwashing (Council of the EU, 2023) among other types of bonds: 'sustainable bonds' and 'sustainability-linked bonds'. It would be too long going over characteristics of all these financial products, so a non-exhaustive summary is offered in Figure 9.1.

While not as large as the traditional bond market, the sustainable debt market has experienced formidable growth, reaching a cumulative value of USD 1 trillion in December 2020 (PwC, 2021). Data available for 2021 and 2022 on CABs

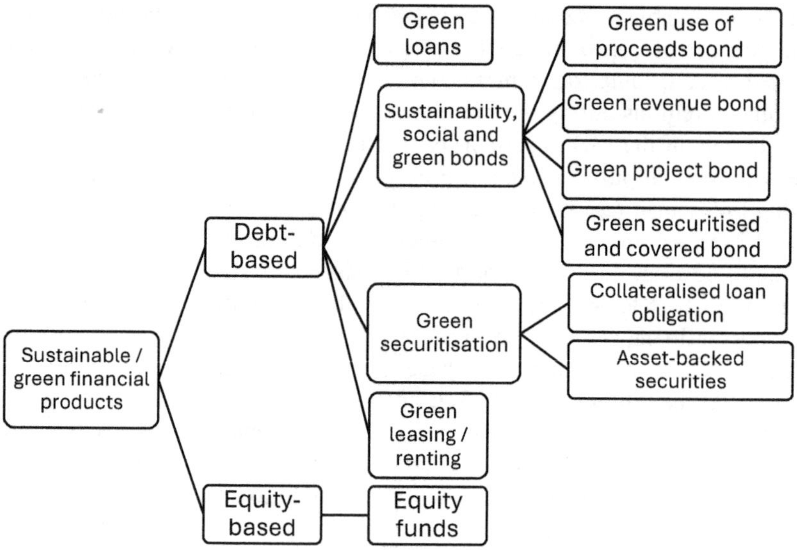

Figure 9.1 Overview of green/sustainable financial products

Source: Author's elaboration.

and SABs indicate that the figure has been widely surpassed since then (Halder, 2023). What is more, Luxembourg has become the centre for the trade of green bonds worldwide, with the Luxembourg Stock Exchange being the most popular Green Bond listing venue (PwC, 2021). In that regard it takes advantage of being the headquarters of the EIB, so it hosts over 95% of the EIB's CABs and SABs issuances. It is also the base of the world's first green exchange (LGX), which is a dedicated platform for listing and trading green, social and sustainable financial products (Halder, 2023).

It is easily observable that when it comes to the geographical distribution of green finance initiatives, Europe takes the lead, particularly with regard to the growth of Sustainable Responsible Investment (GGFC, 2017), but there are also differences with regard to which actors are involved in said initiatives, as well as between countries (EC, 2016). The UK is right now lagging behind (Mittal, 2024) with concerns about lack of investment appearing several years back. In this regard it is particularly suffering from the decision to sell the Green Investment Bank, which appears to have shifted the focus towards international investment instead of domestic one (House of Commons, 2018). Concerns about funding availability after Brexit, and how to attract private investors to the clean energy sector were the main issues the country has been dealing with in this area (House of Commons, 2018), but currently the government own commitment of funding seems to put them under scrutiny (Mittal, 2024). France, however, can be considered a frontrunner, with specific mandatory regulations directed towards the private sector early on (GGFC, 2017). More details about France can be found in Box 9.1.

Box 9.1 Sustainable finance products in France

As mentioned in the main text, France has the highest stock of sovereign green bonds in Europe as of end of 2022 (Eurostat, 2023). France was the first country, together with Poland, in issuing sovereign green bonds in 2017 – early, compared to the rest of Europe, but late, bearing in mind that the first bonds were issued ten years earlier (Cheng et al., 2022). Municipalities and local governments also entered early in the market, with the first issued green bond by Île-de-France (the Paris region) in 2012 (EIB, 2021). Before sovereign bonds, both non-financial corporations and banks were issuing green bonds in France in 2013 (Cheng et al., 2022). In terms of sovereign bonds recently issued, France was the second largest issuer in 2022, with 3.6% of the total, showing also an increase in comparison with the amounts issued in previous years (Eurostat, 2023).

It has already been established that one of the ways of classifying green and sustainable bonds, and financial products in general, is through the use of the proceeds obtained from said products. The use of the process requires a verification process, as well as an impact assessment process, in order to ensure that the products achieve the desired environmental benefits. In the case of France it is an independent committee the one in charge of defining the specifications of the impact report of green bonds (Cheng et al., 2022).

France has also benefited from the EIB green loans. Early in 2024 a €200 million loan was granted for Nantes Métropole to improve the tram infrastructure and provide cycle paths as an alternative to the use of cars (EIB, 2024b). The country was the second beneficiary of the EIB Group financing in 2023 (total financing, not just green) but it was the top beneficiary of climate and environment financing, with 64% of the volume received (EIB, 2024c).

Beyond the mention of France as pioneer and large participant in the market for green bonds, academic literature does not cover a proper evaluation of the effectiveness of the sustainable finance products in the country. So based on statistics we can only confirm that France is ahead of the curve and given the experience by different type of actors (public and private, local and national), it can position itself to benefit not only from the environmental point of view but from the financial point of view, in the future functioning of global green financial markets.

Romania, on the other hand, is struggling, with a private sector and government obliged by European commitments, but far to embed concepts such as social responsibility in their operations (Doval and Negulescu, 2014). In fact, as of 2022 it reported not having issued any green bonds, which is not an exclusive situation, since Bulgaria, Czechia, Estonia, Greece, Croatia, Cyprus, Malta, Portugal, Slovakia and Finland were in the same situation (Eurostat, 2023). Reliability of these data need some consideration, given that other sources (Statista, 2024b) report green bonds issued in 2022 by some of these countries: Finland (7), Slovakia (5), Portugal (3), Romania (2) and Czechia (1). The non-consistencies may be due to the different moments in which the data were collected but also to the fact that Eurostat data refer to government (sovereign) green bonds, while Statista does not specify the type of issuer, which would involve that the corporate sector would probably be the one issuing bonds in these countries. This is worthy of further investigation but there is not sufficient information to extract conclusions at this point. Nevertheless, this offers a picture similar to what other chapters have already portrayed: the fact that with the exception of Finland, it is the newer Member States, together with Portugal and Greece, whose economies traditionally struggle, the ones lagging behind in the development of sustainable finance, adding to the narrative of a two-speed Europe. In the case of the Eastern European Member States, it is understandable to some extent that they are in this situation, since their capital markets are comparatively underdeveloped, and around 55% of companies perceive lack of access to finance as an obstacle (EIB and EBRD, 2022).

One interesting point of analysis is to which extent all these initiatives and products have actually managed to channel private funds to finance sustainability-related projects. The truth is that supranational institutions (such as the EU through the EIB) have dominated the green bond market, though corporates and financial institutions (banks) have become more active since 2012. In the case of corporates (private companies) their proportion of the bond market has been more stable, with banks showing an uneven but growing trend (EIB, 2021). This progression changed as a result of the Covid-19 pandemic, with wider participation again from government-backed entities (PwC, 2021).

These comments introduce another type of classification of sustainable financial products by type of issuer, which can give us variations such as supranational, sovereign (central government), corporate (financial and non-financial), local governments, development banks and public enterprises (Cheng et al., 2022). The latest data available at the time of writing belong to the year 2022. In that year, financial corporate bonds accounted for the highest proportion of green bonds issued in Europe (33%), while non-financial corporate made up 23% (Statista, 2024a). This means that private bonds surpassed public issuance, indicating the desired outcome of the regulators and reversing to some extent the practice began as a result of the pandemic, at least at the national level, given that supranational institutions still have an important role to play. Among the public institution-issued bonds, the ones by central governments keep representing the highest proportion (30%), with government-backed entities (6%) and development banks (5%) making up the rest (Statista, 2024a). Per country, France (35.5%) and Germany (23.7%) hold the highest proportion of government (sovereign) green bonds stock, followed at a distance by Spain, Belgium and Italy (Eurostat, 2023). Sweden, Germany, Italy and Spain issued their first sovereign green bonds during the pandemic, and the EU aims to finance 30% of the NextGenerationEU funds with green bonds (Cheng et al., 2022). The proportion of green, social and sustainability bonds issued by local governments is comparatively very small (PwC, 2021), and only France seems to have made use of this instruments at the local level (Eurostat, 2023). Regional (state) green bonds have been issued by Belgium, Spain and Germany, and at least in 2022, for Spain the proportion of green bonds issued at the state level is bigger than the central government level (Eurostat, 2023). This may be indicative of the decentralisation of financial governance in some countries (Switzerland reflects the extreme case where most of the green bonds are state-issued instead of central government-issued [Eurostat, 2023]), and the level of autonomy of the regions to finance projects in their own geographical demarcation.

In any case, despite the growing figures in green bond markets, in Europe and elsewhere, there needs to be an assessment of their effectiveness not only in attracting capital, particularly private investors to supplement governmental efforts in the sustainability transition, but also to contribute directly to sustainable development, in terms of renewable energy penetration, GHG emissions reduction, and other relevant variables. The problem is that many of the projects these financial instruments support will not show that type of result immediately. In fact, depending on which sector the investment is going to take place, green bonds are issued for periods up to 15 years (Cheng et al., 2022) which means that it is too early for some of the projects to have been completed. Some criticism about how the green bonds market is working (Maltais and Nykvist, 2020) point out that instead of being an innovative financial tool, green bonds are becoming simply a subset of the whole bond market, perceived as a low-risk option for some investors, and not necessarily unlocking new sources of capital or making green investments financially viable if they would not be otherwise.

Reflections on the contribution of green finance to sustainable development and the role of the private sector

There are several conclusions that can be extracted from the previous paragraphs. First of all, that there has been a shift in the rhetoric around green finance, from a purely economic recovery purpose to a full embrace of the sustainable development discourse and a commitment, at least at the highest institutional level, to achieve the UN SDGs set up for 2030. Secondly, it becomes apparent that the contribution of green finance towards said goals has been outlined as key, at the institutional, governmental, and academic levels. However, the progress experienced so far is limited, and there is very little evidence of the real contribution of green finance to sustainable development on the ground. This is because the type of project this type of resources aims to finance, particularly environmental and climate change-related ones, but also biodiversity ones, are necessarily longer in duration, and results on many occasions cannot be observed in the short term. An additional conclusion that appears as evident is that approaches, governance actors, and implementation progress are uneven among geographical areas, with a remarkable division between developed and developing countries (which we have not really covered in this chapter but is implicit in most of the literature consulted), and within Europe (and the EU), between old and new Member States. In general, there is a continuous call for an increased participation of the private sector in green finance, due to the lack of resources available at the governmental level to undertake the investments (particularly big infrastructures) that are necessary, with the implied understanding that governments would still be in charge of defining the regulatory framework and financial policy (UNEP, 2018). Within the private sector there needs to be a focus on the financial sector, which should aim to redeem itself from its role in the economic crisis of 2008, and has potential for more action towards sustainability. The Sustainability Disclosure Regulation and the CSRD, with their respective delegated legislative packages aim to guide the transformation of the financial and corporate sectors with sustainability in mind. It would be expected that initially having to include environmental and social considerations in their decision-making process would be almost a shock to the system, given the fact that financial institutions and markets have been traditionally identified with maximisation of profits, without any concern for social nor environmental aspects (Janicka, 2016). However, green finance has been earmarked as essential for both economic development and sustainability for some time now (Chowdhury et al., 2013). The generalised view at international level (UNEP, 2017), replicated at EU level (EC, 2019a, 2021) is that green finance needs to be scaled up because the current level of investment is insufficient. Even within the G20 countries, progress has been quite uneven among the seven options defined to work towards the modification of the financial sector, with some proposals focusing on voluntary measures (UNEP, 2017) still being developed, as the latest Green Bond Standard Regulation of the EU (OJEU, 2023) attests.

Since there seems to be agreement on the need for the private sector to increase its participation in green finance initiatives, barriers that influence negatively said participation need to be identified. The ones that start emerging, given the early stages of development of sustainable finance products and policies, are linked to the general governance framework and perception of the financial markets up to now. Some of the most commonly mentioned are: market failures, information gaps, undervaluation of natural capital, over-reliance on voluntary commitments and inconsistent policies (Clark et al., 2018). These barriers at international level are the ones that the EU has been trying to address in the last years with what could be considered unprecedented levels of legislative initiatives. The fact that most of the ones mentioned here are approved as Regulations instead of the traditional Directives provides an indication of a shift in the governance framework towards harder governance structures, and towards quicker implementation timelines. In that regard, two aspects seem to confluence: the decrease in the trust that the private sector will act with the necessary pace if relying on voluntary measures, and the sense of emergency to deal with climate change and sustainability challenges.

Bearing in mind all the issues identified in the lines above there is a need for common definitions on green and sustainable finance to be agreed, and international coordination needs to be reinforced in order to provide clarity about which products would fall under the category of green finance. It would also be desirable that, apart from a reform of the financial sector itself, and its regulation, including a more transparent governance framework and accountability system, the focus widens and diversifies to include actors other than banks. Awareness and design of new green financial products needs to be extended, since the main product everyone focuses on is green bonds.

It can be then concluded that green and sustainable finance have the potential to contribute to the achievement of the SDGs, the Paris Agreement, the EGD and the EU climate neutrality goal, but only if effective action is taken by all the actors involved. So far supranational institutions have acted as promoters of both green finance and the SDGs, but implementation on the ground is limited and so are the successful outcomes. Importantly, this is a fast pace and moving market, with continuous changes in the regulatory framework, the type of instruments and the actors involved, both at the EU and international level. This makes unpredictable how future developments will impact investors. Standardisation and interoperability among an increasing number of bodies issuing standards do not seem to satisfy the uncertainty and confusion that most companies face.

The topic of green and sustainable finance has so many ramifications and perspectives under which its analysis can be approached that it would be impossible to cover them here. The overview provided by this chapter aims to offer some clarity on trends and instruments, but acknowledges that there are some issues not even addressed, such as the interest rates and premiums that the different financial instruments may offer and how they may be different to traditional financial instruments, or the fact that even if initially the green financial instruments markets were denominated in Euros, now other markets operate in other currencies like the US Dollar or the Chinese Yuan. So there is plenty for the reader to explore if this area is of interest.

Discussion questions

1 Given the responsibility of developed countries towards the climate crisis affecting developing countries, should green or sustainable finance prioritise the funding for developing countries?
2 To which extent can the approach taken by the EGD with regard to sustainable finance be considered original or unprecedented, bearing in mind what happened with the financial and economic crisis of 2007–2008?
3 Which financial instruments, of the ones explored in the chapter, have more potential to reach positive outcomes for the sustainability transition?
4 Is the new EU Sustainable Finance Strategy fit for purpose, that is, enough to channel the necessary level of green investments?
5 Are sustainable or green finance products helping those Member States who need them the most or is it ‘business as usual’?

Further readings

Bush, D., Ferrarini, G. and Grünewald, S. (eds) (2021) *Sustainable Finance in Europe. Corporate Governance, Financial Stability and Financial Markets.* Springer: This book covers some of the ideas discussed in this chapter in more details, as well as other topics out of the scope of the chapter. These include the area of corporate governance, which will be more relevant to those interested on business management.

Cheung, F. M. and Hong, Y.-Y. (eds) (2021) *Green Finance, Sustainable Development and the Belt and Road Initiative.* Routledge: Though in the title it is mentioned last, the focus of the book is the Belt and Road Initiative. Through its analysis the authors explore its potential to contribute to sustainable development and green finance while looking into the role of China in this international endeavour.

Shahbaz, M., Dong, K., Balsalobre-Lorente, D. and Gedikli, A. (eds) (2023) *Recent Developments in Green Finance, Green Growth and Carbon Neutrality.* Routledge: This extensive work covers the connection between green finance, green growth and carbon neutrality exploring synergies in policies and strategies. It provides a thorough economic-based approach in connection with business management perspectives, with case studies that go beyond Europe to cover its links with Asia.

References

ABN Amro (2024) European investment bank and ABN AMRO to make €500 million available to Dutch businesses. *News Article*, 29 January. Available from: https://esgnews.com/ing-and-eib-provide-e600-million-to-smes-in-the-netherlands-belgium-and-luxembourg-to-boost-sustainability/

Brühl, V. (2022) Green financial products in the EU – A critical review of the status quo, *Intereconomics,* 57 (4): 252–259.

Cheng, G., Ehlers, T. and Packer, F. (2022) Sovereigns and sustainable bonds: Challenges and new options, *BIS Quarterly Review*, September 2022: 47–55.

Chowdhury, T. U., Datta, R. and Mohajan, H. K. (2013) Green finance is essential for economic development and sustainability, *International Journal of Research in Commerce, Economics & Management*, 3 (10): 104–108.

Clark, R., Reed, J. and Sunderland, T. (2018) Bridging funding gaps for climate and sustainable development: Pitfalls, progress and potential of private finance, *Land Use Policy*, 71 (2018): 335–346.

Council of the European Union (2023) European green bonds: Council adopts new regulation to promote sustainable finance. Press Release, 24 October 2023. Available from: https://www.consilium.europa.eu/en/press/press-releases/2023/10/24/european-green-bonds-council-adopts-new-regulation-to-promote-sustainable-finance/

Cui, L. and Huang, Y. (2018) Exploring the schemes for green climate fund financing: International lessons, *World Development*, 101 (2018): 173–187.

Doval, E. and Negulescu, O. (2014) A model of green investments approach, *Procedia Economics and Finance,* 15 (2014): 847–852.

ESG (2023) ING and EIB provide €600 million to SMEs in the Netherlands, Belgium and Luxembourg to boost sustainability. *ESG News,* 19 July. Available from: https://esgnews.com/ing-and-eib-provide-e600-million-to-smes-in-the-netherlands-belgium-and-luxembourg-to-boost-sustainability/

European Commission (2016) Study of the potential of green bond finance for resource-efficient investments. Luxembourg, November 2016.

European Commission (2017) Defining 'green' in the context of green finance. Final Report. October 2017.

European Commission (2019a) Communication from the commission to the European parliament, the European council, the council, the European economic and social committee and the committee of the regions: The European Green Deal. COM (2019) 640 final. Brussels, 11.12.2019.

European Commission (2019b) Sustainable finance: Commission welcomes agreement on a new generation of low-carbon benchmarks. Press Release IP-19-1418. Brussels, 25 February 2019.

European Commission (2021) Communication from the commission to the European parliament, the European council, the council, the European economic and social committee and the committee of the regions: Strategy for financing the transition to a sustainable economy. COM (2021) 390 final. Strasbourg, 6.7.2021.

European Commission (2023) Communication from the commission to the European Parliament, the European council, the council, the European economic and social committee and the committee of the regions: A sustainable finance framework that works on the ground. COM (2023) 317 final. Strasbourg, 13.6.2023.

European Investment Bank (2017) EFSI: EUR 500 billion to build a Europe that's fit for the future. Factsheet – An online course for regional and local authorities. 15 January–23 February 2018. EIB 12/2017

European Investment Bank (2021) Evaluation of the EIB's Climate Awareness Bonds. April 2021.

European Investment Bank (2022) Promoting clarity to facilitate sustainable investment. Sustainability Lending – Sustainability Funding. October 2022.

European Investment Bank (2023) What is sustainable finance? Available from: https://www.eib.org/en/stories/what-is-sustainable-finance

European Investment Bank (2024a) Spain: EIB and Iberdrola agree a €700 million green loan for power grid expansion. Press Release, 18 March. Available from: https://www.eib.org/en/press/all/2024-112-eib-and-iberdrola-agree-a-eur700-million-green-loan-for-power-grid-expansion-in-spain

European Investment Bank (2024b) France: EIB lends €200 to Nantes Métropole to back sustainable mobility investment. Press Release, 12 February. Available from: https://www.eib.org/en/press/all/2024-065-la-bei-prete-200-meur-a-la-metropole-de-nantes-pour-soutenir-ses-investissements-dans-les-mobilites-durables

European Investment Bank (2024c) EIB group invests nearly €12 billion in France in 2023. Press Release, 1 February. Available from: https://www.eib.org/en/press/all/2024-038-le-groupe-bei-a-investi-pres-de-12-milliards-d-euros-en-france-en-2023-copy

European Investment Bank and European Bank for Reconstruction and Development (2022) Business Resilience in the pandemic and beyond. Adaptation, innovation, financing and climate action from Eastern Europe to Central Asia.

Eurostat (2023) Green and sustainability bonds issued by governments. Statistics explained. June 2023.

Flammer, C. (2020) Green bonds: Effectiveness and implications for public policy, *National Bureau of Economic Research*, 5 (2020): 95–128.

GGFC (2017) Global and European Green Finance Policy Directory. Global Green Finance Council. July 2017.

Gilchrist, D., Yu, J. and Zhong, R. (2021) The limits of green finance: A survey of literature in the context of green bonds and green loans, *Sustainability*, 13 (2021): 478. https://doi.org/10.3390/su13020478

Global Environment Facility (2017) Introduction to green finance. Available from: https://www.thegef.org/sites/default/files/events/Intro%20to%20Green%20Finance.pdf

Grönroos, J. (2023) Green equity: Supporting the transition towards sustainable business models. *Focus,* December. World Federation of Exchanges. Available from: https://focus.world-exchanges.org/articles/green-equity-lamor

Halder, K. (2023) Climate and sustainability awareness bonds: Driving true sustainable finance. *Delano,* 11 July. Available from: https://delano.lu/article/climate-and-sustainability-awa

Hall, P. A. (2016) The Euro crisis and the future of European integration. BBVA, In Search of Europe, Madrid, 2016.

House of Commons (2018) Green finance: Mobilising investment in clean energy and sustainable development. Environmental Audit Committee, Sixth Report of Session 2017-19. HC617.

International Finance Corporation (2017) *Green Finance. A Bottom-Up Approach to Track Existing Flows*. Washington, DC: World Bank Group.

International Organization for Standardization (2022) Green and Sustainable Finance. October 2022.

Janicka, M. (2016) Financial markets and the challenges of sustainable growth, *Comparative Economic Research,* 19(2): 27–41.

Kamau, P. (2021) EIB backs Ørsted with €500m loan agreement to boost green energy in the Netherlands. *Marketing Report,* 30 September. Available from: https://marketingreport.one/brand-and-sustainability/eib-backs-orsted-with-500m-loan-agreement-to-boost-green-energy-in-the-netherlands.html

Lindenberg, N. (2014) Definition of Green Finance. German Development Institute, April 2014.

Maltais, A. and Nykvist, B. (2020) Understanding the role of green bonds in advancing sustainability, *Journal of Sustainable Finance& Investments,* https://doi.org/10.1080/20430795.2020.1724864

Mittal, S. (2024) 'Embarrassing failure': UK ranks last in green spending among major European economies. *Edie,* 5 March. Available from: https://www.edie.net/embarrassing-failure-uk-ranks-last-in-green-spending-among-major-european-economies/

Official Journal of the European Union (2019) Regulation (EU) 2019/2088 of the European parliament and of the council of 27 November 2019 on sustainability-related disclosures in the financial services sector. L317, 9.12.2019.

Official Journal of the European Union (2020) Regulation (EU) 2020/852 of the European parliament and of the council of 18 June 2020 on the establishment of a framework to facilitate sustainable investment, and amending Regulation (EU) 2019/2088. L198, 22.6.2020.

Official Journal of the European Union (2023) Regulation (EU) 2023/2631 of the European parliament and of the council of 22 November 2023 on European Green Bonds and optional disclosures for bonds market as environmentally sustainable and for sustainability-linked bonds. L68, 30.11.2023.

PwC (2021) Green, Social and Sustainability (Linked) Bonds. The role of a verifier/certifier. Luxembourg Office.

Schütze, F. and Stede, J. (2024) The EU sustainable finance taxonomy and its contribution to climate neutrality, *Journal of Sustainable Finance & Investment,* 14 (1): 128–160.

Shmelev, S. E. and Speck, S. U. (2018) Green fiscal reform in Sweden: Econometric assessment of the carbon and energy taxation scheme, *Renewable and Sustainable Energy Reviews,* 90 (2018): 969–981.

Statista (2024a) Distribution of green bonds issuance in Europe in 2022, by issuer type. Available from: https://www.statista.com/statistics/754858/green-bonds-issued-by-issuer-europe/

Statista (2024b) Volume of green bond issuance in selected European countries in 2022. Available from: https://www.statista.com/statistics/1090928/green-bonds-issuance-volume-europe/

Storm, S. (2018) Financialization and economic development: A debate on the social efficiency of modern finance, *Development and Change,* 49 (2): 302–329.
UN (2015a) Transforming our world: The 2030 agenda for sustainable development. Resolution adopted by the General Assembly on 25 September 2015.
UN (2015b) Paris Agreement. Resolution adopted on 12 December 2015.
UNEP (2009a) *Global Green New Deal. Policy Brief.* March 2009.
UNEP (2009b) *Global Green New Deal. An Update for the G20 Pittsburgh Summit.* September 2009.
UNEP (2014) Demystifying private climate finance. UNEP Finance Initiative. December 2014.
UNEP (2016) Inquiry: Design of a Sustainable Financial System. Definitions and Concepts. Background Note. *Inquiry Working Paper* 16/13.
UNEP (2017) Green Finance. Progress Report. Inquiry: Design of a Sustainable Financial System, July 2017.
UNEP (2018) Greening the rules of the game. How sustainability factors are being incorporated into financial policy and regulation. Inquiry: Design of a Sustainable Financial System. *Working Paper* 18/1, May 2018.
UNEP and World Bank (2017) Roadmap for a sustainable financial system. Inquiry: Design of a Sustainable Financial System. November 2017.
Voica, M. C., Panait, M. and Radulescu, I. (2015) Green investments – Between necessity, fiscal constraints and profit, *Procedia Economics and Finance*, 22 (2015): 72–79.
World Federation of Exchanges (2023) The WFE green equity principles. 23 March 2023.

10 Reflections and suggestions for the future ahead

Is the social pillar of sustainability lost in translation?

When the book began offering definitions of concepts related to the sustainability transition it spoke of the three (four if the UNESCO cultural pillar is included) well-known pillars: economic, social and environmental. While the conceptualisation of sustainable development and those three pillars have been mentioned throughout the chapters, a parallel connotation, sometimes used as synonym, has not been addressed. That is the 'triple bottom line' coined by Elkington in the 1990s referring to the need of combining 'economic prosperity, environmental quality and social equity as an integrated method of doing business' (Arowoshegbe and Emmanuel, 2016). What we have with this term is an approach from the business perspectives to sustainability, which has been used hand in hand with terms such as corporate social responsibility (CSR) or business ethics (see Crane and Matten, 2010). It is worth mentioning this perspective here because businesses are very important stakeholders in the sustainability transition. They are the actors at the centre of economies' productive systems, and even if the SDGs talk about sustainable production and consumption (SDG12), most of the initiatives that the EU, national governments, and other supranational institutions have enacted are aimed at changing the way in which business (i.e. production) is done. Said initiatives, whether regulatory or voluntary, have created a major link between the private sector and the government, as the two main components of an integrated system.

From the business literature we also get the notion of 'triple helix' model of innovation (Vaivode, 2015) which establishes the importance of knowledge in post-industrial societies to achieve economic development (not just growth). This adds academia and research as part of the loop initially constrained to government and businesses. But the model has evolved further into a 'quadruple helix' (Cai and Lattu, 2022) that involves media-based and culture-based public and civil society into the innovation equation, going beyond the previous perspectives to advocate for a knowledge society and knowledge democracy. It is this model that integrates the social pillar of sustainability, and the one that has wider acceptance as opposed to the 'quintuple helix' (Carayannis et al., 2012) that would complete the equation integrating the environment and ecosystems as the outer part of a nested system. From the business point of view, authors (Cai and Lattu, 2022) argue that there is

DOI: 10.4324/9781003224785-13

less acceptance of the quintuple helix because the integration of the environment is not easy. But from a sustainability point of view, the quadruple helix would be missing its environmental pillar. Visually, the nested model presents parallelisms with the strong sustainability system (see Chapter 1) but in more recent representations (Carayannis et al., 2019) the nest has lost its layered shape to be represented with more loosely established connections between the different stakeholders (helices), similarly to what a weak sustainability approach would look like. This development calls for a new question: are we moving backwards and towards disintegration of the stakeholders' connections or is this a natural progression?

In the journey through the sustainability transition pathway that the book has been analysing, the message has been that within the evolution of the governance framework, a reasonable integration of the economic and environmental pillars of sustainability has been achieved, but to the detriment of the social pillar. In theory, with the EGD there has been a transformation of the discourse to make the transition work for citizens and leave no one behind, following the motto of the UN SDGs and correcting to some extent the lower level of priority given to the social component in the past. However, even the EGD discourse goes backwards, and the Energy Union Package seemed to be more ambitious (Fernandez, 2021: 93) with regard to active participation of citizens and communities.

The academia or research helix of the innovation model could be represented, for instance, by the role of the EEA providing evidence to inform policy, in addition to all the research funded by Horizon Programmes over the years. But as the previous chapters have confirmed, there is a mismatch between the environmental focus that the EEA is advocating and the economic focus that regulators are using. This is an additional reason to find a dichotomy between discourses and actions (Kovacic and Benini, 2022), and a lower level of ambition reflecting the political compromises required to move forward. As a researcher, this author finds that the connection between academia, business and government is patchy at best, but however this relationship is, the connection between any of these stakeholders and civil society is far from optimal. For instance, evaluation of universities' role in the communities they are part of tend to highlight how much they contribute to the economy of the area (Marrocu et al., 2022: 1106), instead of aiming for real engagement between the general public (local communities) and the researchers.

Citizens' engagement in the sustainability transition

In light of the statements made in the previous paragraphs, it becomes apparent that there is a need for a wider bottom-up approach in the policy process at EU level, which signifies a need for change in the current multi-level governance system. This in turn involves that citizens' participation cannot be limited to consultations during the planning process of projects or initiatives. This conclusion is not new. The observation of what happened in the first-ever global citizen deliberation process, hosted in 2009 during COP15 in Copenhagen, already pointed to the limited impact that citizens' participation had in climate policymaking (Rask and Worthington, 2012: 3). But if that was the conclusion then, ideally something should have changed to increase both citizens' engagement and the impact of said engagement. Citizens need to be active participants throughout, and when policies establish monitoring and evaluation processes the communities affected need to be heard too, instead of using aseptic measures, perhaps, of how many GHG emissions have been avoided in a particular period of time. Indeed, the participation should not be limited to receiving the feedback or report of certain results (which would be what many research actions do through the so-called dissemination activities and outputs). Evidence suggests (Trischler et al., 2023: 2093–2094) that citizens' knowledge can be the source of innovation for sustainability transition initiatives, which would make them essential actors in the quadruple and quintuple helix models described in the previous section. We are in a delicate moment, with European elections recently held, and if the EU does not want to be accused again of democratic deficit or elitism and living too far away from people's real lives, something will have to change. Once again, the EEA acknowledges this need (EEA, 2023) but also argues that the EGD supports this discourse and the positioning of citizens as the driving force of the sustainability transition. However, it also recognises that on the one hand, the tools for true citizens' empowerment have not been created, and on the other hand, deeper transformation of institutional frameworks needs to occur to create the enabling environments for active participation, moving beyond the establishment of 'tools' (EEA, 2023: 13). Advocacy in this regard calls for co-creation as a form of active participation and engagement, but some (Leino and Puumala, 2021) warn of the need to acknowledge the heterogeneity of citizens and citizens groups to prevent the perpetuation of issues such as exclusion of those with less resources, so that social justice can be served.

Answering the book's research questions

The book started asking the question of how the EU has been dealing with the allocation of resources to foster the sustainability transition. Effectively, Chapters 2–9 have answered this question by providing examples of how the allocation of resources through the EU budgets has evolved, with the EGD committing to specific proportions of the revenue collected being dedicated to climate and biodiversity-related actions. This represents a positive move insofar those percentages or figures did not feature in previous policies, but as already evidenced by the Commission's own behaviour, one thing is to commit resources and something different is to actually spend those resources in the designated actions. We have also seen that the process of allocation of resources is not straightforward, and a myriad of policies within the EU remit compete for a finite volume of resources. The trend observable has been the initial increase in the budget dedicated to environmental purposes over time, including through the creation of specific instruments or programmes (such as LIFE). Several circumstances have led to slowing down or halving this increasing trend: chronologically, the enlargement of the EU to Eastern Europe involved more countries and citizens entitled to funding without a proportional increase in the budget, which limited the resources available for everyone. This was followed by the economic crisis of 2007–2008, which left the finances of a significant number of Member States in tatters, and contributed to a period of self-imposed austerity as a method for damage control. But this led to unthinkable social consequences which put into question for some the validity of the European integration process as a whole. Addressing social aspects of sustainable development became a requirement for policy action, parallel to international commitments to tackle climate change and biodiversity loss. These circumstances compounded the emerging discourses that advocated for the move from increasing resources to 'streamlining' the resources available. All this in a climate of sluggish economic growth at a time when the EU intended to become the most competitive economy in the world. Hence, the reinforcement of the message that the transition involves everyone and the recognition that public finances cannot deal with everything, and private sector resources are very necessary too.

This situation takes us to the second and third research questions that this book addresses: how are the additional transformations required by the 'climate emergency' going to be financed? And, which actors (businesses, governments, citizens) are going to pay for it and how? The EU found itself in a situation of limited resources and increased number of policy priorities. The decision then was to become 'creative' and instead of attempting to increase the available budget significantly, it shifted approach to bring funds from someone else – the business sector. On the one hand, the discourse about the need for businesses to get involved and be accountable for their socio-environmental impacts got translated into regulations that took a harder approach than in the past (as the Directive and Delegated Regulation on sustainability reporting, or the modifications on the ETS Directive attest). On the other hand, and given the limited impact that voluntary action over the private sector has achieved, a discourse appealing to the investment opportunity that climate action can bring became prominent. It could be argued that a 'carrot and stick' approach has been used with this particular group of stakeholders. The creative side of the approach also involves the EU taking an indirect financing role: instead of providing funding through grants, loans, structural funds and others, it becomes a 'guarantor' so that the private sector feels reassured and the private investment can take place. All this transferred somehow to the hands of the European Investment Bank as the so-called Climate Bank. In this regard we have a more prominent role of the 'technical' EU institutions as opposed to the more politically constrained ones, as it occurs with the Commission. The answer to the second question becomes: through a mix of streamlining of existing funds, creation of new instruments (taxes) and the expectation of private funding contributions labelled as investments.

Answering the third question becomes more complicated. As the previous paragraphs have highlighted, the EGD and its related initiatives aim at increasing the participation of both citizens and businesses in the sustainability transition. But while the policy initiatives have traditionally focused on regulating the behaviour of the private productive sector (businesses) the recent increase in energy prices and the concerns over energy security in trying to decouple the EU Member States from Russia's fossil fuel provision, have turned things around and there is a little bit more interest on seeing behavioural change in consumers. The latest initiatives actively try to promote a decrease in energy consumption, at the same time that the levels of energy poverty across Europe have increased. This is not an isolated problem, with issues related to food supply and inflationary pressures that have also made food poverty present across European countries, something that not long ago EU authorities rejected as a possibility. The onus has been placed on citizens to change habits, sometimes without providing real affordable alternatives. The previous chapter also touched upon the access to financial instruments by citizens, as private actors who can participate in the transition asking for 'green loans' if those green loans are offered by retail banks. This is something still not developed by the EU and has only been hinted in one of the Commission Communications in 2023, so it is unlikely that any change in this area will happen in time to contribute to the 2030 targets.

One must question though, if this message is compatible with the ones that call for living within someone's means, which is parallel to the sustainable and circular economy messages calling for respecting ecological limits. There is a danger that in this push for increasing the participation in the financial markets we end up promoting a type of consumerism that in theory the sustainability transition should avoid. Hence the question about to which extent is reasonable and ethical to financialise every aspect of our lives (Storm, 2018). This does not seem to be the type of message that promotes inclusiveness and living no one behind. What is more, it reinforces something that economic theory has been explaining for a long time: no matter if a tax is imposed over consumers or producers, consumers will end up paying a share of that tax through what is called 'burden sharing'. It then becomes apparent that if the EU budget coming from Member States contributions emanate from what the citizens of each Member State pays one way or another; if the private productive sector is going to pass at least part of their costs (whether as taxes or funds invested) to consumers and it is expected that consumers directly will invest their savings into sustainability projects – it is citizens, it is all of us (we are all consumers) who will pay for the sustainability transition. The question then becomes if that 'share' of the burden is fair and to which extent we are really building a just transition – as the EGD and overarching institutional discourses claim.

Reflection on the findings of the previous chapters – challenges and the future ahead

There are several conclusions that can be reached from the previous chapters of this book: one of them is that the economic component of the sustainability transition keeps being the one given priority by EU institutions and national governments alike. The cost of living crisis caused by the Covid-19 pandemic and the energy prices hike provoked by the war in Ukraine keep pushing the economy in the political agenda. But as a difference with the economic crisis of 2008, when austerity measures crippled large segments of society, the reaction to this new crisis has been: spend and invest. Both of them with the same background banner of 'let's move our economies towards a green path and transform them into low-carbon economies that function with renewable energies'. That part of the discourse has not changed.

What has now become more apparent is that for all the transformations to happen, extensive amounts of financial resources are necessary, and it has long past the time in which governments at any level could afford to pay for all those costs through public funding. So the discourse about the need to involve private actors in the sustainability transition is recurrent throughout the EGD and all its delegated initiatives. It is business-related regulation the one that has progressed more rapidly and more intensely, for the production processes and the investment decisions of businesses to change. In trying to answer the main question of the book (summarising the previous section), which is who and how is going to pay for the necessary changes, the truth is that it is all of us – whether through taxes over things that did not use to be taxed in the past, or through higher prices for the products we buy (which would have been increased by producers to transfer any extra cost they may face), the resources that governments and supranational institutions get come from all of us. It would be fair then that citizens and communities have a bigger voice in the decision-making process about our future. The EGD established Climate Ambassadors, but their role has not been one of decision making. Importantly, the circular economy that we are supposed to be aiming for calls for doing things locally, using local resources (reducing dependencies and emissions) and in any case policy implementation happens at the local level. However, what the book has left clear is that the smaller actors, the local actors, are not benefiting from the new programmes and financial instruments, and the resources keep going to the same large players.

We also had the opportunity to confirm that EU institutions use the terms green and sustainable sometimes in a confusing manner, and even if not reaching what would account for greenwashing, if the narrative is that the priority on environmental fiscal reforms is to maintain a stable stream of revenue instead of improving environmental conditions, the use of the terms environmental or green is misleading. However we consider it, from a business, economy or policy perspective, we tend to find that the discourses aim to portray a commitment with a version of sustainability that is a hybrid between a weak and strong one, but with much more work to do particularly to integrate the social pillar, at least at the same level than the economic and environmental ones. This means that in reality it is possible that in some sense we do not even reach the 'weak' connotation of sustainability.

In sum, with all the developments brought by the EGD to guide the EU towards climate neutrality and a sustainable path, we have seen that the measures so far have been classified as insufficient, and not providing the desired results. The inefficacy of the ETS, for instance, and the long winding journey to reach reasonable prices to incentivise innovation and change, shows that the EU is slow in its learning by doing approach and as it stands it will not reach its goals. The pandemic and the war in Ukraine have proved once more that the EU tends to act in a reactive manner instead of a proactive one, even if long-term goals exist. What is more, there is still a big gap between 'old' and 'new' Member States' level of integration with the overarching messages and direction of travel, and it seems that in the sustainability transition journey we are going to be, once again, a two-speed Europe. This implies that if no one is to be left behind, whether more resources are put forward for those currently lagging, or everyone else slows down. The latter is not an option given the challenges ahead – climate emergency, international conflicts, etc. The term 'resilience' has been used frequently in the EGD discourse, but it does not seem that the EU is there yet, and it is debatable if it will be, on time.

References

Arowoshegbe, A. O. and Emmanuel, U. (2016) Sustainability and triple bottom line: An overview of two interrelated concepts, *Igbinedion University Journal of Accounting,* 2 (2016): 88–126.

Cai, Y. and Lattu, A. (2022) Triple helix of quadruple helix: Which model of innovation to choose for empirical studies? *Minerva,* 60 (2022): 257–280.

Carayannis, E. G., Barth, T. D. and Campbell, D. F. J. (2012) The quintuple helix innovation model: Global warming as a challenge and driver for innovation, *Journal of innovation and Entrepreneurship*, 1 (2012): 2. Available from: https://www.innovation-entrepreneurship.com/content/1/1/2

Carayannis, E. G., Iftimie, I. A. and Iftimie, M. C. A. (2019) Energy security in a quintuple helix innovation system. *Ipsonet.* Available from: https://ipsonet.org/wp-content/uploads/2021/04/Iftimie_2019.pdf

Crane, A. and Matten, D. (2010) *Business Ethics* (third edition). Oxford University Press.

European Environment Agency (2023) *The Case for Public Participation in Sustainability Transitions*, Briefing no. 18/2023.

Fernandez, R. (2021) Community renewable energy projects: The future of the sustainable energy transition? *The International Spectator*, 56 (3): 87–104.

Kovacic, Z. and Benini, L. (2022) Striking the balance: Sustainability and institutional transitions in the European environment agency, *Futures*, 141 (2022): 102984. https://doi.org/10.1016/j.futures.2022.102984

Leino, H. and Puumala, E. (2021) What can co-creation do for the citizens? Applying co-creation for the promotion of participation in cities, *Environment and Planning C: Politics and Space*, 39 (4): 781–799.

Marrocu, E., Paci, R. and Usai, S. (2022) Direct and indirect effects of universities on European regional productivity, *Papers in Regional Science*, 101 (5): 1105–1133.

Rask, M. and Worthington, R. (2012) Towards a new concept of global governance. In Rask, M., Worthington, R. and Lammi, M. (eds) *Citizen Participation in Global Environmental Governance.* Abingdon: Earthscan by Routledge: 3–29.

Storm, S. (2018) Financialization and economic development: A debate on the social efficiency of modern finance, *Development and Change*, 49 (2): 302–329.

Trischler, J., Svensson, P. O., Williams, H. and Wikström, F. (2023) Citizens as an innovation source in sustainability transitions – Linking the directionality of innovations with the locus of the problem in transformative innovation policy, *Public Management Review*, 25 (11): 2093–2115.

Vaivode, I. (2015) Triple Helix Model of university–industry–government cooperation in the context of uncertainties, *Procedia – Social and Behavioural Sciences,* 213 (2015): 1063–1067.

Index

Note: **Bold** page numbers refer to tables; *italic* page numbers refer to figures and page numbers followed by "n" denote endnotes.

Kolibri 360 GmbH
Ferdinand-Jühlke-Straße 7
99095 Erfurt, Deutschland
produktsicherheit@kolibri360.de